Twenty Questions That Shaped World Christian History

Twenty Questions That Shaped World Christian History

Derek Cooper

Fortress Press
Minneapolis

TWENTY QUESTIONS THAT SHAPED WORLD CHRISTIAN HISTORY

Cover design: Rob Dewey

Library of Congress Cataloging-in-Publication Data

Print ISBN: 978-1-4514-8771-8

eBook ISBN: 978-1-5064-0269-7

The paper used in this publication meets the minimum requirements of American National Standard for Information Sciences — Permanence of Paper for Printed Library Materials, ANSI Z329.48-1984.

Manufactured in the U.S.A.

This book was produced using PressBooks.com, and PDF rendering was done by PrinceXML.

Contents

What's in a Question?

A man living on a small but significant stretch of land in the Middle East was walking with a ragtag group of fellow Jews in what is now the Golan Heights. There, in the Roman city of Caesarea Philippi, surrounded by shrines dedicated to pagan gods, the man eyed his companions and asked a question, "Who do people say that I am?"[1] The men accompanying Jesus of Nazareth responded this way and that way before the most outspoken of the crew, a fisherman named Cephas, blurted out what he thought was the right answer to his rabbi's question.

Christianity is a religion that raises more questions than it answers. Though theologians wax eloquent about the doctrines of the church, Christianity is a religion rooted in mystery. Its core beliefs—that God is three persons yet one nature, that Jesus is human yet divine, and that he rose from the dead three days after being murdered—begs for more explanation, more understanding, more clarity. If Christianity were a sentence, it would be followed by a question mark.

According to Socrates, an unexamined life is not worth living. The records of church history confirm this to be true. From one

1. Literally, the passage says, "Who do people say the Son of Man is?" which was Jesus' unique way of referring to himself, especially as made clear by the following verses in the passage. Other than substituting "I" for "the Son of Man," I am using the NRSV. I am following the version given in Matt. 16:13–16.

perspective, the history of Christianity is nothing but a series of questions asked by people committed to a life of intense scrutiny. All generations of Christians ask their own questions as they examine their Christian identity and search for meaning in their lives. From our historical vantage point, it's quite right that Christians continually ask new questions and regularly revisit old ones. We could say that asking questions is in our religious DNA. Besides praying, serving, and believing, perhaps asking is what Christians do best. Jesus, after all, was the consummate question asker who often responded to people's questions by asking his own, suggesting to Christians nearby and far away that few things are as sacred as asking questions. During his short ministry on earth, the questions he asked were penetrating and provocative:

What are you looking for?

What will it profit [people] if they gain the whole world but forfeit their life?

Why do your disciples break the tradition of the elders?

Why does this generation look for a sign?

My God, my God, why have you forsaken me?[2]

Taking our cue from the way that Jesus taught his disciples, this book queries whether the story of world Christianity is best told followed by a series of question marks than by semicolons, periods, or, worse yet, exclamation marks. Out of an endless array of questions from which to choose, this book will narrate the history of Christianity by responding to twenty key questions in the church's past. Each chapter begins with a story that provokes one overarching question for discussion. The remaining chapter provides responses to each question from writers of that century, with a conclusion attempting to shed light on the possible outcomes to the question

---

2. These questions come, respectively, from John 1:38, Matt. 16:26, Matt. 15:2, Mark 8:12, and Matt. 27:46.

posed. For the purposes of order and clarity, each chapter typically represents only one century, meaning that the twenty chapters in this book correspond to the first twenty centuries of the church. We all know, of course, that centuries are blocks of time devised by historians to serve as mental placeholders, but they also provide an agreed upon structure useful for understanding the past.

So, what were twenty questions that shaped world Christianity? Needless to say, it has not been an easy task to select only one question for each century—and the reasons why I have isolated one question over another are not unassailable. But nor are they arbitrary. It is best not to think that each chapter's framing question was *the only* question asked and debated that century, that it fully embodied the ethos of the age, or that it represented all of the vast geographic and theological sectors of the church. Naturally, no one question can exemplify an age. Nor can it epitomize a movement as globally and socially diverse as Christianity. Nonetheless, the questions isolated in each chapter do emerge from contemporary sources—even if they would not have been asked in the same exact way—and I cite in each chapter how secondary sources assume the importance of such questions for each particular century.

When reading this book, allow yourself to be drawn into the questions and responses. Imagine living in this or that century. Listen to the way contemporary writers responded in their own words to questions that we ask them today. Recognize their responses as windows into the past. Some of the questions that we formulated from contemporary concerns are long gone, suffering loss in the sands of time, while others are slowly being unearthed. Some, in fact, are as fresh today as they were centuries ago. But, at the end of the day, we must not forget that these were real people we are talking about, struggling to understand Christ in a meaningful way within their own time periods. Whether in Africa or America, Europe or

Asia, these individuals simply responded to the real-life conditions they faced—religious or otherwise. Then as today, religious issues never exist in a vacuum; they are always inextricably linked to everything else in society, and so we will survey Christian responses to a whole host of social concerns such as death, power, science, sex, slavery, and war. As we do so, we will not only learn about the past but the present as well. We will learn that our questions today are shaped by a welter of contemporary concerns, which sometimes have little to do with those of Christian communities living elsewhere in the world. How do you think your understanding of Christianity will be affected as we take this journey together? And which questions will you resonate with from the past?

1

What's the Relationship between Christianity and Judaism?

It was the year 48. Almost twenty years had passed since Jesus had died and reportedly risen from the dead. While fasting and in prayer, the leaders of the fledgling Christian community in Antioch, the city where Christians first received their name, set aside and anointed two Jewish men to spread the message of Jesus Christ outside of the region. Their names were Barnabas and Saul. Their first destination was Cyprus, Barnabas's homeland. In what would become a standard practice, these two men initially preached their message to Jews before then "turning to the Gentiles" (Acts 13:46). According to the book of Acts, the missionary duo eventually traveled to the southwestern part of the island of Cyprus. There, in Paphos, they met with the Roman governor—a man named Sergius Paulus—explaining to him and his court how a Jewish criminal crucified by the Romans was the *Soter mundi*, or Savior of the world.

It was at this point in the story when two interrelated events occurred: the conversion of the Roman governor to Christianity and the change of Saul's name. The conversion of Sergius Paulus signaled a great change in the history of Christian mission, for this governor was not only a Gentile but also the most powerful Christian man currently living in the Roman Empire. In fact, one New Testament scholar goes so far as to suggest that Saul departed Cyprus earlier than anticipated since conversion at "the highest level of society" all but guaranteed the conversion of the island without the apostle's presence.[1] It was also at this time that Saul changed his Jewish name to Paul in the presence of the governor, Sergius Paulus. Given the venue of the name change and the larger cultural Roman practice of patronage, it's possible that Saul formally adopted the *cognomen* or family name of his new patron, Paulus (or Paullus). Such a theory is bolstered by the fact that Paul and Barnabas, now under the patronage of the governor, immediately set sail from Cyprus for Pisidian Antioch, the hometown of Sergius Paulus. The governor likely sent Paul and Barnabas along with letters of introduction to individuals in that very important city in the Roman province of Galatia. In order to indicate this shift of wind in Christian mission, one of the greatest of the apostles, Saul, would henceforth be known not by his Jewish name but by one of his Roman ones, Paulus.

Figure 1.1. Understanding Roman Names

Many Roman citizens had three names (*tria nomina*). These are commonly referred to as the (1) *praenomen*, (2) *nomen*, and (3) *cognomen*:

1. *Praenomen* – Personal name chosen by the parents of the child
2. *Nomen* – Family name of Roman citizen (shared with other family or clan members, passed on generationally)
3. *Cognomen* – Additional name used to identify child's relation to other family or clan members. It's possible that the apostle Paul adopted the *cognomen* Paul (in Latin: Paulus or Paullus) after coming under the patronage of the Roman governor Sergius Paulus.[2]

---

1. Eckhard Schnabel, *Early Christian Mission*, vol. 2, *Paul and the Early Church* (Downers Grove, IL: InterVarsity, 2004), 1088.
2. Naturally, scholars debate whether Saul had always had the name Paulus as one of his names since he was a Roman citizen or whether he later adopted it.

The Question of the Parting of Ways

It comes as no surprise that the so-called Jerusalem Council, convened to formulate a policy on how to address conversions of Christianity by non-Jews (called Gentiles), came at the heels of Saul's name change to Paulus and his conversion of a powerful Roman governor. Though emerging out of Judaism, it was now clear that Christianity was more than a Jewish sect. At the same time, it was not at all clear what requirements were expected of Gentiles who affirmed Jesus as their *Dominus et Deus*—their Lord and their God. As one early Christian historian wrote, "it is relatively easy to see that the movement Christ started was in conflict with Judaism from the beginning."[3]

In this chapter, we will engage the first of our twenty questions that shaped world Christian history. Our focus will be the following question: What was the relationship between Christianity and Judaism? This question, amply discussed and alluded to in the New Testament documents, consumed the thinking and writing of the earliest Christians. It was, in fact, a question that loomed over the formation and development of Christian churches all across the Mediterranean world. From the Gospels, to Paul's letters, to the Council of Jerusalem, and to the destruction of the Jewish temple, we will sift through various Christian responses to this most fundamental of questions during the first century of the Christian era.

Jesus in the Gospels: A Foreshadowing of an International Ministry

Jesus was raised in Nazareth, a three-day journey from Jerusalem. In the first century CE, Nazareth was an insignificant Jewish village

---

3. James Leonard Papandrea, *Reading the Early Church Fathers: From the Didache to Nicea* (Mahwah, NJ: Paulist Press, 2012), 1.

of only a couple of hundred people. Nazareth was surrounded by Gentile populations and was located on the outskirts of a large Roman-influenced city known as Sepphoris. We know next to nothing of Jesus' early childhood. According to the gospel accounts, in his late twenties or early thirties Jesus abandoned his craft as a "woodworker" and spent the last years of his life preaching and healing in the Palestinian backwaters of Galilee, earning the reputation of a great wonderworker and teacher.

The climax of Jesus' ministry occurred in Jerusalem the last week of his life. According to each of the New Testament Gospels, Jesus made a pilgrimage to Jerusalem for Passover like many other pious Jews. There, in the city where all prophets were destined "to be killed" (Luke 13:33), Jesus openly rebuked Jewish authorities in the temple precincts, arousing their ire and jealousy. New Testament historian N. T. Wright suggests that Jesus was ultimately killed for redefining the people of God in a way that threatened and offended Jewish authorities as well as common Jewish people alike:

> Jesus seems to have believed himself to be the focal point of the real returning-from-exile people, the true kingdom-people; but that kingdom, that people and this Messiah did not look like what the majority of Jews had expected. Jesus was summoning his hearer to a different way of being Israel. We now have to come to terms with the fact that he believed himself called to go that different way himself as Israel's anointed representative and to do for Israel—and hence also for the world—what Israel could not or would not do for herself.[4]

It is certainly significant that the "different way" Jesus went about as Israel's representative favored religious inclusivity. We get a glimpse of the different way of Jesus when he was almost stoned to death by the villagers of Nazareth one day as a result of lauding God's provision of Gentiles (and not Jews) during the days of Elijah and

---

4. N. T. Wright, *The Challenge of Jesus* (Downers Grove, IL: InterVarsity, 1999), 81.

Elisha (see Luke 4:16–30), two wonderworking prophets whom Jesus emulated. As New Testament scholar E. P. Sanders argues, "All the authors of the gospels favoured [Jesus'] mission to Gentiles." Not surprisingly, therefore, these authors hunted for "all the pro-Gentile material that they could"[5] find to include in their biographies of Jesus. And, according to many scholars, it was Jesus' radical redefinition of who was included in the kingdom of God—Gentiles as well as Jews—that played a large part in his execution.

The belief that Jesus' racially inclusive teaching contributed to his death need not conflict with select passages from the Gospel of Matthew, traditionally believed by early Christians to be written for a largely Jewish audience. Jesus' saying in the Gospel of Matthew that he "was sent only to the lost sheep of the house of Israel" (15:24; see also 10:5–6) should be tempered by other passages in that gospel indicating that Jesus was understood to be a light to the Gentiles whose birth was good news for non-Jews (e.g., 2:1; 4:15–16; 8:10; 12:18–21; 28:19). As best as we can reconstruct, Jesus regarded himself as the inaugurator of God's reign, the one whose death would usher in a divine (and eschatological) kingdom encompassing Jews *and* Gentiles. Such a calling gives us the context for Jesus' famous statement in the Sermon on the Mount, "Do not think that I have come to abolish the law or the prophets; I have come not to abolish but to fulfill" (5:17). Rather than abolish the Torah or condemn the Jewish people God had called, safeguarded, and "entrusted with the oracles of God" (Rom. 3:2), Jesus fulfilled the Torah in his own person. In this way, Matthew's community regarded Jesus not merely as the most authoritative interpreter of Torah in relation to the scribes or other Jewish leaders but as the personification of the Torah, as Matthew's many formula citations indicate (1:22; 2:5, 15, 17, 23;

---

5. E. P. Sanders, *The Historical Figure of Jesus* (London: Penguin, 1993), 192.

4:14; 8:17; 12:17; 13:14, 35; 21:4; 27:9). In short, Jesus came to fulfill the mission for which Israel had always existed but had not always recognized—to be the collective channel of God's salvation to the entire world.

The Ministry of the Apostle Paul (40s to 60s CE)

The apostle Paul based his ministry on the conviction that Jesus brought to an appropriate fulfillment the story of God's dealing with humankind. "Paul, a servant of Jesus Christ, called to be an apostle," words Paul dictated to his scribe Tertius in his most famous of letters, believed that he had been "set apart for the gospel of God, which he promised beforehand" (Rom. 1:1–2). The gospel or "good news" that Paul proclaimed centered on the offer of salvation made available to people of all ethnic backgrounds and religious persuasions due to the life, death, and resurrection of Jesus. Though God's covenant was previously restricted to the nation of Israel, God was bringing to completion this covenant in order to invite all other nations into the covenant as well. As historian Peter Brown succinctly writes, Paul's "mission had been to bring pagans into the kingdom."[6] Israel was meant to bless the world and become the means by which the rest of the world gained salvation. Paul, as the self-styled "apostle to the Gentiles" (Rom. 11:13), worked tirelessly to establish and shepherd Gentile and Gentile-Jewish Christian communities.

As we survey the journeys of the apostle Paul in the book of Acts, we surmise that he did not regard Christian identity as in any way tied to the land of Judea. Nor do any of the New Testament authors appear to do so. On the contrary, after his encounter with the risen Christ, Paul rarely spent time in Judea or in the holy city of Jerusalem. Instead, the majority of his ministry was devoted to establishing and

---

6. Peter Brown, *The Body and Society: Men, Women, and Sexual Renunciation in Early Christianity* (New York: Columbia University Press, 1988), 45.

nurturing Christian communities across the Mediterranean world, oftentimes in Gentile-dominated regions in modern Turkey and Greece. According to the so-called three missionary journeys of Paul narrated in the book of Acts, Paul always preached to Jews and Gentiles, but it was his preaching to Gentiles that caused the greatest controversies. Paul minced no words with Jewish Christians in Galatia who attempted to strong-arm Gentile and Jewish Christians into fully observing the Law of Moses while professing belief in Christ: "Listen! I, Paul, am telling you that if you let yourselves be circumcised, Christ will be of no benefit to you" (Gal. 5:2).

Although Paul was, of course, a Jew—and a rather proud one that at that (see Phil. 3:4–6)—he confounded many Jews by the ease with which he moved from the Jewish and Gentile worlds. In the matter of a few hours, it seems, Paul would preach in a synagogue, be stoned, shake the dust off his sandals, and proceed to spend the night with Gentiles. The next day he would do it all over again. In many ways, Paul was a conundrum. He refused to circumcise Titus by matter of principle, but forced his companion Timothy to undergo circumcision. He boldly asserted that Jesus was the end of the law, but was persuaded to undergo a Jewish ritual at the temple in Jerusalem. He argued that Jesus broke down the barrier dividing free people from slaves, but ordered slaves to be obedient to their masters. He commanded Christians to be good citizens and obey the authorities, but had a prison record longer than any two-bit criminal in the Roman Empire. And yet, through all these apparent contradictions, Paul was the one destined to move the Christian message forward into the Gentile world like no one else before him. For him, at any rate, Gentiles were full partners with Jews in the plan of salvation. Although he struggled greatly with how to implement this conviction from context to context, he went to the grave believing that Jesus' death destroyed the centuries-long division between Jews and Gentiles. Through baptism into the community of faith, all ethnic, gender, and social distinctions that formerly caused division were stripped away. The individual's baptism into the church was a symbolic death to racism, exclusivism, and social bigotry.

The Jerusalem Council (49 or 50)

Paul's work among Gentiles precipitated concerned questions from many Jews, a people long accustomed to stark division existing (in diet, clothing, religion, and lifestyle) between Jews and *goyim*, that is, Gentiles. Were Gentiles able to become full participants in what God was doing through Christ? If so, what was expected of them? Although the book of Acts reported that Peter had received a revelation that effectively abrogated the continuation of dietary restrictions between Jews and Gentiles in the 30s CE, the issue was anything but settled. Indeed, as Paul crowed in his Letter to the Galatians, possibly written just months before the Jerusalem Council convened, he condemned Peter to his face for backing off table fellowship with Gentile Christians.

Each of the major players of Jewish Christianity was present at the Jerusalem Council: James, Peter, Paul, and Barnabas. Although they did not know this at the time, the council members were establishing a precedent of epic proportions, as each generation of Christian leaders since this time has held councils to settle church disputes on the basis of this one in the first century. The first words of the council were, not surprisingly, spoken by the impetuous Peter, while the last words came from James, who, true to form as one who is "quick to listen, slow to speak" (James 1:19), wisely spoke only after weighing everyone else's testimony. Barnabas and Peter shared personal stories emerging from their work as missionaries.

The ruling of the council was settled on the basis of a novel Christ-centered interpretation of the Hebrew Bible as well as on the experiences of Christian leaders. In short, the experiences of Peter, Paul, and Barnabas confirmed—in light of Jesus' ministry and teaching—that Gentiles were to be included in the work that God was doing in the world among the Jewish people. The council determined that circumcision and the keeping of the law was unnecessary for Gentile converts. Gentiles were only required to refrain from blood, fornication, sacrificing food to idols, and from things strangled—basic requirements of Gentiles who converted to Judaism based on passages in Leviticus 17 and 18.

Although the Jerusalem Council is the basis for all subsequent councils in the history of Christianity, its rulings were surprisingly short-lived. It's true that Paul delivered the ruling to the church in Syrian Antioch, but it does not appear that he really took the rulings to heart. If it's true that Paul wrote his Letter to the Galatians before the council convened, the deliberations would have been anti-climactic. He had already decided how to handle the issue of contention. What need was there to receive the approval of mortals when Jesus Christ had personally appeared to him, commissioning him to the great task of Gentile missions? As Paul poignantly wrote to the Galatian Christians, "I died to the law" (2:19). For Paul, this was no figure of speech; he was fully persuaded that Jesus had ended observance of the law. He even went so far as to egg on those Jewish Christians adamant about demanding badges of Jewish identity such as circumcision: "I wish those who unsettle you would castrate themselves!" (5:12).

When viewed from hindsight, it's apparent that the Jerusalem Council was anything but definitive. It did not resolve how Jewish

Christians were to relate to the Law of Moses. If anything, it seemed to presuppose that Jewish Christians continued observing the law—but to what extent, it is not exactly clear. At the same time, the council did extend the door that Paul and others had opened in their evangelization of the Gentiles. Although Gentiles did not have to become Jews to become Christians, they were not on equal footing with Jewish Christians. Such were the conclusions of Jewish Christians living in the heart of Judaism amidst a fully operational temple—but this would not always be the case.

The First Jewish War (66–70)

The First Jewish War and the destruction of the Jewish temple were watershed events in the history of Christianity. Before the temple's destruction in 70 CE, even the apostle Paul, the very man who so strongly avowed that those who clung to observance of Jewish rituals were making null and void the work of Christ, fulfilled a Nazarite vow in deference to James decades after becoming a Christ-follower. Of course, Paul's presence in the Jewish temple caused a riot—demonstrating not only Paul's penchant for provoking controversy but also his apparent urging for Jews to "forsake Moses, and . . . [other Jewish] customs" (Acts 21:21). According to the early church historian Eusebius, relations between Jews and Jewish Christians had deteriorated to such an extent that the threat of the temple's destruction, the holiest site on earth and the throne of God in the eyes of the Jews, did not compel them to remain at home and fight with their fellow Jews against the pagan Romans. Nor did the Christians feel obliged to pay the temple tax now that they were no longer bound to the sacrificial system. It appears that there was already a growing division between Jews and Jewish Christians.

Figure 1.2. Timeline of the First Jewish War

- Begins in Caesarea when Roman soldiers stand by as Jews are killed (66)

- Gains force as Jewish priests cease to make (required) offerings for Roman emperor (66)

- Escalates as General Vespasian enters Palestine and attacks Jewish forces (67)

- Halts as Emperor Nero commits suicide and Rome is in an uproar (68)

- Continues as Vespasian leaves Israel to become emperor—the fourth in a year (69)

- Culminates when Vespasian's son, Titus, takes over as general and utterly destroys Jewish rebels, their land, and, finally, the temple (69–70)

- Comes to finale as a hardened band of Jewish rebels commits suicide at Masada rather than die at the hands of Romans (73)

The First Jewish War, which lasted roughly from 66 to 70 CE, was an inevitable battle that had been brewing in the in the minds and hearts of Jews since the Romans annexed Judea in the year 6 CE. The mounting animosity between Jews and Romans serves as the backdrop to some of the stories in the Gospels, though New Testament scholars disagree to what extent Jesus was influenced by this Jewish-Roman hostility. According to the first-century Jewish general Josephus, who later became a spy for the Romans and who retired to a life of leisure and writing in Rome after the war ended, the culmination of the war came when General Titus, the son of the newly proclaimed Roman Emperor Vespasian, entered Jerusalem in the year 70, set up Roman standards, made pagan sacrifices, and proceeded to destroy the temple.

While those Jews who escaped death watched their holy furnishings cavalierly handled by Roman soldiers and their temple's walls burned to the ground, the Jewish Christians of the Jerusalem church were safely in a city called Pella in the region of Perea, about sixty miles northeast. According to Eusebius, the Christians in

Jerusalem had been directed to flee "the judgment of God [which] at last overtook [the Jews] for their abominable crimes against Christ and His apostles."[7] For Eusebius, whose thinking was drawn in part from Paul's First Letter to the Thessalonians (2:14–16), God used the Romans to condemn the Jewish people and their most prized possession, the temple, in accordance with Jesus' prophecy in the Gospels. In the eyes of Eusebius, the destruction of the temple did several things simultaneously: it confirmed the prophecies of Christ; illustrated Christianity's final break with Judaism; and demonstrated the patience of God, who "for forty years after [the Jews'] crime against Christ delayed their destruction" in order to provoke the Jewish people toward repentance so that "they might obtain pardon and salvation."[8]

> Eusebius of Caesarea is an important figure in early Christianity. Eusebius was bishop of Caesarea (capital of the Roman province of Judea, where the governors formally lived—now an ancient site in Israel) from the year 314 until his death in c. 340. He wrote the first major history of the church (as well as several other books) and was a client of the first Christian emperor of the Roman Empire, Constantine, under the so-called patronage system. Eusebius later wrote a book that lauded Constantine as a man of faith who protected Christianity.

However the early Christians interpreted this event, the destruction of the Jewish temple was clearly a turning point for Jews and Gentiles. As one early historian wrote, "the period after the destruction of the Temple certainly saw a worsening of relations between Christians and non-Christian Jews."[9] For Jews, the absence of a temple obviously made full observance of the Jewish law impossible since so many laws were dependent on the continuation of the sacrificial system. The war had also decimated the populace

---

7. Eusebius, *The History of the Church* 3.5 (London: Penguin, 1989), 68.
8. Ibid., 75.
9. Jonathan Hill, *Christianity: How a Tiny Sect from a Despised Religion Came to Dominate the Roman Empire* (Minneapolis, MN: Fortress Press, 2011), 70.

and destroyed many Jewish groups. Such groups included the Sicari, a radical Jewish sect that committed suicide at the citadel of Masada in 73 CE; the Sadducees, who were the Jewish elite connected to the temple and part of the Sanhedrin; and the Essenes, who had retreated to the Dead Sea and were responsible for the Dead Sea Scrolls. For Jewish Christians in Palestine, the church became increasingly Gentile in orientation since Jews in Judea were unable to enter the area, especially after the Second Jewish War ended in 135.

The Thought and Practice of the Ebionites

Although virtually none of their writings have outlived their own time period, there was a fringe group of Jewish Christians from the first century who would have responded to the question of the relationship between Judaism and Christianity differently than many other Christians such as the apostle Paul and what we may call the proto-orthodox group of Christians—those whose views would become the majority. They were called Ebionites. Like the apostle Paul, the Ebionites believed that Jesus was the Jewish Messiah and that he fulfilled prophecies in the Hebrew Bible. In contrast to Paul, however, the Ebionites did not regard Jesus as God; nor did they believe that Jewish Christians had to observe the Law of Moses in order to be in relationship with God. As a result, the Ebionites—though Christians—followed the law of the Hebrew Bible in full, even though they understood the Law very differently than non-Christian Jews did.

Like the pious child of a Jewish mother and a Christian father, Ebionites observed the rituals of both parents. As Jews, they took daily ritual baths while, as Christians, they performed baptism; as Jews, they kept the Sabbath from Friday to Saturday afternoon while, as Christians, they observed the Lord's Day on Sunday. Unlike Gentile Christians, however, they revered the city of Jerusalem and

13

faced its direction while in prayer; and unlike Jews, they believed that Jesus' death had ended the sacrificial system. They were "in" the worlds of both Christianity and Judaism, but "of" neither.

From what we can gather, the Ebionites disagreed vigorously with the apostle Paul on many points of doctrine. Although in the first century there was no such thing as a "New Testament" as we conceive of it today, Paul's letters would never have been included in the Ebionite canon of Scriptures. Nor would Paul have tolerated their views of Christ had he known about them. Paul would have regarded their theology on par with the Judaizers of Galatia—and thus a gospel-free theology—while, on the other hand, the Ebionites would have considered Paul a heretic for urging Jews to cease observing the Law of Moses and instead urging faith in Jesus on the supposition that "Christ is the end of the law" (Rom. 10:4). The Ebionites also objected to Paul's teaching that Jesus was the ultimate sacrifice of God who was slaughtered like a lamb in order to save the world. On the contrary, we know from a third-century document called "The Letter of Peter to James" that the Ebionites considered Paul thoroughly mistaken. As the letter states, Paul is considered the "enemy" of Peter who distorted Peter's message. In clear contrast to Paul's teaching, the Ebionite letter indicates that only "a man who … has been circumcised is a believing Christian."[10]

Although the Ebionites appeared to flourish for a season, the Ebionite movement died out in the centuries to come. As the Christian church in the Roman Empire become predominantly Gentile, Jewish Christians such as the Ebionites found themselves in the minority and out of favor. Yet not all of the theology of the Ebionites disappeared. Although the Ebionite church perished, one of their distinct beliefs—that Jesus was adopted by God at some point

10. "The Letter of Peter to James and Its Reception," in Bart Ehrman, *After the New Testament: A Reader in Early Christianity* (Oxford: Oxford University Press, 1999), 137–38.

in his ministry—would strike a chord with various Christian groups in the years that followed. Such Christian "adoptionists," though not part of what we may regard as mainstream Christianity, have always had a following in the history of Christianity, even to this day. Although movements come and go, ideas, especially controversial ones, are often recycled during some other period in history.

Conclusion: Christianity and Judaism as Separate Religions

Despite the presence of fringe groups such as the Ebionites, by the close of the first century there was a mounting consensus that Christianity and Judaism were quite distinct. Perhaps early church historian W. C. H. Frend summed it up best when he wrote, "After circa AD 100 there was . . . more of a tendency to contrast Christianity and Judaism as separate religions."[11] Over time, this tendency has only accelerated. Likely written at the end of the first century, the *Didache* urged Christians to fast on different days of the week than did "the hypocrites," that is, the Jews, in order to demonstrate the clear separations of these two religions. Likewise, we cannot overestimate how significant it was that early Christians moved their day of worship from the Sabbath (Friday to Saturday afternoon) to Sunday, the day when Jesus was reported to have risen from the tomb.

Writing in the second century, the Gentile Christian Justin Martyr captured the division between Jews and Christians by boldly declaring to his Jewish dialogue partner Trypho that the Law of Moses was "already obsolete." Whereas circumcision was only given to "you Jews," Justin asserted, the message of Christ was intended "for all men."[12] Justin argued that Gentiles who adopted the Law of

---

11. W. C. H. Frend, *The Rise of Christianity* (Minneapolis, MN: Augsburg Fortress, 1986), 124.
12. Justin Martyr, "Dialogue with Trypho 11," in *The Fathers of the Church*, vol. 6, *A New Translation*, trans. Thomas Falls (Washington, D.C.: The Catholic University of America Press, 1977), 164.

Moses would not be saved, nor would any Jews who did not believe in Christ. Justin went on to declare to Trypho:

> Aren't you acquainted with [the words of the prophets like David and Moses], Trypho? You should be, for they are contained in your Scriptures, *or rather not yours, but ours*. For we believe and obey them, whereas you, though you read them, do not grasp their spirit.[13]

Taking into consideration the argument of Justin Martyr in the second century, we see that the parting of ways between Judaism and Christianity was essentially complete by the second century, if not before.[14] Although it is true, as historian Jaroslav Pelikan once wrote, that "Virtually every major Christian writer of the first five centuries either composed a treatise in opposition to Judaism or made this issue a dominant theme in a treatise devoted to some other subject,"[15] such treatises were effectively intellectual exercises. Most early Christians understood themselves to be the inheritors of God's promises in the Old Testament and thus the rightful possessors of the Hebrew Bible. While the Jews read the Hebrew Bible in a carnal way—their eyes covered as if by a veil, wrote the apostle Paul (2 Cor. 3:14)—the Christians read it spiritually and hence saw Christ everywhere. Though sharing a common heritage, Judaism and Christianity were really different religions whose beliefs and practices have only diverged over time.

---

13. Justin, "Dialogue with Trypho 19," 191 (italics added).
14. As New Testament historian James Dunn writes in *The Parting of Ways: Between Christianity and Judaism and Their Significance for the Character of Christianity*, 2nd ed. (London: SCM Press, 2006), 318, "by the end of the second Jewish revolt, Christian and Jew were clearly distinct and separate."
15. Jaroslav Pelikan, *The Christian Tradition: A History of the Development of Doctrine*, vol. 1, *The Emergence of the Catholic Tradition (100-600)* (Chicago and London: University of Chicago Press, 1971), 15.

2

What Makes Someone a Heretic?

It was the year 165. In the region of Phrygia, in what is today central Turkey, a Christian man named Montanus was heralding himself as the mouthpiece of the Holy Spirit. He spoke in a frenetic manner, enamoring some but alarming many others. Quite controversially, Montanus had two female colleagues, Priscilla and Maximilla. These women had left their husbands and families in order to proclaim the coming of the Lord. Like Montanus, these women spoke as if intoxicated with alcohol. Reports of their prophecies were sometimes incomprehensible, but always interesting. According to a fourth-century bishop named Epiphanius, Montanus was reported to have said: "I am the Lord God, the Almighty, dwelling in a man." Montanus also purportedly stated, "Neither angel nor messenger, but I the Lord, God the Father, have come." To Epiphanius, deeply suspicious of novelty, such words were clear proof that "this pathetic little man, Montanus"[1] was an arch-heretic—a man to be resisted as if he were Satan incarnate.

Although there were several others who agreed with Epiphanius's hostile assessment of Montanus, other Christians lauded Montanus's

---

1. *The Panarion of Epiphanius of Salamis: Sects 47–80, De Fide* (Leiden, The Netherlands: Brill, 1994), 16–17.

teaching and conduct. A second-century North African named Tertullian, a prolific writer who later joined the Montanist church, retorted that Montanists were hated not because of their theology but because of their rigorism. As he wrote about the Montanists in his book *On Fasting*, "they plainly teach more fasting than marrying."[2] Today, many scholars agree with Tertullian's assessment of the Montanist movement over Epiphanius's. Such scholars believe that far from claiming divinity, Montanist prophets simply used first-person speech in the same way that the biblical prophets did. Such practices, in addition to their belief in the full continuation of the prophetic gifts, focused on moral purity and discipline, and it's likely that their clash with a hardening church structure precipitated their censure among more mainstream churches in the decades to follow.

The Question of Authority and Orthodoxy

The movement that Montanus started, called "the New Prophecy" by insiders and "Montanism" by outsiders, was popular among the common people, but a great threat to Christian leaders. The clash between the Montanist church and what later came to be seen as the Catholic or Orthodox Church brings together all kinds of questions about early Christianity, particularly about its leadership and authority. As historian of antiquity Christopher Haas writes, "The period on either side of 200 was an age when questions of apostolic succession, teaching authority, and the definition of orthodoxy came to dominate the work of churchmen."[3] To state the issue more broadly, we may frame a question for discussion as follows: How does the church distinguish between orthodox Christians and heretical

---

2. Tertullian, "On Fasting," in *The Ante-Nicene Fathers*, ed. Alexander Roberts and James Donaldson, vol. 4 (Peabody, MA: Hendrickson, 1994; reprint), 102.
3. Christopher Haas, "Alexandria," in *Early Christianity in Contexts: An Exploration across Cultures and Continents*, ed. William Tabbernee (Grand Rapids, MI: Baker, 2014), 208.

ones? In this chapter, we will examine select second-century Christian responses to this question of leadership succession, authority, and orthodoxy.

The Bishops as Successors to the Apostles in the Letters of Clement and Ignatius (Late First and Early Second Centuries)

Two of the earliest Christian documents we have outside of the New Testament were written by highly respected bishops overseeing Christians in two of the largest cities in the Roman Empire, Rome and Antioch.[4] Bishop Clement of Rome wrote his letter (called *1 Clement*) to the church in Corinth at the very end of the first century. Ignatius, the bishop of Antioch, wrote a series of seven letters to local churches and leaders in the first or second decade of the second century on his way toward death in Rome. As we read through these ancient documents, we get the sense that the early church was just as prone to division as it is today, and that questions of authority were very much on the minds of church leaders and laypeople as a means of settling church disputes.

Beginning with *1 Clement*, this letter opens with strong allusions to division and schism, alerting later readers that not much seems to have changed since the apostle Paul's dealings with that church four decades earlier. In the first chapter, Clement described how he distinguished between true and false teachers and churches—a view that would become fairly standardized over the centuries. For him, living "in accordance with the laws of God" (1:3) meant submitting to the leaders of the church—laypeople to officers of the church, younger men to older men, and women to their husbands. Toward the end of the letter, Clement provided more detail about his views

---

4. There is scholarly debate on whether early bishops, such as those in Rome, were single bishops or more of a chairman of a council of priests. See Alistair Stewart, *The Original Bishops: Office and Order in the First Christian Communities* (Grand Rapids, MI: Baker, 2014).

of authority and church structure. Like officers in the military, there was a straightforward chain of command: God → Christ → apostles → bishops → deacons → laypeople (41:1; 42:1–5).

Clement's most sustained attention to church authority came in the second half of the book. He wrote:

> Our apostles likewise knew, through our Lord Jesus Christ, that there would be strife over the bishop's office. For this reason, therefore, having received complete foreknowledge, they appointed the officials mentioned earlier and afterwards they gave the offices a permanent character; that is, if they should die, other approved men should succeed to their ministry (44:1–2).[5]

This is probably the earliest claim for apostolic succession—a theory holding that there is an unbroken line and direct descent from Christ to bishops. The authority of these bishops, far from deriving from the dictates of human beings, comes from Christ through succession from the apostles. In the last verses of this letter, Clement, as if to emphasize that many of the problems the Corinthians faced had to do with their refusal to submit to the deacons and bishops, asserted that it was right and just for the Corinthians "to bow the neck and, adopting the attitude of obedience, to submit to those who are the leaders of [their] souls" (63:1) in order to gain peace in the church.

Only separated by about ten years, the next earliest series of Christian documents we have come from Bishop Ignatius of Antioch around the year 107. Like Clement, Ignatius was the bishop of a church with a noble heritage. Not only did Christians receive their name in Antioch, but Peter himself was regarded as the first bishop of that cosmopolitan city. His chair (as a symbol of his authority) was still on display well beyond the time of Ignatius. To his impressive credit, Ignatius was rumored to have been a disciple of the apostle

---

5. I am using the translation from *The Apostolic Fathers*, 2nd ed., ed. Michael Holmes (Grand Rapids, MI: Baker, 1989), 52.

John, and he was already given the stature of a "confessor" (one who confessed his faith to the authorities, often undergoing bodily harm) and thus was well respected among the Christian community. Of Ignatius's seven letters, he wrote four of them in Smyrna and three in Troas—both cities in what is now in the nation of Turkey.

The letters of Ignatius built upon the understanding of authority as found in Clement's letter to the Corinthians. In order to bolster his opposition against so-called Docetists (Christians who believed that Jesus only appeared to be human) and Judaizers (Christians who demanded observance of the Jewish law), Ignatius held that church authority was exercised by bishops who could trace their heritage back to one of the original apostles of Christ. In this way, the unity of the church was preserved by bishops who could not trace their spiritual descent back to the apostles.

Many contemporary readers of Ignatius are surprised to learn how resolutely Ignatius defended the authority of bishops:

"Let us, therefore, be careful not to oppose the bishop, in order that we may be obedient to God" (Eph. 5:3).

"It is essential, therefore, that you . . . do nothing without the bishop, but be subject also to the presbytery as to the apostles of Jesus Christ" (Trall. 2:2).

"You must all follow the bishop, as Jesus Christ followed the Father, and follow the presbytery as you would the apostles; respect the deacons as the commandment of God. Let no one do anything that has to do with the church without the bishop. Only that Eucharist which is under the authority of the bishop . . . is to be considered valid. Wherever the bishop appears, let the congregation be; just as wherever Jesus Christ is, there is the catholic church. It is not permissible to either baptize or to hold a love feast without the bishop" (Smyrn. 8:1–2).

"It is good to acknowledge God and the bishop. The one who honors the bishop has been honored by God; the one who does anything without the bishop's knowledge serves the devil" (Smyrn. 9:1).[6]

Ignatius understood the bishop to be the representative of the Lord. Simply put, no bishop, no church. Although it's easy to get lost in the forest of Ignatius's thought, we may properly regard him as a man "set on unity" (Phil. 8:1), a unity which had quickly degenerated into division, schism, and splits after the time of Christ. For Ignatius, the most tangible way to bring about unity was for the church to rally around legitimate bishops who had safeguarded the true doctrines and practices of Christ as handed down to them from the apostles themselves. Anyone who submitted to the authority of such a bishop was truly part of what Ignatius called the "catholic church" (the first use of this term in recorded history). By contrast, anyone who denied or subverted the authority of a valid bishop was a servant of Satan, and thus part of a heretical or, at least, schismatic church.

Secret Knowledge, Human Reasoning, and Spiritual Ecstasy in the Theology of Valentinus, Marcion, and Montanus (Early Second Century)

Despite the development of the office of bishop, disputes did not subside. From the second century onward, we see nothing but an increase in schisms and splits, and a proliferation of so-called heresies. In this section, we will examine three Christian men in the second century who came to be regarded as heretics: Valentinus, Marcion, and Montanus. These three men, though different from one another in many important ways, eventually found themselves on the fringes of mainstream Christian society. Their writings are no longer extant, having either been destroyed or lost over the centuries. This means, regrettably, that our information about these men is mostly derived from their opponents—who, in this case, were mainstream Christian authors such as Clement of Alexandria, Epiphanius, Hippolytus, Irenaeus, and Tertullian.

6. *The Apostolic Fathers*, 88, 98, 113.

We will begin our discussion with Valentinus, an Egyptian born in the year 100. In terms of pedigree, Clement of Alexandria, a contemporary Christian opponent, wrote that Valentinus claimed to be a follower of Theudas who, in turn, was a disciple of Paul himself. Like many other so-called Gnostics—those who claimed special knowledge handed down to them privately and who were scornful of the material world—Valentinus claimed to possess secret wisdom coming from the apostle Paul—a man whose private encounters with the Lord were as renowned as they were recondite (see Acts 9:9–10 and 2 Cor. 12:2–4).

Sometime in the 130s, Valentinus left Alexandria for Rome. He was highly regarded among the Roman Christians and was once considered for the office of bishop. The theology of Valentinus, not easy to reconstruct, was complex and multilayered. His theology envisioned a series of worlds and celestial beings. Jesus Christ was not a human being, but was part of a Trinity. According to the *Gospel of Truth*, a second-century document possibly written by Valentinus that was only discovered in Egypt in 1945, people live in a "fog" due to their ignorance of the Father. Jesus' appearance on earth and his death on the cross were meant to bring knowledge to humans. As the document states:

> Knowledge of the Father and the revelation of his Son gave [human beings] the means of knowing. For when they saw and heard him, he let them taste him and smell him and touch the beloved Son. He appeared, informing them of the Father, the illimitable, and he inspired them with what is in the thought, doing his will.[7]

After Jesus "swallowed" death, he returned to the so-called Pleroma—the Fullness—while the church transmitted the knowledge

---

7. "The Gospel of Truth," in *The Nag Hammadi Scriptures: The International Edition*, ed. Marvin Meyer (New York: HarperOne, 2007), 42.

that the Savior gave to human beings and initiated them into the rites of the church. After Valentinus's death in the 160s, a Christian school of thought called Valentinianism coalesced around his ideas. The different churches associated with Valentinianism were heavily influenced by Greek philosophy. They shared similarities with other Christian gnostic groups and churches. In fact, from what we can piece together from a Valentinian liturgy discovered in 1945, Valentinian Christians observed the sacraments of Baptism and the Eucharist. Despite mounting opposition in the years to come, the Valentinian church persisted till the seventh century, if not later.[8]

The second controversial Christian leader we will look at in this section is Marcion, who was actually a contemporary of Valentinus in Rome. Like Valentinus, Marcion immigrated to Rome in the late 130s or early 140s. According to various reports, Marcion was a businessman from the city of Sinope in Pontus (along the Black Sea in northern Turkey). There he was the son of a Christian bishop. Upon moving to the Eternal City, Marcion made a sizeable donation of 200,000 sesterces to the Roman church. He was apparently in good standing among the leaders before being excommunicated in the year 144. There were several charges laid against Marcion by the Roman church. One of them was that Marcion was teaching that the God of the Old Testament was different from the God of Jesus Christ. A common belief among gnostic teaching, the lesser God of the Old Testament was called the Demiurge. As the one responsible for the creation of the world, the Demiurge was the creator of evil and material things, while the God of Jesus was loving and merciful. Another charge against Marcion was that he removed large portions of the Gospel of Luke and ten letters of Paul (he excluded 1 and 2 Timothy and Titus). Believing that later scribes had corrupted these

8. See Ismo Dunderberg, *Beyond Gnosticism: Myth, Lifestyle, and Society in the School of Valentinus* (New York: Columbia University Press, 2013), 7.

documents, Marcion stripped his biblical canon (the first such biblical canon, as far as we can tell) of those verses referring to the God of the Old Testament, Jesus' birth, or fulfilled prophecy. Marcion's Bible was an assortment of passages from Luke and Paul divorced from their Old Testament context.

Though certainly a product of his own times, Marcion was also an original thinker—something that got him into trouble with many other Christians. As his opponent Tertullian later wrote of him, "Marcion had an unhealthy interest in the problem of evil—the origin of it—and his perceptions were numbed by the very excess of his curiosity" (*Against Marcion* 1.2). Whereas his opponents believed that authority derived from an unbroken line of bishops who taught "the one faith" handed down to them from their forebears, Marcion reasoned away the continuity of the Hebrew Bible with the Gospels and Paul's letters. Marcion believed that the former spoke of a God who authored evil while the latter spoke only of the author of the good.

According to Marcion, there was no knowledge of Jesus before his appearance in the first century. Marcion believed that the prophecies of the Hebrew Bible were to be fulfilled in the future by the God of the Jews—not the God of Jesus Christ. These two Gods were as different as day and night, as far away from each other as good is from bad. Jesus came to earth in a body (though he was not a human being like you and I) to pay the penalty for our sins. By simply believing in Jesus, one could escape the God of the Jews and instead have eternal life with the God of Jesus—a good and kind God whose love trumped judgment.

It took about five years before the Roman church decided to excommunicate Marcion. In 144, his sizeable donation was given back to him in full to signal that the Roman church had shaken off the dust of Marcion's heresy from their sandals. Now independent of the Roman church and with seed money to boot, the Marcionites established Christian churches across the Roman Empire. From what we can tell, the Marcionite churches were similar in many ways to mainstream churches, but differed from them by believing in two Gods, rejecting most things Jewish, practicing extreme forms of asceticism, using water instead of wine in the Eucharist, allowing women to administer sacraments, and favoring the doctrine of reincarnation over resurrection.

It was immediately after the time period in which Marcion and Valentinus were active that another charismatic and controversial Christian leader was spreading his views. His name was Montanus, a man we discussed briefly in the introduction. According to later reports, Montanus began making claims about the Holy Spirit around the year 165 in the city of Pepouza. The church that Montanus founded referred to itself as the New Prophecy, or simply the Prophecy. It emphasized charismatic gifts, strict morality, the imminent return of Christ, and martyrdom. As was the case above with Valentinus and Marcion, most of the information we have about Montanus comes from his opponents—some of which emerged in the second century when he was active, but most of it coming after the Roman Empire became increasingly hostile toward non-conforming Christian bodies in the fourth century.

It is possible that Montanus was a pagan priest before becoming a convert of Christianity. What is clear, however, is that Montanus formed a group of disciples that celebrated gender equality when it came to leadership. In particular, there were two women who accompanied Montanus on his travels named Priscilla and Maximilla. Far from being his assistants, these women were colleagues who carried the same amount of authority as Montanus did. In fact, women were ordained to the office of priest in Montanist churches, just as men were. According to the Montanists, the Holy Spirit was the source of their authority, whose work was no respecter of gender.

Some scholars have interpreted Montanism as a remnant of the Christian community inspired by the book of Revelation, a book that first circulated near the province of Phrygia in Turkey. Just as Revelation lauded prophecy and visions, asceticism, and martyrdom for one's faith in Christ, so, too, the Montanists emphasized these spiritual concerns in their churches. Although Montanism has been lumped together with other Christian groups eventually dubbed heretical and out of favor with mainstream churches, they probably shared more similarities with orthodox churches than differences. One important place of difference, however, was authority. As we saw from Clement and Ignatius, the orthodox consensus was that authority derived from bishops who held the power of life and death based on their link to the apostles. The Montanists, by contrast, considered ecstatic prophets the true spiritual heirs and power brokers of the church. Bishops claiming apostolic succession were welcome to teach in Montanist churches, but the real authority was the Holy Spirit's presence in the words of prophets and prophetesses. It was this issue of authority and organization, in other words, which "led to the struggle and the eventual breach" between the catholic and Montanist churches.[9]

The Montanist church spread quickly outside of modern Turkey and into Rome and North Africa. As it did so, it clashed with the Catholic Church, which was suspicious of the charismatic leaders of the movement. Despite ample criticism, Montanist churches existed for centuries after their founding in the second century. From the third century onward, there were Montanist bishops overseeing their own cluster of churches. Yet, over time, the number of Montanist

---

9. Rex Butler, *The New Prophecy and "New Visions": Evidence of Montanism in The Passion of Perpetua and Felicitas* (Washington, D.C.: The Catholic University of America Press, 2006), 17.

churches declined. The real "death-blow" of the Montanist churches came in the sixth century. What happened then? In the year 550, the bishop of Ephesus "entered Pepouza . . . , destroying the shrine containing the bones of Montanus, Maximilla, and Priscilla, and confiscating the Montanist cathedral and all other Montanist property"[10] in behalf of the imperial church under the Byzantine Emperor Justinian. Montanism was wiped off the face of the map.

Counterattack in the Writings of Irenaeus and Tertullian (Early and Late Second Century)

Although each the three Christian leaders discussed above attracted a considerable following, they had their detractors. Irenaeus and Tertullian denounced both Valentinus and Marcion, condemning the churches they founded as seedbeds of Christian heresy. The same cannot be said consistently of Montanus, however. It is debatable how heretical the Montanist church was in relation to Gnostic and Marcionite churches.[11] Tertullian, in fact, joined the Montanist church later in his life, just as many Montanist churches joined Catholic Churches in the decades to come. For this reason, and because Montanism was briefly discussed in the introduction, this final section we will concentrate on how Irenaeus and Tertullian responded to Valentinus and Marcion.

Irenaeus was a native of the Roman province of Asia, and he grew up within the historic Christian community in what is now Turkey. Although Irenaeus found himself in Rome in the middle of the second century, he was selected bishop of Lyons in modern France after the current bishop, Pothinus, was martyred in 177. A prolific writer, Irenaeus's most well-known work was called *Against*

---

10. William Tabbernee, *Fake Prophecy and Polluted Sacraments: Ecclesiastical and Imperial Reactions to Montanism* (Leiden, The Netherlands: Brill, 2007), xxxi.
11. For exceptions to this notion, see Tabbernee, *Fake Prophecy and Polluted Sacraments*, 41.

Heresies, a document written in about the year 185 that greatly impacted the development of Christianity. For our present purposes, the document is important due to its ample discussion of church authority. Irenaeus not only affirmed apostolic succession, but he also appealed to tradition and a complete canon of Scripture as proof that any given church was legitimate.

According to Irenaeus, the church professes the one Christian faith based on the teachings of Christ as they had been passed down faithfully from the apostles. As if to gain victory in his verbal sparring match with his opponents, Irenaeus launched into his argument in the very first lines of his book by unrolling the historic faith of the church—and thereby condemning any person who contradicted it, whether Valentinus in his denial of an incarnate Savior or Marcion in his belief in two Gods:

> The Church, though dispersed through the whole world, even to the ends of the earth, has received from the apostles and their disciples this faith: (She believes) in one God, the Father Almighty, Maker of heaven, and earth, and the sea, and all things that are in them; and in one Christ Jesus, the Son of God, who became incarnate for our salvation; and in the Holy Spirit, who proclaimed through the prophets the dispensations of God, and the advents, and the birth from a virgin, and the passion, and the resurrection from the dead, and the ascension into heaven in the flesh of the beloved Christ Jesus, our Lord, and His (future) manifestation from heaven in the glory of the Father "to gather all things in one," (Ephesians 1:10) and to raise up anew all flesh of the whole human race (1.10.1)[12]

Regardless of whether a church exists in Germany, Ireland, Egypt, Libya, or Iran, "the faith is one and the same,"[13] and there is nothing that can be added or taken away from it. Irenaeus also argued that

---

12. This is based on the translation in Kevin Kaatz, ed. *Voices of Early Christianity: Documents from the Origins of Christianity* (Santa Barbara, CA: Greenwood, 2013), 171.

13. Ibid., 172.

there are only four valid gospels, which must be accepted in their entirety: Matthew, Mark, Luke, and John. Envisioning someone in his mind such as Marcion who only accepted bowdlerized parts of the Gospel of Luke, Irenaeus went on to criticize those who judge Scripture: "When [perceived heretics] are refuted by Scripture, they turn to accuse the Scriptures themselves—the text is not good, they are not authentic, they contradict each other."[14]

Irenaeus went on to claim that groups like the Gnostics and Marcionites are not "in agreement either with Scripture or with Tradition."[15] Instead, these rival churches cobble together pieces of the Scriptures advantageous to their distinct beliefs while rejecting others that contradict them. What's more, rather than accepting the public and manifest faith of the apostles, the "heretics" have devised their own doctrines like slippery snakes, slithering away from the one true faith. For Irenaeus, making a case against heretics was rather basic: for even "if the apostles themselves had not left us the Scriptures, should we not have been obliged to follow the order of tradition which they handed down to those to whom they committed the churches?"[16] Rather than follow the clear teachings of the apostles or that of the Scriptures, Irenaeus regarded heresies as recent inventions, hatched decades after the true faith had been handed down to the faithful churches and safeguarded by legitimate bishops. For him, Scripture and tradition—as preserved by legitimately ordained bishops—guaranteed right doctrine and practice.

The arguments of Irenaeus were ably taken up by Tertullian. Tertullian was one of the most prolific authors in the early church. Trained in philosophy and law in Rome, Tertullian returned to his

14. *The Library of Christian Classics*, vol. 5, *Early Latin Theology*, trans. S. L. Greenslade (Philadelphia: The Westminster Press, 1961), 67.
15. Ibid., 68.
16. Ibid., 69.

native Carthage in the 190s. Although Tertullian wrote many books against his opponents, we will focus on his books *Against Marcion* and *Prescription against the Heretics*, both written around the year 200. Tertullian, like Irenaeus's work from which he constructed many of his arguments, attacked Marcion's belief in two Gods rather than one, his disdain for the Old Testament, his penchant for human reasoning and novelty, and his use of select portions of the New Testament. To a larger extent, Tertullian attacked heretics in general for deviating from what he considered to be the standard norm of Christianity.

In Tertullian's estimation, Marcion encapsulated what it meant to be a heretic. Formerly in good standing with the church and under its authority, Marcion later rejected that one true faith for one of his own invention. In his book *Against Marcion*, Tertullian wrote that "a heretic may from his case be designated as one who, forsaking that which was prior, afterwards chose out for himself that which was not in times past."[17] The same notion is found in *Prescription against the Heretics*. "We Christians," Tertullian argued, "are forbidden to introduce anything on our own authority or to choose what someone else introduces on his own authority. Our authorities are the Lord's apostles, and they in turn chose to introduce nothing on their own authority."[18]

Like Irenaeus, Tertullian understood authority to derive from "a deposit of faith" that was preserved and transmitted from the time of Christ to the present. While Tertullian focused less on this transmission of faith from apostles to legitimate bishops, he clearly divided right theology from wrong theology, Christian theology from pagan philosophy. "What has Jerusalem to do with Athens," Tertullian famously asked in *Prescription against the Heretics*, "the

---

17. Kaatz., ed., *Voices of Early Christianity*, 177.
18. Bart Ehrman, ed., *After the New Testament: A Reader in Early Christianity* (New York and Oxford: Oxford University Press, 1999), 212.

Church with the Academy, the Christian with the heretics?"[19] Nothing at all. Authority in the Christian church came from the acceptance and teaching of the tradition handed down from the time of Christ, while novelty and human speculation was reserved for pagan philosophers. For orthodox Christians, Tertullian continued, "we begin believing that there is nothing else which we have to believe."[20] We have Scriptures as well as what he and many other early Christians called "the rule of faith," the tradition roughly equivalent to the deposit of truth coming from Christ and the earliest Christians. Heretics, by rejecting both Scripture (whether in part or in whole) and the rule of faith, forfeit the right to claim any ownership of these twin sources since they are cut off from the source of their authority, Christ himself.

Tertullian regarded the theology of Valentinus and Marcion as opposite sides of the same heretical coin. Whereas Marcion was the equivalent of a theological butcher who discarded the edible portions of the Bible's meat in favor of the gristle and undesirable parts, Valentinus evinced a juvenile understanding of how to read a piece of literature as well as offering a perverted way of systematizing theology. As Tertullian wrote of the two Christian men:

> One man [Marcion] perverts Scripture with his hand, another [Valentinus] with his exegesis. If Valentinus seems to have used the whole Bible, he laid violent hands on the truth with just as much cunning as Marcion. Marcion openly and nakedly used the knife, not the pen, massacring Scripture to suit his own material. Valentinus spared the text, since he did not invent scriptures to suit his matter, but matter to suit the Scriptures. Yet he took away, and added more, by taking away the proper meanings of particular words and by adding fantastic arrangements.[21]

19. Ibid., 213.
20. Ibid., 213.
21. Ibid., 217.

Pressing Paul's dictum to "become all things to all people" (1 Cor. 9:22) to its absurd limits, Tertullian criticized perceived heretics like Valentinus and Marcion for not adequately distinguishing baptized Christians from catechumens, and catechumens from non-Christians. To their shame, "They are in communion with everyone everywhere,"[22] and thus, in Tertullian's estimation, with no one nowhere.

Conclusion: Apostolic Succession Legitimizes Churches

In the past several decades, our understanding of the early church has changed considerably. Due to the discovery of ancient documents and the recovery of artifacts, scholars now have a better understanding of the widespread diversity of the early church. Far from being a one-size-fits-all institution, churches and Christian figures advanced all kinds of rival theories about God and what it meant to be a "Christian." When it comes to the issue of authority in the early church—an escalating concern from the second century onward—we have seen that there was no one single response to the question of who has authority in the church. While the so-called Gnostic Christians accentuated secret knowledge, Marcionite Christians lauded human reasoning, and Montanist Christians reveled in spiritual ecstasy, more mainstream Christians derived their authority from bishops and the so-called rule of faith.

From the second century onward, this mainstream group of Christians, who later came to be called catholic or orthodox Christians (and only later, as today, Catholic and Orthodox Christians), prevailed in the Roman Empire. Their victory over the perceived heresies of Gnosticism, Marcionism, and Montanism (as well as others) was apparent in many ways, not least in the fact

22. Ibid., 217.

that we have precious little of the writings from these groups and a treasure-trove of writings from mainstream Christians. Despite initial diversity, the mounting consensus was that authority derived from legitimate bishops who could trace their spiritual lineage all the way back to the apostles, who had safeguarded the precious and unchangeable doctrines of the church handed down to them from generation to generation like a chain with no missing links. Any teaching that deviated from the doctrinal consensus of authoritatively ordained bishops flirted with heresy, and those who openly rejected the authority of such bishops were considered heretics.

3

What Happens to Christians Who Backslide?

It was the year 203. Two women from the city of Carthage in North Africa, Perpetua and Felicitas, were arrested along with three other men by Roman authorities. The two women were catechumens, meaning that they had yet to be baptized into the church. Perpetua was a Roman noblewoman, and Felicitas was her slave. Both were willing to die for their Christian faith, but there was a problem: Roman law did not allow execution of pregnant women, and both were expecting. It is a testimony of their unwavering faith that both women ignored pleas for them to make pagan sacrifice in order to deliver their children and raise them in safety. Shortly after entering prison, Perpetua delivered her child, and Felicitas, in answer to prayer, gave birth earlier than expected.

At this early time in the church's past, the title of "confessor" was being used to describe a Christian who risked imprisonment or death by confessing his or her faith and refusing to make pagan sacrifices. Confessors were so highly regarded among early Christians that they were considered martyrs even before being killed. Because of her status as a confessor, Perpetua was told that God would respond in favor to her request for a vision. This God did. It was revealed that she would become a martyr. In the spring of 203, in the public arena in the large city of Carthage, Perpetua and Felicitas were delighted to be mauled by wild animals and finished off by gladiators.

The Question of Backsliding

The story of Perpetua and Felicitas was a highly celebrated one. These two young Christian women were venerated as martyrs and believed to possess the ability to intercede for Christians living on earth. The same cannot be said, however, for many other Christian women and men prosecuted in the early church. Despite the many Christians who resolutely pursued martyrdom, there were many more who backslid, that is, who renounced their faith in the face of hardship. In this chapter, we will explore responses to the following question: what is to be done with those who lapse in their faith at the threat of arrest, death, or some other punishment? Although prosecution of Christians occurred across the ancient world, we will concentrate on North Africa. As we do so, we will learn that backsliding precipitated a great schism in the North African church. It led to profound disagreements about whether, or in what way, Christians could be brought back into the good graces of the church.

A Short History of Christianity in North Africa

The earliest evidence we have of Christianity in the northwestern part of Africa is dated to the late second century. We know, of course, that the church in Africa was much older than this, with origins likely going all the way back to the second half of the first century. The context for our earliest report of the church in this area is that of prosecution. It was the summer of 180. Five women and seven Christian men from the village of Scilli, near Carthage, had been arrested. Each of their names suggests that they were local Africans, not immigrant Christians. The Roman proconsul, a man named Vigelius Saturninus, interrogated these twelve Christians for refusing to swear by the Roman emperor and offered them pardon if they cooperated. Upon their refusal, they gave thanks to God for the honor to become martyrs and they were each speedily beheaded.

Although Christians were not constantly hunted down in the Roman Empire, there were bursts of prosecution. The first such burst occurred in the year 202. According to the *Augustan History* (17.1), a history of the Roman emperors written during the second and third centuries, Emperor Severus issued an edict prohibiting conversion to Christianity. It was possibly this edict that led to the condemnation and death of Perpetua and Felicitas in the year 203. The next burst of prosecution occurred in the year 250. The emperor was a man named Decius, who ruled from 249 to 251. At this time in Roman history, the empire was fragmented, the economy was faltering, and morale was low. In order to jumpstart a failing empire and unite what was once an invincible kingdom, Decius issued an edict requiring all citizens to make public sacrifices to the Roman gods.[1]

Because Emperor Caracalla had made all inhabitants of the Roman Empire citizens in the year 212, Christians were required to obey the edict. Although the edict was not directed against the church as a whole, many Christians fell victim. Authorities apparently targeted well-known clergymen; each of the bishops of Antioch, Jerusalem, and Rome was arrested and killed. According to the edict, citizens who complied with the ritual were given a certificate, called a *libellus* in Latin. We have dozens of these certificates from this time period, letting us know that many people complied with the emperor's edict.

---

1. According to Eusebius (*History of the Church* 6.39), Decius required the sacrifice out of hate for Emperor Philip, whom Decius had just defeated, on account of Eusebius's belief that Philip was the first Christian emperor. It's also possible that Decius was requiring the empire-wide sacrifice as a celebration of Rome's one-thousand year anniversary.

Those who refused to comply with the edict risked banishment, forced labor, imprisonment, or death. A few years later, in 257, Emperor Valerian renewed the prosecution under Decius, though it was short lived due to the emperor's premature death.

The next empire-wide prosecution occurred in the years 303 and 304 under the reign of Emperor Diocletian, a man believed to be married to a Christian but whose possible fear of the future emperor, Galerius, led to his edicts. Diocletian ordered the destruction of churches, the banning of services, and the imprisonment of Christian clergy. (As such, it is sometimes called the "Great Persecution.") By this time in Rome's history, the empire was only a glimmer of its former glory. Many attributed Christian refusal to acknowledge the Roman gods as the cause of the empire's moribund state, so an empire-wide edict was issued requiring citizens to placate the gods and attempt to salvage the once-mighty Roman Empire.

Response to North African Prosecution in the Thought of Tertullian (Early Second Century)

In order to better understand the cause of backsliding in the North African church, we will briefly examine the writings of the most prolific author in Carthage: Tertullian, a man we met in Chapter Two since his life spans the second and third centuries. In response to the question of what to do in the midst of Christian prosecution, Tertullian wrote a treatise in the year 212. As was typical of Tertullian, he offered a no non-sense approach to the issue. For Tertullian, everything that happens in life is a result of God's will. If God permits prosecution of Christians, it is because God wants to sift through individual believers, "separating the grain of the martyrs from the chaff of the deniers" (1.4).[2] Whoever flees from prosecution,

---

2. Tertullian, *De Fuga in Persecutione*. References in the body of the text will be given based on the translation from this source: http://www.tertullian.org/anf/anf04/anf04-23.htm.

therefore, is attempting to stymie God's will for his or her life. As Tertullian reasons, "if persecution proceeds from God, in no way will it be our duty to flee from what has God as its author" (4.1).

Regarding the question of whether prosecution is the work of God or the devil, Tertullian argues that both are at work. First, it is God who wills prosecution of the church in order to strengthen it. For after the church is prosecuted, the church's faith is "more zealous in preparation, and better disciplined in fasts, and meetings, and prayers, and lowliness, in brotherly-kindness and love, in holiness and temperance" (1.6). But although prosecution is imputed to God for the betterment of the church, prosecution proceeds from the devil, who is bent on destroying the church in vile and violent ways. The devil destroys the church through his own power, given by God, and by appropriating power given by free human beings, including Christians. In this way, God is the origin of Christian prosecution while the devil is the agent of this prosecution.

Tertullian then proceeds to address the major issue at hand, namely, what the correct response should be to those who flee during prosecution. In short, Tertullian asserts that those who flee, though trying to persuade themselves of their good intentions, have effectively denied their faith. As he writes, "If you are not willing to confess, you are not willing to suffer; and to be unwilling to confess is to deny" (5.2). To flee is to follow one's own will, while to remain and confess one's faith is to submit to God's will. And as if to make his case unassailable, Tertullian then lists various passages in the New Testament, all of which confirm that Jesus and the Spirit-filled apostles always endured prosecution in accordance with God's will rather than "take to our heels" and flee out of harm's way (9.2). By fleeing and thereby giving oneself over to the devil, Christians deny the very one who bought them and thereby become slaves all over again rather than free people in Christ. Finally, for those who attempt to bribe authorities for certificates of compliance, they are no different from those who made the sacrifice themselves. As Tertullian gave as his parting words,

> It is not asked who is ready to follow the broad way, but who is ready to follow the narrow way. . . . And they who have received [God] will neither stoop to flee from persecution nor to buy it off, for they have the Lord Himself, One who will stand by us to aid us in suffering, as well as to be our mouth when we are put to the question (14.3).

Tertullian was a man of principle. He did not mince words when it came to the issue of prosecution in the church. Although later Christians in North Africa would build upon the thought of Tertullian, they would face new challenges that required slightly different responses to the issue at hand. We might say that Tertullian's writing represented the Christian ideal, though many Christians fell short of this. As we shall see below, the fact that most Christians in North Africa took a different approach to prosecution—that is, they compromised their faith, according to Tertullian—meant that Christian leaders faced any number of practical issues during the third century about how to reconcile backsliders to the church, if at all.

The Classification of Backsliders during the Decian Persecution (250s)

The emperor Decius issued an edict requiring citizens to given an offering, say a prayer, offer incense, or pour a libation to Roman gods on January 1, 250. The command to make sacrifice to a pagan god was a clear act of idolatry and apostasy in the eyes of many in the church. As such, many men and women confessed their faith and therefore risked censure and death. These confessing Christians lost property, suffered torture, died in prison, or were banished to work in the mines in faraway lands.

Did most Christians backslide or remain steadfast? It's impossible say with complete accuracy, but it appears that many compromised their faith. It was not unheard of to see bishops guiding their clergy, fathers gathering their families, and patrons leading their clients toward the forum to offer animal sacrifices, pour out libations, or burn incense to the Roman gods in front of the authorities. In the year 250, Bishop Dionysius of Alexander, who went underground when the edict was issued, indicated in a letter to the bishop of Antioch how cowardly many Christians conducted themselves in the face of this ordeal:

> Summoned by name, [many Christians] approached the unclean, unholy sacrifices. Some came white-faced and trembling, as if they were not going to sacrifice but to be sacrificed themselves as victims to the idols, so that the large crowd of spectators heaped scorn upon them and it was obvious that they were utter cowards, afraid to die and afraid to sacrifice. Others ran more readily towards the altars, trying to prove by their fearlessness that they had never been Christians. Of these, the Lord had declared long before with complete truth that they would be saved with difficulty.[3]

There were various names for those who complied with the Roman edict, leading to a veritable caste system of Christian apostasy. The general term for Christian backsliders was *lapsi*, "apostates." With a greater degree of precision, those who actually made a pagan sacrifice, such as the "cowards" Bishop Dionysius referred to, were called *sacrificati*, "sacrificers." The individuals who refused to make a pagan sacrifice but who nevertheless bribed authorities for a certificate or simply forged one were called *libellatici*, "certificate buyers." The Christians who only offered incense on the altar before statues of pagan gods were called *thurificati*, "incense burners."

3. Quoted in Eusebius, *History of the Church* 6.41 (London: Penguin, 1989), 212.

Finally, those who, for whatever reason, were not publicly called upon to obey the edict were called *stantes*, "those remaining" in Latin.

Which of these Christians had committed the worst crime, and what were their punishments? As might be imagined, there were no immediately agreed upon answers to these questions. Although some of the *lapsi* never returned to the church, there were plenty who did. And when the *lapsi* returned, the bishops had to decide how, if at all, these backsliders could again become children of Mother Church. What was church leadership to do?

One of the ways that the *lapsi* reentered the church was by appealing to their Christian counterparts—the *confessores*, "confessors," and the *martyres*, "martyrs." As mentioned above, confessors were those who had "confessed" their faith under pressure. They regularly underwent punishment and torture as a result. Confessors who were condemned to die were regarded as living martyrs. As Bishop Cyprian, who fled Carthage during the Decian persecution out of self-described "affection" for his flock said to confessors in prison awaiting death: "although you are still placed in the flesh, it is the life not of the present world, but of the future, that you now live."[4] After these confessors became martyrs, it was understood that they were welcomed into heaven as celebrities with spiritual privileges. Although dead and without a body, the early church believed that martyrs were close to God and that they could intercede for human beings on earth. Prayers were offered to martyrs by the living, and the martyrs could answer these prayers. It was a divine transaction. The martyrs were the patrons, and those Christians praying to them for favors were their clients.

4. Cyprian, *Epistle* 15. http://www.newadvent.org/fathers/050615.htm.

Figure 3.1. Names and Descriptions of Groups during the Persecution	
Names in Latin	**Description**
Episcopi ("bishops") and *presbyteri* ("priests")	According to clergy and laypeople, could forgive sin of *lapsi* based on apostolic succession
Confessores and *martyres*	According to laypeople (but not necessarily clergy), could forgive sin of *lapsi* based on holiness under prosecution
Sacrificati, libellatici, and *thurificati*	Had to have sin forgiven by clergy or by confessor before being allowed reentry into the Catholic Church
Stantes	Those who were never called on to make any sacrifices during prosecutions and so remained silent

In order to reenter church, some of the *lapsi* begged forgiveness from confessors. These *lapsi* requested letters of peace under the conviction that approval by a confessor was sufficient for readmission into the church. Although this worked for some, some bishops, including Bishop Cyprian, ignored the letters and only allowed the truly penitent *lapsi* to return to the church at the moment of death or during a severe illness.

As one historian of early African Christianity understated, "The bishop's authority was certainly put to the test through these events."[5] Between the years 251 and 254, there were four councils that met in the city of Carthage to address the very practical matters facing the North African churches. Although priests and deacons accompanied each bishop, bishops wielded the authority. By matter of principle, these various councils encouraged the *lapsi* to make public penance for their sins of denying their faith while under pressure. At the council in 251, it was decided that the *libellatici*, those who either bribed authorities for a *libellus* or who simply forged one, were to be immediately readmitted into the church upon penance. The *sacrificati* and *thurificati*, by contrast, due to the seriousness of their sins, were

5. Francois Decret, *Early Christianity in North Africa*, trans. Edward Smither (Eugene, OR: Cascade, 2009), 55.

only to be reunited with Mother Church at the moment of death. At the next council meeting in 252, however, the bishops agreed to let the *sacrificati* and *thurificati* back into church based on continued penance since their lapse in faith. At the same time, the *sacrificati* and *thurificati* who were clergy were barred from the priesthood.

Disagreement About What to Do with Christian Backsliders (250s)

The most outspoken and influential bishop during this third-century ordeal in North Africa was a nobleman named Cyprian. A recent and very wealthy convert to Christianity, Cyprian had become bishop the same year Decius assumed the Roman throne, the year 249. As was the case in other parts of the world, the bishops of leading cities—such as Alexandria, Antioch, Constantinople, Carthage, Rome—tended to be more highly regarded than those of less significant cities. Partly due to the prestige associated with his office and partly due to his own temperament and aristocratic background, Cyprian came to dominate many of the discussions on what to do with the *lapsi*. Well aware that the Decian persecution was targeting prominent bishops—indeed, Bishop Fabian of Rome had just been killed—Cyprian made the controversial decision of fleeing from the city rather than risking arrest. Along with some local clergy and laymen, Cyprian departed Carthage just as a warrant for his arrest was being issued. From a safe distance, Cyprian corresponded with his flock through a spate of letters over the course of fifteen months.

Although Cyprian was well-respected among North African churches, he had his naysayers. One of them was a clergyman named Novatus, who had many friends that likewise opposed Cyprian's rule. In the absence of Bishop Cyprian, a schismatic church emerged that offered a different approach to the whole backsliding controversy. At first, this rival church took a much more lenient posture toward the apostates. Rather than the more time-consuming process required by Cyprian and many other bishops, this rival church offered immediate forgiveness to the *lapsi*. There was also another rival Christian contention in Carthage. This group was associated with a priest named Novatian, who was serving as the active bishop of Rome after the death of Bishop Fabian in January of 250.

Before long, there were three claimants to the office of bishop in Carthage: Cyprian, the lawful bishop who had fled; a man named Fortunatus who urged leniency in the matter of the *lapsi*, mostly since he himself had fled and because most of the Christians under his care were *lapsi*; and a man named Maximus, who was part of a more rigorous schismatic church associated with the Novatianists—those who wanted to maintain the purity of the church by excommunicating the *lapsi*. When Cyprian returned to Carthage in March of 251 after fifteen months of hiding, he encountered a fragmented church. He convened a council of bishops in April of that year, which excommunicated the two rival bishops of Carthage (illegitimate claimants to the office of bishop were called antibishops), Fortunatus and Maximus. However, this did not at all end the controversy surrounding the *lapsi*. Now there were primarily two Christian sets of churches that strongly disagreed with one another over the matter at hand. We may refer to them as the Catholic Church and the Novatianist church. While the former were the moderates regarding the issue of the backsliders, the latter were rigorists.

The most prominent representative of the moderates was Bishop Cyprian of Carthage. The moderates were supported by the majority of bishops. These men regarded Novatian and the church he founded as schismatic. Moderates also appealed to the story of Saint Peter, whom Jesus rehabilitated after Peter backslid during Jesus' trial after denying three times that he was associated with Jesus. Rather than rebuke and excommunicate Peter, Jesus admitted Peter back into fellowship after his resurrection. The moderates were also guided by Jesus' words in his so-called parable of the weeds. In this parable, when askedwhether the weeds should be uprooted from the garden, Jesus replied:

> No; for in gathering the weeds you would uproot the wheat along with them. Let both of them [wheat and weeds] grow together until the harvest; and at harvest I will tell the reapers, Collect the weeds first and bind them in bundles to be burned, but gather the wheat into my barn. (Matt. 13:29–30)

According to the moderates, the church was destined to be full of wheat and weeds—*confessores* and *lapsi*, the faithful and the faithless—until the time Jesus would return. However, it was not the task of the church to uproot the weeds before harvest time but to allow them to grow side-by-side with the wheat. In fact, it was arguable that the *lapsi* were not weeds at all since they were repentant of their sins.

According to Bishop Cyprian, "the bride of Christ cannot be made an adulterous. She is undefiled and chaste." For Cyprian, one of the major points of contention between the Catholics and the Novatianists was more about unity and division than about purity or impurity (though the two were related, to be sure). Cyprian believed that the sin of schism was far worse than the sin of apostasy. As he wrote, "To break the peace and concord of Christ is to go against Christ."[6] While apostasy could be forgiven, separation could not for the simple reason that schismatics were outside of the bounds of the church. Therefore they were unable to perform the requirements

---

6. Cyprian, *On the Unity of the Church* 6, in *Early Latin Theology*, vol. 5, *Selections from Tertullian, Cyprian, Ambrose, and Jerome*, trans. S. L. Greenslade (Philadelphia: Westminster Press, 1956), 127–28.

necessary to be restored to the community. As Cyprian famously declared, "outside of the church, there is no salvation."[7]

On the other side of the controversy was the Novatianist church. This was the more rigorous of the two main groups. The Novatianist church was connected to Novatian. It was this man who had been consecrated as a rival bishop in Rome in the spring of 251 after the vast majority of bishops selected someone known to be more lenient when it came to backsliders, named Bishop Cornelius. Although some Novatianists eventually reentered the Catholic Church, many refused—sowing the seeds of a separatist church that outlived Novatian by several centuries. This Novatianist church was regarded as schismatic by the Catholic Church and, over time, Novatian was unjustly objectified as Satan incarnate.

According to the Novatianists, the church was the holy bride of Christ. Impurity was not to be tolerated, and it was incumbent upon the leaders of the church to guard its purity before the Lord. The Novatianists were all too aware of the moral laxity of the church. It was their belief that a return to the simpler and more rigorous disciplines of the first generation of Christians was needed to safeguard the church's holiness. Like the moderates, the rigorists appealed to many passages in the Bible. One of their more prominent passages was found in Heb. 6:4–6:

> For it is impossible to restore again to repentance those who have once been enlightened, and have tasted the heavenly gift, and have shared in the Holy Spirit, and have tasted the goodness of the word of God and the powers of the age to come, and then have fallen away, since on their own they are crucifying again the Son of God and are holding him up to contempt.

7. Cyprian, *Epistle* 72.21.

For the Novatianists, these verses from the book of Hebrews were crystal-clear proof that backsliders could not repent and gain salvation after falling away from the faith. By allowing apostates back into the church, they were debauching the body of Christ.

Both Novatian and Cyprian were strong-willed men whose feud was only cut short by death. Novatian went to the grave believing that Cyprian was part of an impure church, while Cyprian believed that Novatian was part of no church at all. Their feud notwithstanding, Emperor Valerian renewed prosecution of Christians in the year 257. As before, prominent bishops were targeted, and so both Cyprian and Novatian were arrested. Both of them confessed their faith and died in the year 258 as martyrs.

Conclusion: Backsliders Allowed under Most Conditions

Despite some fringe groups like the Novatianists, there was nevertheless a mounting consensus forming among mainstream Christians that backsliders could be readmitted into the church provided that they do so under appropriate authority and according to strict regulations. In the end, the bishops (particularly Catholic or [Eastern] Orthodox bishops) were the real victors of the debate about whether, or in what way, to rehabilitate those who had lapsed in their faith. There was a long tradition holding that the unity of the church was found in the "college" of the bishops. This proved to be the case when it came to deciding what to do about Christian backsliders. As Cyprian stated in one of his letters, "the Church is made up of the bishops and clergy and all who stand firm."[8] The bishops were the foundation of the church who alone determined how the *lapsi* would be restored.

---

8. Cyprian, *Epistle* 33.

The resolve of the bishops to readmit the *lapsi* into the fold of the church led to the development of the penitential system. Christians who re-sought full communion with the church were given a very clear set of steps to follow. These steps of rehabilitation were prescribed and supervised under the authority of legitimate bishops. Over time, there came to be four classes of penitents, each of which class was progressive in nature: (1) *weepers*, who had to remain outside of church services and weep for their sin; (2) *hearers*, who were allowed to stand in the back of a service but dismissed before the administration of the sacraments; (3) *kneelers*, who were able to attend church services but were to remain kneeling at all times; and (4) *bystanders*, who were allowed full participation in the church other than the Eucharist. Depending on the gravity of the sin—in this case, the sin of apostasy—penitent believers could progress from being a weeper to a bystander and then to becoming a full member of the church community over the course of several weeks to several years.

4

Are Jesus and the Holy Spirit Divine?

It was the year 318. A Christian senior priest was presenting his views about God to his bishop, a man named Alexander. They were both living in the cosmopolitan city of Alexandria, Egypt, where tradition held that John Mark had preached the gospel of Jesus Christ in the first century. It was in the Baucalis section of Alexandria that John Mark was believed to have been martyred for the faith, the very neighborhood where this senior priest lived and ministered, possibly at the very parish that housed the relics of John Mark.

The relationship between this respected priest, named Arius, and his presiding bishop was deteriorating. After listening to a sermon by the bishop, Arius accused him of teaching the existence of two Gods, God the Father and God the Son. Arius felt that his suspicions were confirmed after hearing Bishop Alexander repeat the interesting phrase, "always a God, always a Son." Although Alexander was attempting to preserve the Son's divinity, this phrase struck Arius as heretical. It was unthinkable to him that God had an equal. As he later wrote in a letter to a former classmate who was now a prominent bishop, "we are persecuted because we have said the Son has a beginning but God has no beginning."[1]

In order to resolve this dispute, Alexander convened a synod of around one-hundred Egyptian bishops who promptly excommunicated Arius. The bishops composed a detailed retraction of each of Arius' theological statements that defied orthodox teaching. Despite the clear ruling by the bishops, however, this matter was not at all resolved. Arius, after all, was a man of passion, and he had friends in high places. Before long, the feud between Arius and Alexander spilled over into the entire Greek-speaking church. Churches divided and violence ensued. For the welfare of the empire, the emperor was forced to bring a resolution to this theological issue.

The Question of Divinity

The controversy between Arius and Alexander was one of the greatest in the early church. This argument went to the core of Christianity—the nature of salvation—eliciting responses from the most gifted and learned theologians in the fourth century. Discussion about the deity of the Son was so foundational to Christianity that it quickly flowed into discussion about the deity of the Holy Spirit. In short, the question before the church was the following: were Jesus and the Holy Spirit of the same stuff as God the Father? That is, were these two divine? In this chapter, we will break this larger question into two smaller parts: first, the more urgent question about whether Jesus was God and, then, the question emanating out of that one, whether the Holy Spirit was God. We will see that there were a

---

1. Because most of Arius's writing was destroyed, we are reliant upon his opponents, who preserved portions of his writings in their treatises directed against him. Quoted in Theodoret, *Church History* 1.5. See http://www.fourthcentury.com/index.php/urkunde-1.

variety of Christian responses given to this larger question, though a consensus was reached by the end of the fourth century.

The Theology of Arius (c. 320s–330s)

Arius was probably born in Libya in the middle of the third century. Ancient reports indicate that he was intelligent, disciplined, popular among the people, and well connected. According to a contemporary description, Arius "spoke gently, and people found him persuasive and flattering."[2] Arius was a gifted thinker who had studied under a man named Lucian of Antioch while in Syria. Several years before his dispute with Alexander, Arius had returned to his native Africa and become a parish priest in Alexandria. The theology of Arius was informed by common sense and the biblical text. Arius's axiomatic conviction was that God was one, and that he was absolutely transcendent. As he and his supporters wrote in a letter to Bishop Alexandria around the year 320, "We acknowledge One God, alone unbegotten, alone everlasting, alone without beginning, alone true, alone having immortality . . . , unalterable and unchangeable."[3] Based on his prior conviction of the existence, oneness, and unchangeableness of God, Arius appealed to various passages in the Bible hinting at Jesus' subordination and begotten-ness, such as the following:

> As he was setting out on a journey, a man ran up and knelt before him, and asked him, "Good Teacher, what must I do to inherit eternal life?" Jesus said to him, "Why do you call me good? No one is good but God alone." (Mark 10:17)

---

2. Quoted in Rowan Williams, *Arius: Heresy and Tradition* (Grand Rapids, MI: Eerdmans, 1987; reprint), 32.
3. Quoted in Athanasius, *On the Synods* 16. See http://www.fourthcentury.com/index.php/urkunde-6.

"If you loved me, [Jesus said to his disciples], you would rejoice that I am going to the Father, because the Father is greater than I." (John 14:28)

Biblical passages such as these made it clear to Arius that the Son was neither co-eternal with God the Father nor of the same exact substance. To the chagrin of his opponents, Arius had many more biblical passages (such as Prov. 8:22, Acts 2:36, Heb. 1:2, etc.) in his arsenal that he used to emphasize the subordination of the Son to the Father.

The Theology of Arius in a Nutshell

1. God is one and indivisible.
2. The Son is a creature—though a perfect creature.
3. The Son was created outside of time and before anything else was created.
4. The Son was not "truly God."

According to Arius, the Son was the highest of creation, born outside of time and before the ages existed. Based on the Son's unique position within creation, he was the inheritor of all things, though he was not fully God. As Heb. 1:2 put it, the Son was "appointed heir of all things, through whom he also created the worlds." Arius further explained his theology in a letter to his bishop by stating that the Son

> was begotten apart from time by the Father, and created and founded before the ages, was not in existence before his generation, but was begotten apart from time before all things, and he alone came into existence from the Father. For he is neither eternal nor co-eternal nor co-unbegotten with the Father, nor does he have his being together with the Father.

If the Son was of the same essence as the Father, Arius reasoned, this would constitute two divine beings, not one. It would be the end of monotheism. Although Arius did speak in terms of a Holy Triad of Father, Son, and Spirit, neither the Son nor the Spirit was of the same substance of the Father. It was a lopsided triad—a Trinity of unequal partners. The Son could be called God's Son in a certain sense, but the Son was "not truly God."[4]

Arius was a passionate man whose theological beliefs spilled over in song. The catchy Greek hymn that he composed was sung loudly and proudly along the streets of Alexandria by his supporters.

> He who is without beginning made the Son a beginning of created things.
> He produced him as a son for himself by begetting him.
> He [the son] has none of the distinct characteristics of God's own being
> For he is not equal to, nor is he of the same being (*homoousios*) as him
> …
>
> So there is a Triad, not in equal glories.
> Their beings are not mixed together among themselves.
> As far as their glories, one infinitely more glorious than the other.
> The Father in his essence is a foreigner to the Son, because he exists without beginning.[5]

The decision to put theology to song was an effective way to communicate this theology and also to garner support from the populace.

The First Council of Nicea (325)

The Council of Nicea was convened by Emperor Constantine in the year 325 to address, in part, the widespread controversy caused by the theology of Arius. The emperor selected Nicea (current Iznik, Turkey) as the location so that he could remain close by during the deliberations, and it is reported that he actually oversaw the first and last sessions. Even though Constantine invited all of the Christian

4. Quoted in J. N. D. Kelly, *Early Christian Doctrines*, rev. ed. (New York: HarperSanFrancisco, 1978), 229.
5. Quoted in Athanasius, *Orations against the Arians* 1. See http://www.fourthcentury.com/index.php/arius-thalia-intro.

bishops within his vast empire, there were only around 300 who attended the council. Most of these bishops were Greek speakers from the East. (Constantine, though proficient in Greek, oversaw the deliberations through a Latin translator and had difficulty following along.)

The Council of Nicea was the first international event of its kind, and it's doubtful that any of the bishops knew how significant the council would be in the history of Christianity. Several of the bishops bore scars from Roman authorities, and now they found themselves cordially invited to address important theological matters under the auspices of the emperor himself. The bishops produced twenty canons of legislation on church practice, but the most prominent deliberations centered on the Arian controversy. Of the hundreds of bishops present, there were roughly three theological camps when it came to this issue, which we may loosely label as: (1) pro-Arian, (2) anti-Arian, and (3) non-Arian or semi-Arian. This first group of bishops was staunchly in agreement with the thought of Arius. These bishops believed that the Father and the Son were of a different substance or essence, and that the Father existed before the Son. The most prominent of the so-called Arian bishops were Eusebius of Nicomedia and Theognis of Nicea. Eusebius had been a classmate of Arius's under Lucian of Antioch, and they had both drunk deeply from the well of their master's thought. In fact, Arius ended the only existing letter he wrote to Eusebius as follows: "I pray that you fare well in the Lord, remembering our tribulations, fellow-Lucianist."[6] Arius never considered himself to be an independent theological renegade, but one who was part of a venerable Christian tradition.

The second group at the council was composed of anti-Arians. This group was equally matched in numbers with the pro-Arians. Arius's own bishop, Alexander of Alexandria, was of course anti-

6. http://www.fourthcentury.com/index.php/urkunde-1.

Arian, as was the unbending deacon from Alexandria named Athanasius, who would become bishop of Alexandria and the bitterest opponent of Arian thought. There were also other vocal anti-Arian bishops, including Marcellus of Ancyra and Eustathius of Antioch. As a foreshadowing of where imperial Christianity was headed, each of these men—Athanasius, Marcellus, and Eustathius—would later face exile or condemnation as a result of their dogged rejection of Arianism after the council. Finally, the last major group of bishops at the council could be considered non-Arian or semi-Arian. The men comprising this group were the majority of the bishops. They were not aware of the Arian controversy before the council, but nonetheless regarded Arius's theology as out of step with what they had learned from their bishops and with what they taught in their dioceses.

At the end of the council, a creed was formulated that delineated the essential doctrines of Christianity, particularly in reference to the Son's relationship to the Father. The creed was a clear victory for the anti-Arian party. It held that Jesus Christ was "of the same [or 'similar'—since it could mean both] exact substance" (in Greek, *homoousios*) of God the Father, that he was therefore "true God," and that he was "begotten, not made." In short, Jesus was God, and he was worthy of all the worship given to God the Father. In order to make the carefully worded language even more unassailable, the creed was punctuated with condemnations of the theology of Arius and his proponents:

> And those who say, "There was when he was not," and "Before he was begotten he was not," and that "He came into being from what is not," or those that allege, that the son of God is "of another substance or essence," or "created," or "changeable," or "alterable," these the Catholic and Apostolic Church anathematizes.[7]

7. W. H. C. Frend, *The Early Church* (Philadelphia: Fortress Press, 1987), 141.

Emperor Constantine ordered all bishops present to sign the document. While all of the anti-Arians and non-Arians were pleased to do so, some of the pro-Arian party was reluctant. Two of Arius's friends flatly refused, and Constantine excommunicated them. Two other of Arius's friends, Eusebius of Nicomedia and Theognis of Nicea, signed the creed grudgingly but did not endorse the concluding anathemas against Arius, thus finding themselves (temporarily) out of favor with the emperor.

Despite the weight of its pronouncement and the support of the emperor, the theology of Nicea would not be universally enforced in the decades to come. In hindsight, we can see that the church now found itself in a precarious position. For the first time in its history in the Roman Empire, the fate of the church was intertwined with that of the state. Depending on the religious persuasion of the emperor, Nicea was ignored, disregarded, or enforced. The church became a political plaything in the hands of Roman rulers. Emperors, adroit in matters of politics, played bishops against one another in accordance with their own interests.

But the emperors were not the only ones with political savvy. As early historian of Christianity Robert Louis Wilken explains,

> The fourth century would go down in Christian history as a time of learned and sophisticated theological debate joined with low, dirty, partisan politics, of councils opposing or contradicting other councils, of disputes over the election of bishops, and of the exile of controversial bishops.[8]

Between the years 325 and 381, factions of bishops politicked for their theological positions like parliamentarians trying to push through a bill. Bishops argued with one another endlessly about terms and even single letters in words (see Figure 4.1 below). Even

---

8. Robert Louis Wilken, *The First Thousand Years: A Global History of Christianity* (New Haven and London: Yale University Press, 2012), 94–95.

though such arguments appear abstruse to readers today, to fourth-century bishops such nuances were the stuff of right and wrong, orthodoxy and heresy, life and death. Salvation itself was at stake. Even laypeople, the vast majority of whom could neither read nor write, were invested in the arguments about Christ. As the bishop of Sasima (a small city in modern Turkey) famously wrote about the people in the city of Constantinople around the year 380:

> The whole city is occupied with these conversations . . . the clothes-sellers, the money-changers, the food vendors. If you ask for change, they philosophize about the Begotten and the Unbegotten. If you ask the price of bread, the answer is: "The Father is greater and the Son inferior." If you ask, "Is the bath ready?" [the bath attendant] will answer, "The Son was created from nothing."[9]

Though surely an example of poetic license, the bishop's description of the theological mood of the times indicates just how consuming the arguments about the Godhead were in the fourth century. In some cities, there were rival bishops—one might be a pro-Arian and the other an anti-Arian. Bishop Athanasius of Alexandria, a noted Homoousian (see Figure 4.1 below) and anti-Arian, was exiled five separate times for his theological positions, while Bishop Eusebius of Nicomedia, a noted Homoean and pro-Arian, was banished but later promoted: after baptizing Emperor Constantine, he was transferred from the diocese of Nicomedia to the imperial capital, Constantinople, where he became a trusted advisor to the imperial court.

9. Gregory of Nyssa, *On the Divinity of the Son and the Holy Spirit*, quoted in *The Acts of the Council of Chalcedon*, vol. 1, ed. Richard Price and Michael Gaddis (Liverpool: Liverpool University Press, 2005), 8.

Figure 4.1. Four Views about Christ Emerging after the Council of Nicea			
Group	Greek Meaning of Term	Belief	Bishop(s) Who Advocated Belief
Homoousians	"of the same substance"	Supported Nicene Christology and believed Christ was of the same substance as the Father	Athanasius of Alexandria
Homoiousians	"of a similar substance"	Wanted to preserve the distinction among the Godhead and so maintained that Christ was of a similar substance of the Father	Basil of Ancyra
Homoeans	"like"	Opposed the use of the word "substance" since it was not a biblical term	Acacius of Caesarea and Eusebius of Nicomedia
Anomeans	"unlike"	Believed that Christ was unlike the Father in divinity	Eudoxius of Antioch

The Theology of the Cappadocians (Late Fourth Century)

It was in the midst of this great theological and political turmoil that three bishops gained notoriety for the way they answered an increasingly important question that flowed out of the discussion about Christ's relationship to the Father: was the Holy Spirit divine? Because the question of Christ's divinity overshadowed that of the Spirit's, it was not until the second half of the fourth century that detailed attention was focused on this question. Although Athanasius and Bishop Cyril of Jerusalem had discussed (and affirmed) the Spirit's divinity and role among the Trinity, the most influential writers on this subject were Basil of Caesarea, Gregory of Nazianzus, and Gregory of Nyssa. Basil and Gregory of Nyssa were brothers, and they were friends with Gregory of Nazianzus. Each of them came from the spectacular region of Cappadocia in central Turkey, and they are therefore known as the Cappadocian fathers. Their writings about the Trinity deeply influenced the development of Eastern

Christianity, particularly regarding the question of the divinity of the Holy Spirit.

Due to the prominence of the question of the Son's divinity, the creed drafted by the bishops at Nicea included a mere five words about the Holy Spirit: "and in the Holy Spirit." This was incredibly vague. Not surprisingly, there was any number of conjectures about who or what the Holy Spirit was, each of which views appealed amply to Scripture in support of its position. In short, Athanasius argued that the Holy Spirit was fully God and of the same substance of the Father and the Son; Eusebius of Caesarea relegated the Spirit to a sort of third power among the Trinity; Arius regarded the Spirit as the pinnacle of the Son's creation (and thus inferior to both the Father and the Son); while another group (called the Tropici by Athanasius) conceived of the Spirit as a powerful angel. Amid this flurry of contrary interpretations, there were two main groups taking shape: what we may call the Pneumatomachians ("Spirit fighters") and the Athanasians or Cappadocians. While the former rejected the divinity of the Holy Spirit, the latter group affirmed it.

Due to the lack of adequate source material surviving from the Pneumatomachians, we will concentrate on the theology of the Cappadocians. We will begin our discussion of the Cappadocians with the most well known, Basil of Caesarea (coming from the major city in Cappadocia, not the one in Palestine). Like the other Cappadocians, Basil received an excellent Greek education and was deeply shaped by Platonic thought. A shrewd politician, Basil appointed many of his friends and relatives to the office of bishop in order to counter the large number of Arian bishops in the East. Basil was a learned theologian who wrote a treatise called *On the Holy Spirit* in the second half of the fourth century as well as several individual letters dealing with theology.

Basil's treatise *On the Holy Spirit* was written in opposition to those who objected to his use of a doxology lauding the Holy Spirit as an equal member of the Godhead: "Glory be to the Father, with the Son, jointly with the Holy Spirit." In his argument, Basil made use of Scripture, Greek philosophy, and church tradition. After turning to biblical passages pointing to the divinity of the Holy Spirit, Basil wrote:

> We are compelled to advance in our conceptions to the highest, and to think of an intelligent essence, in power infinite, in magnitude unlimited, unmeasured by times or ages, generous of Its good gifts, to whom turn all things needing sanctification, after whom reach all things that live in virtue, as being watered by Its inspiration and helped on toward their natural and proper end. (9.22)[10]

Later Basil argued that "we speak of Him [the Holy Spirit] singly, conjoined as He is to the one Father through the one Son, and through himself completing the adorable and blessed Trinity" (18.45). The fact that the Father "begot" the Son did not at all devalue the Son's divinity since the terms were relational ones, not marks of rank.

One of Basil's greatest contributions to Trinitarian theology was his articulation of a notion that has since become the mainstream view among historic Christians—namely, that the Trinity is one being, essence, or substance (*ousia* in Greek; *essentia* or *substantia* in Latin) and three distinct subsistences, properties, or personalities (*hypostases* in Greek; *personae* in Latin). As he famously wrote:

> The distinction between *ousia* and *hypostasis* is the same as that between the general and the particular, as, for instance, between the animal and the particular man . . . in the case of the Godhead, we confess one essence or substance . . . but we confess a particular *hypostasis*, in order that our conception of Father, Son and Holy Spirit may be without

---

10. Basil of Caesarea, *On the Holy Spirit* 9.22. See http://www.newadvent.org/fathers/3203.htm.

confusion and clear. . . . [For instance,] the Godhead is common; the fatherhood is particular. (*Letter* 236.6)[11]

From such thinking, Basil reasoned that although each member of the Trinity shares the same one essence of divinity within the single Godhead, each has a distinct property and particular role.

Figure 4.2. The Theology of the Cappadocians in a Nutshell

1. Each of the members of the Trinity is fully God.
2. In God, there is one *ousia* (divine essence equally shared by each member of the Trinity) and three *hypostases* (the individual subsistence of the Father and of the Son and of the Spirit).
3. Like a chain, the Trinity is relational; discussion of one member of the Trinity always involves the others.

Gregory of Nyssa, the younger brother of Basil who was selected by him to serve as bishop in a small town in Turkey, picked up where his older brother left off. He argued against the Pneumatomachians just as his brother had done in such treatises as *On the Holy Trinity*, *On Not Three Gods*, and *Against Eunomius* (directed against a man who was a noted opponent of Basil). Like the other Cappadocians, Gregory was charged with polytheism by is opponents. How could the Father, Son, and Spirit not be understood as three different Gods?

Gregory was a more mystical thinker than the other Cappadocians, and he appealed to the utter transcendence of God. It was often more appropriate, he maintained, to speak of how or what God was *not* rather than to speak of how or what God *is*. As he wrote, "For in speaking of the mysteries, we acknowledge three Persons and recognize there is no difference in nature between them."[12] For

---

11. Basil of Caesarea, *Letter* 236.6. See http://www.newadvent.org/fathers/3202236.htm.
12. Gregory of Nyssa, *An Answer to Ablabius: That We Should Not Think of Saying There Are Three Gods*, in *Christology of the Later Fathers*, ed. Edward Rochie Hardy (Louisville, KY: Westminster John Knox, 1954), 257.

Gregory, every operation of the one and united Godhead may be said to "have its origin in the Father, proceed through the Son, and reach its completion by the Holy Spirit."[13] In this way, everything related to the Godhead was always issued by the Father, actualized by the Son, and perfected by the Spirit. The Godhead does not work independently but always jointly.

Gregory of Nazianzus, friend to brothers Basil and Gregory, was the bishop of a small city named Sasima (and briefly of Constantinople). For Gregory, as with the other Cappadocians, the Godhead was one but consisted of three persons of undivided and equal glory, honor, and substance. His most cogent case for the full deity of the Holy Spirit is found in his *Theological Orations*, delivered in Constantinople on the eve of the Council of Constantinople. In these orations, Gregory argued for the distinct role each equal member of the Trinity played—the Father was the Father of the Son; the Son was begotten by the Father; and the Holy Spirit proceeded from the Father. In every way other than these, the three members of the Trinity were one and known in relation to the other members. The Godhead was perfect, and if there were a time when God the Father did not exist—because the Godhead is one and united—then there was a time when neither the Son nor the Spirit existed. And such was not possible. As he responded to his opponents, "if you overthrow any of the three you will have overthrown the whole."[14]

Of the Cappadocian fathers, Gregory of Nazianzus was probably the one who best responded to the argument posed by the Pneumatomachians that the Holy Spirit could not be divine based on the silence of Scripture on that matter. Even though Gregory argued vigorously that there were plenty of biblical passages supporting the divinity of the Spirit, he is most famous for the following retort:

13. Ibid., 262.
14. Gregory of Nazianzus, *The Theological Orations* 5.12, in ibid., 201.

The Old Testament proclaimed the Father openly, and the Son more obscurely. The New manifested the Son, and suggested the deity of the Spirit. Now the Spirit himself dwells among us, and supplies us with a clearer demonstration of himself. For it was not safe, when the Godhead of the Father was not yet acknowledged, plainly to proclaim the Son; nor when that of the Son was not received, to burden us further (if I may use so bold an expression) with the Holy Ghost. (*Theological Orations* 5.26)[15]

Applying the concept of progressive revelation (that God is revealed to humanity gradually and in steps over time—during the Old Testament, the New Testament, and the age of the church), Gregory argued that the deity of the Holy Spirit was unveiled only after the deity of the Father and of the Son were clearly indicated and people were capable of receiving this profound truth. In this way, the Spirit's divinity was confirmed over time in fulfillment of Jesus' words to his disciples: "the Holy Spirit, whom the Father will send in my name, will teach you everything" (John 14:26).

The Council of Constantinople (381)

The theology of the Cappadocian fathers was extremely influential in the proceedings of the church's next international council (Gregory of Nazianzus was even temporarily the president of the council). Like each of the so-called Ecumenical Councils (seven in total, from the years 325 to 787), the Council of Constantinople was comprised mostly of Greek-speaking bishops in the East. The bishops were strongly opposed to Arianism, and they rejected each of the previous councils of the past half century led by Arian sympathizers. Nicene theology was thus squarely affirmed, but this council went even further than Nicea did.

15. Ibid., 209–10.

After including the original wording of the creed drafted at Nicea in 325, "And in the Holy Spirit," the Council of Constantinople filled in what was formerly missing:

> And [we believe] in the Holy Spirit, the Lord and the Life-giver, that proceeds from the Father, who with Father and Son is worshipped together and glorified together, who spoke through the prophets.

The council members proposed this article based on explicit biblical passages (such as 2 Cor. 3:6, 17; John 6:63 and 15:26) as well as on teaching from the Cappadocians. As they wrote, the Son is begotten of the Father while the Spirit proceeds from the Father, yet both members share equal glory with the Father. It was not exactly clear what all of this language meant about begetting and proceeding, but the council endeavored to protect the mystery of the Godhead rather than define it too precisely.

At the same time, not all of the bishops were agreed that the Spirit was to be worshiped as God in the same way as the Son and the Father were. Centuries later in the West, Latin-speaking Christians would add one word that would lead to a serious showdown (and eventual split) between East and West: *filioque* ("and the Son"). Dissatisfied with the language offered at the Council of Constantinople, the Westerners changed the wording in the sixth century to: the Holy Spirit "proceeds from the Father *and the Son*" [*qui ex Patre* Filioque *procedit*], a change that was popularized under the so-called Carolingian Renaissance of the early ninth century. Nonetheless, the creed re-drafted at Constantinople has become perhaps the most definitive declaration of the Christian faith of all times. Known as the Nicene Creed (officially the Niceno-Constantinopolitan Creed), this theological pronouncement has endured the ages as the international creed of the Christian world.

Conclusion: Jesus and the Holy Spirit as Fully Divine

During the fourth century, the church struggled with two related theological questions: are the Son and the Spirit divine? As we have seen, this question yielded a variety of contradictory responses from Christians. Although groups of Christians who denied both the full divinity of the Son and the Spirit continued well beyond the fourth century, there was a mounting consensus in the church that both the Son and the Spirit were full and equal members of the Trinity. Not only did the Son and Spirit share the same substance with God the Father, but each of these members was also in existence from the beginning along with the Father. All of the operations of the Godhead, though not fully revealed in the Bible but only gradually over time, were carried out by the joint and holy work of God the Father, God the Son, and God the Spirit.

Although our investigation of this question has concentrated on Greek-speaking Christians in the East, it should be noted that a similar answer was reached in churches in the West and beyond the Roman Empire. In the West, a whole host of venerable Latin-speaking theologians addressed the question at hand with great vigor, and concluded that each of the three members of the Trinity was God—*una substantia et tres personae* as classically formulated: a God of one substance and three persons, each to be honored and worshiped.

5

How Many Natures Does Christ Have?

It was the year 428. A new patriarch[1] had just been appointed to Constantinople, the leading patriarchal see in the Christian East, which was also the location of the imperial capital of the Byzantine (or East Roman) Empire. The new patriarch's name was Nestorius. A Syrian born around the year 382 in what we could now call Turkey, Nestorius received a sound Greek education and was highly regarded for his impressive sermons and austerity as a monk. He was likely chosen as patriarch of Constantinople as a man who would rise above the petty politics that characterized the imperial capital and bring about some type of unity—a tall order, to be sure.

Once consecrated as patriarch, Nestorius went to work quickly. In his inaugural sermon, he boasted to the emperor, "Purge, O Caesar, your Kingdom of heretics, and I in return will give you the Kingdom of Heaven. Stand by me in putting down the heretics and I will stand by you in putting down the barbarian Persians."[2] After only

---

1. The highest-ranking bishops in early Eastern Christianity came to be called *patriarchs* rather than simply *bishops*. The term *patriarch* applies specifically to the patriarchates (that is, bishoprics or dioceses of Constantinople, Alexandria, Antioch, and Jerusalem). Bishops of lower-ranking dioceses, such as that of Caesarea or Edessa, were called *bishops*."

five days on the job, he incited a riot that burned an Arian church to the ground. Before long, Nestorius was leading the charge against any church that showed the faintest degree of Christian schism or divergence from mainstream Christianity. Within the year, he had turned his attention to a theological controversy about Christ. Although the title *Theotokos* had been used by Constantinopolitans for decades to describe the Virgin Mary as the "Mother of God," Nestorius was convinced that this term smacked of heresy—how could a young woman, however honorable and pure, be the mother of the God of the universe? It didn't make sense.

Though not rejecting the term in every instance, Nestorius believed that the people of Constantinople had raised the pedestal of Mary too high. Instead of the word *Theotokos*, Nestorius preferred a much more theologically appropriate term, *Christotokos*, which meant "bearer of Christ." Yes, he reasoned, "In his divinity [Christ] was brought forth by the Father, in his humanity by the Holy Virgin."[3] These two separate natures were not to be mingled willy-nilly. Unprepared for the politics of imperial living, historian Philip Jenkins argues that Nestorius "did not understand the minefield he was entering."[4] Nestorius's detractors included not only the emperor's clever sister, the military, monks, and laypeople, but important bishops outside of Constantinople, including the bishops of Alexandria and Rome, who turned their attention to Nestorius's sermons and letters with the aim of discrediting his theology and reputation. Before long, an inquiry was made into Nestorius's beliefs

2. Quoted in Mar Bawai Soro, *The Church of the East: Apostolic and Orthodox* (San Jose: Adiabene Publications, 2007), 227.
3. Quoted in Christoph Baumer, *The Church of the East: An Illustrated History of Assyrian Christianity* (London: I. B. Tauris, 2006), 47.
4. Philip Jenkins, *Jesus Wars: How Four Patriarchs, Three Queens, and Two Emperors Decided What Christians Would Believe for the Next 1,500 Years* (New York: HarperCollins, 2010), 137.

and the emperor was forced to convene an ecumenical council to deal with the international dispute that his new patriarch was causing.

The Question of Christ's Natures

The question of Christ's natures, sparked by how Christians should refer to Mary, was a question of immense controversy and disunity in the body of Christ. Despite the conclusions drawn by the first two Ecumenical Councils in the fourth century, the question of how to understand the person of Jesus Christ vexed Christians well into the fifth century. Although mainstream Christianity had reached consensus that Christ was both human and divine, there was no agreement about how these two natures united—if they did at all. In this chapter, we will explore three major responses to the question of how Christ's natures were to be understood vis-à-vis the Councils of Ephesus (431) and Chalcedon (451). We may reconstruct the question as follows: how many natures does Christ have?

A Short History of the Orthodox Churches

Although it is customary, especially in the West, to speak of Orthodox Christianity as a monolithic system of thought and practice, there are actually various strands of Orthodoxy. Each of these strands is traced back to the earliest centuries after Christ, and they are grouped together, in part, based on their different understandings of the natures of Christ. In this section, we will offer a short history of the three major divisions of Orthodox churches from the first to the fifth centuries in order to provide needed context to the Christological disputes in the 400s.

We will begin our study of early Orthodox Christianity by discussing what has eventually come to be called the Church of the East. Confusingly, it is a church known by many other names:

the East Syriac Church, Assyrian Church, Persian Church, and the Nestorian Church. The Christians whom we group as part of the Church of the East were influenced by Syriac theology and practice. Early records suggest that Christianity entered Edessa (now Urfa, Turkey), the Syriac-speaking capital of the Osrhoene Kingdom, at the end of Jesus' ministry via Syrian Antioch, where both Peter and Paul were active. Antioch had served as the original missional outpost for the evangelization of the Middle East, including many ancient kingdoms and city-states in Mesopotamia such as Osrhoene, Adiabene, and Palmyra.

Syriac was closely related to the language in which *Yeshua* (Jesus) spoke, taught, and prayed, and it has been the liturgical language of the Church of the East since the first century. Syriac Christians referred to themselves as *Nazarenes* (the term still used by Semitic-speaking Christians today), and they produced some of the earliest Christian documents, liturgical prayers, chants, hymns, schools, and monastic centers. Headquartered in what is now Iraq, historian Dietmar Winkler believes that the Church of the East "achieved the greatest geographical scope of any Christian church until the Middle Ages."[5] East Syriac Christians were ubiquitous in Iran and Iraq, southeastern Turkey, Syria, and parts of India, China, and Central Asia. In this regard, the Church of the East was most active *outside* of the East Roman or Byzantine Empire. It always existed as a minority religious community under the political reign of non-Christian kingdoms. In the fifth century in what is now Iraq, the Church of the East codified its doctrine during a series of church councils under the direction of the Persian shah (who was a Zoroastrian, not a Christian). Although the Church of the East fully supported the Councils of Nicea (325) and Constantinople (381), it

---

5. Wilhelm Baum and Dietmar Winkler, *The Church of the East: A Concise History* (London and New York: RoutledgeCurzon, 2003), 1.

did not affirm later church councils. The ecclesiastical head of the Church of the East was the catholicos of Seleucia-Ctesiphon, who eventually oversaw churches from Iraq to India and China. As far as Christology is concerned, the Church of the East preferred to speak of Christ as having two natures (and were thus called Diophysites, "two natures" in Greek) that were loosely united in one person.

In addition to the Church of the East, there was another large cluster of Orthodox Christians that eventually found itself out of favor with Byzantine theology. This cluster of churches is now referred to as the Oriental Orthodox Church. This group largely included Coptic Christians from Egypt, Armenian Christians from Armenia, Aksumite Christians from Ethiopia, Nubian Christians from Sudan, St. Thomas Christians from India, and Jacobite Christians from West Syria. Each body had its own ecclesiastical head: for instance, the patriarch of Alexandria for the Copts, Ethiopians, and Nubians; and the catholicos of Etchmiadzin for the Armenians. What these diverse bodies of Orthodox Christians shared is a similar understanding of Christ as having one united nature after the incarnation (and thus these Christians were called Miaphysites, "one nature" in Greek). Like the Church of the East, the Oriental Orthodox Church affirmed the first two Ecumenical Councils but ignored later ones. Increasingly after the fifth century, the Oriental Orthodox Church came to develop its own theology in contradistinction to the Church of the East and the Eastern Orthodox Church.

The Eastern Orthodox Church was the state religion of the East Roman or Byzantine Empire. There was no one ecclesiastical head over the churches in this empire, though the patriarch of Constantinople was always prominent. Although the Byzantine Empire was technically the political sovereign over many parts in the West (including Rome), over time it diminished considerably. It later came to exert influence mostly over Turkey, Sicily, the Balkans, the Holy Land, and Georgia. Byzantine Christianity (another way to refer to this branch of Orthodoxy) was inextricably linked with the politics of the Byzantine Empire, under whose authority each of the so-called Seven Ecumenical Councils were convened, financed, and ratified. When compared with the Church of the East and the Oriental Orthodox Church, the Eastern Orthodox Church was backed by a stronger and more united political machine, and came to be the victor in the Christological disputes of the fourth centuries and following. As we will discover below, Byzantine Christians deemed the Church of the East and the Oriental Orthodox Church as heretical, particularly in regard to their seemingly deficient understanding of the relation of Christ's human and divine natures.

Figure 5.1. Three Major Clusters of Early Orthodox Churches	
Theological Tradition	**Understanding of Christ (on the Relation between his Humanity and Divinity)**
Eastern Orthodox (Also known as: Byzantine, Nicene, Chalcedonian, Melkite, Imperial)	Two (human and divine) natures of Christ that come together in one hypostatic union without confusion, change, division or separation; "Two natures in the incarnate Jesus, and one *hypostasis*"
Church of the East (Also known as: Assyrian, East Syrian, Diophysite, Nestorian, Persian)	Two natures of Christ: a human one (from Mary) and a divine one (from God) that are united without being mixed; "Two natures in the incarnate Jesus with their two *Qnomi* and one *Parsopa*"
Oriental Orthodox (Also known as: West Syrian, Jacobite, Miaphysite, Monophysite)	One nature of Christ whose humanity and divinity were united after the incarnation; "One nature of the incarnate Word of God after the union and one *hypostasis*"[6]

6. The phrases in quotations for each section come from Suha Rassam, *Christianity in Iraq: Its Origins and Development to the Present Day* (Leominster, UK: Gracewing, 2005), xxviii–xxix. See figure 5.2. for more about these technical terms.

The Council of Ephesus (431)

When it came time for the Third Ecumenical Council, named the Council of Ephesus, each of the three clusters of Orthodox Christians discussed above was involved. Naturally, such divisions were still taking shape at this time, and it would only be decades and centuries later that we can clearly discern each of the subtle differences existing among them. Also as mentioned above, it was the dispute over how to refer to Mary, an issue over which Patriarch Nestorius of Constantinople notoriously fumbled, that was the indirect cause of the Ephesian Council. Of course, there were other issues in the background as well, including nationalist rivalries—Egyptian Copts were not generally favorable to foreign Greek rule, the cities of Alexandria and Antioch had become bitter intellectual foes, and Patriarch Cyril was possibly attempting to create a diversion from his own controversies back in Egypt.

In total, about 250 bishops were present at the Council of Ephesus. Nestorius received a very cold reception. Many bishops interpreted his idea to take away the title Theotokos from the Virgin Mary as tantamount to stripping Christ of his divinity. As Cyril wrote, Nestorius was keen to "wrinkle the holy and all-pure Virgin, bringing her down to the unseemly rottenness of [his] own ideas."[7] The bishop of Ephesus, a man named Memnon, actually closed the doors of his parishes to both Nestorius and his supporters. No Mary-hater would dare darken the sanctity of his churches, especially in the city where the Holy Virgin is reported to have lived with the apostle John after Jesus' resurrection. The hostility toward Nestorius was so severe that he had to have bodyguards protect him from the holiest men in the Christian world. To say the least, the deck of cards was heavily stacked against Nestorius. In order to guarantee his

7. Cyril, *Five Tomes against Nestorius* (Oxford: James Parker & Co., 1881), 6.

victory, Cyril, who had become the fiercest opponent of Nestorius as early as 429, brought a gang of thugs along with dozens of Egyptian bishops and monks. Against the wishes of almost seventy bishops, Cyril demanded the commencement of the council despite the fact that many bishops supportive of Nestorius (those of Syria who were connected to Antioch) had yet to arrive. Believing that he would be reviled and fearful for his life, Nestorius refused to attend the council; those who did attend it summarily condemned him as an arch-heretic. Nestorius was called "the new Judas." As an exiled and defeated man years later, Nestorius wrote in his memoirs:

> Who was judge? Cyril. And who was the accuser? Cyril. Who was bishop of Rome? Cyril. Cyril was everything. Cyril was the bishop of Alexandria and took the place of the holy and saintly bishop of Rome ... What need was there for a Council, when this man was everything?[8]

When Nestorius's supporters arrived several days later, rather than attending the straw-man council in session they formed their own council and condemned Cyril! The Ephesian Council only concluded when the Byzantine Emperor tired of the charade and arrested both Nestorius and Cyril—the former of whom resigned as patriarch and was exiled while the latter bribed his way back to Egypt, where he remained patriarch until his death. Although there was reconciliation between the Alexandrians and the Antiochenes in the so-called Formula of Union (433), Nestorius was the scapegoat who was banished out of the Middle East to Egypt, where he lived in the desert for two more decades as a theological pariah.

The Feud between Cyril and Nestorius

Part of the controversy at the Council of Ephesus had to do with the political and intellectual rivalry between the historically significant

---

8. Nestorius, *The Bazaar of Heracleides* (Eugene, OR: Wipf & Stock, 2001; reprint, 1925), 132–33.

cities of Antioch and Alexandria. Such a feud was personified in Nestorius (who, though patriarch of Constantinople, was from Antioch) and Cyril, whose Alexandrian theology clashed with Antiochene theology and who was also resentful of the growing prestige of the patriarchy of Constantinople. It was Cyril who was the first to pounce on the writings of Nestorius. Beginning around the year 429, we have a number of exchanges between him and Nestorius, which contain a patina of courtesy underneath mutual loathing. Cyril was adamant that Mary was the mother of Christ the Word:

> [It is proper to call Mary Theotokos] not as if the nature of the Word of his divinity had its beginning from the holy Virgin, but because of her was born that holy body with a rational soul, to which the Word being personally united is said to be born according to the flesh.[9]

For Cyril, the notion that Mary only gave birth to Christ's humanity was tantamount to separating the Word into two beings rather than understanding the human-divine unity of the Word after the incarnation. Nestorius, in turn, believed that Cyril's theology smacked of Apollinarianism, the heresy that so emphasized Christ's divinity that it swallowed up his humanity. Nestorius was concerned that Cyril's logic undercut the humanity of Christ and led to the frightful conclusion that God died on the cross. According to Nestorius's logic, if Mary was the "Mother of God," and Christ was the "Son of God," then Christ was Mary's grandson! Obviously, the two were worlds apart in their thinking. Nestorius probably overemphasized Christ's human-divine distinctions while Cyril overly accentuated Christ's divinity.

The victors from the Council of Ephesus were the Miaphysites associated with Cyril of Alexandria, while the losers were the

---

9. Quoted in Jenkins, *Jesus Wars*, 143.

Diophysites associated with Nestorius. Although the Church of the East was not represented by any bishops at the Council of Ephesus, it came to be called "Nestorian" for its later refusal to condemn Nestorius. Somewhat inaccurately, the Byzantine Church came to equate the theology of Nestorius with the Church of the East even though Nestorius's contemporary Theodore the Interpreter, bishop of Mopsuestia from 392 to 428, held more influence over the theology of the Church of the East. The division between the Eastern Orthodox Church and the Church of the East was compounded by geographic, linguistic, political, and philosophical differences. The Church of the East thought and worshiped in Syriac, and there were no one-to-one correspondences between Syriac and Greek terms when referring to Christ's natures and persons.

The Council of Chalcedon (451)

While the Council of Ephesus provoked the separation of the Church of the East from the larger Orthodox family, the Council of Chalcedon two decades later led to the condemnation of the Oriental Orthodox Church branch. Regrettably, failure to agree on how to understand the union between Christ's humanity and divinity still proved the basis of the controversy. In contrast to the views of Nestorius, who, many Christians maintained, essentially made Christ into two persons by emphasizing too strict a separation between Christ's humanity and divinity, there were some who argued just the opposite. Among these was a fifth-century archimandrite (that is, one in charge of abbots) named Eutyches. From the imperial capital of Constantinople, Eutyches had gained popularity for advancing the theory that Christ only had a divine nature *after* the incarnation: "I admit that our Lord was of two natures before the union, but after the union one nature."[10]

Although Eutyches was condemned as a heretic for denying the human nature of Christ after his incarnation, he had powerful allies. One of them, named Dioscorus, was patriarch of Alexandria from 444 to 454 (who was Cyril's successor). Dioscorus infamously convened what has come to be known as the Robber (or "Gangster") Synod of 449. As the president of this raucous-filled council, he condemned all those who were not vocal enough against Nestorius and he even rehabilitated his old friend Eutyches. The mockery of this council drove the Byzantine Empire into action.

At the Council of Chalcedon in 451, Christians such as Dioscorus and Eutyches who subscribed to the so-called Alexandrian School of Thought, which emphasized the divinity of Christ over his humanity, had the tables turned on them. Eutyches was condemned anew, and Dioscorus was removed from office. In his place, the Byzantine emperor installed a Greek patriarch. Although the council was decidedly against Eutyches and Dioscorus—representatives of Alexandrian thought—the council was also deeply hostile toward the theology of Nestorius, who represented Antiochene thought. In this regard, the specters of Eutyches, Dioscorus, and Nestorius hung over the deliberations. What really drove the discussions forward at Chalcedon was the so-called Tome of Leo, an impressive document written by the pope that provided a sort of middle way between Alexandria and Antioch. This tome at once protected the mystery of Christ from the perceived heresies of Nestorianism (Christ has two natures and two persons) and Eutychianism (Christ has one nature and one person). As the Chalcedonian Definition came to be worded:

> [Christ is] recognized in two natures, without confusion, without change, without division, without separation; the distinction of natures

10. Quoted in *Documents of the Christian Church*, ed., Henry Bettenson, 2nd ed. (Oxford: Oxford University Press, 1963), 49.

being in no way annulled by the union, but rather the characteristics of each nature being preserved and coming together to form one person.[11]

Though an inaccurate moniker, the Christians casting their lot with the Alexandrians were lumped together as Miaphysites (technically Monophysites, that is, supporters of the one divine nature of Christ). A more careful interpretation of the Alexandrian position, however, recognizes that most Alexandrians believed that Christ had one fully human and divine nature after his incarnation—not just a divine nature. As Egyptian scholar Aziz Atiya explains:

> The Copts [Christians of Egypt] consistently repudiate the Western identification of Alexandrine Christianity with the Eutychianism [theology coming from Eutyches] which originated in Constantinople, and which they have always regarded as a flagrant heresy, since it declared the complete absorption of Christ's manhood in His single divine nature, whereas the Copts clearly upheld the doctrine of the two natures—divine and human—mystically united in one, without confusion, corruption, or change.[12]

Whatever the case, the Miaphysites were the losers at the Council of Chalcedon, a council that "was the cause of much further controversy."[13] By the end of the Council of Chalcedon, the Byzantine Empire had deemed the theology of the Church of the East and of the Oriental Orthodox Church as not only deficient but heretical. Such theology was not welcome within its realms. Constantinople rose in prominence as a patriarchal see while Alexandria diminished. There were attempts at compromise as well as downright persecution of Christians within the Byzantine Empire who failed to comply with the theology drawn at Chalcedon. For

---

11. Quoted in Bettenson, *Documents of the Christian Church*, 51.

12. Aziz Atiya, *History of Eastern Christianity* (Notre Dame, IN: University of Notre Dame, 1967), 69.

13. Sebastian Brock, *Fire from Heaven: Studies in Syriac Theology and Liturgy* (Aldershot and Burlington: Ashgate, 2006), 2.

the most part, this only affected the Oriental Orthodox Church, since the Church of the East was outside of the Byzantine Empire. Back in Egypt, a veritable civil war was brewing between the Coptic Christians and the Byzantine Christians, which was only ended with Arab Muslim control of the region beginning in the seventh century.

Understanding the Terminology Used

So, which one of these three groups of Christians was truly "orthodox"? What is illuminating about the Christological disputes is that each cluster of Christians believed that they alone were right in understanding the mystery of the incarnation, and that the other ones were wrong. Such is world Christian history in a nutshell. Each group, in fact, was prepared to risk their lives for their beliefs. Many scholars today, however, are not only critical of the proceedings and deliberations of the fifth-century councils, but think that the three Orthodox bodies are actually a good deal closer in thought than formerly realized. Syriac scholar Sebastian Brock believes that much of the dispute over the natures of Christ "lay in the different understandings given to certain of the key terms."[14]

These key terms, used as a litmus test of orthodoxy, were "nature," "hypostasis," and "person." Unfortunately, different authors and communities used the same words in different ways—which their opponents read as clear signs of heresy. Behind the first of these words, "nature," stand the Greek words *ousia*, *physis*, and the Syriac word *kyana*. They each generally refer to a specific type of category—such as the nature of the Godhead or of humanity—but they each have different connotations and ranges of meaning. Depending on the circumstance, the Syriac word *kyana* could be translated by the Greek word *ousia* or *physis*. What was especially

14. Brock, *Fire from Heaven*, 6.

problematic in the Christological disputes was the Greek word *hypostasis*, which was translated as *qnoma* in Syriac. This term covered an ample range of meaning—nature, individual manifestation, concrete realization. Put bluntly, Cyril and Nestorius, though both writing in the same Greek language, used the term in different ways. Finally, the word "person," *prosopon* in Greek and *parsopa* in Syriac, refers to the external appearance of someone. By way of example, Nestorius believed that Christ had two *ousiai*, two *hypostaseis*, and one *prosopon*. For Cyril, influenced by Plato, it was not possible to have two *hypostaseis* without two *prosopa*. The Byzantine Christians agreed, though they ultimately found fault with Cyril's theology, which did not appear to protect the mystery of Christ's incarnation as fully human and fully divine.

Figure 5.2. Three Key Terms Used in the Christological Disputes		
Greek Term	**Syriac Term**	**English Description**
Ousia (pl. *ousiai*) or *Physis* (pl. *physeis*)	*Kyana* (pl. *kyane*)	General species or type of being
Hypostasis (pl. *hypostaseis*)	*Qnoma* (pl. *qnome*)	Inner reality of a person; individuality
Prosopon (pl. *prosopa*)	*Parsopa* (pl. *parsope*)	External appearance of a person

Conclusion: No Consensus on Christ's Natures

As historian Christoph Baumer wrote, "Christology [was] the centrifugal force which broke Christian unity into three mutually antagonistic ecclesiastical organizations."[15] Far from uniting the Christian world, the ecumenical councils of the fifth century created further division. While each of the three Orthodox bodies discussed above were in seed form during the fourth and fifth centuries, after

15. Baumer, *The Church of the East*, 32.

the Council of Chalcedon they continued to grow apart and into three noticeably different bodies. The Byzantine Christians established orthodoxy in their realms, which has generated the most influence over Europeans and Westerners since Eastern Orthodox, Catholics, and Protestants have all followed the definitions given at the Councils of Ephesus and Chalcedon—most notably that Christ has a fully human and fully divine nature that is united in one person without change or division. Throughout Asia, however, where the Church of the East was always strongest in the early and medieval time periods, it has been customary to adopt the formulation of Babai the Great, who lauded the two distinct natures of Christ within two *qnome* (*hypostaseis* in Greek) and one person. Meanwhile, the Oriental Orthodox Church, with a large contention in Egypt as well as Eastern Africa, Roman Syria, and Armenia, preferred to speak of Christ as the one incarnate Word. Despite the many similarities that these three Orthodox bodies shared, their inability to come to a consensus on how to understand Christ's incarnation has kept them divided to this day.

6

What Does It Mean to be Holy?

It was close to the year 600. A man named John, possibly born in Syria, was just installed as the abbot (or head monk) of the famous monastery at St. Catherine's in Egypt. St. Catherine's Monastery was one of the most renowned monasteries in the Middle East, constructed at the base of Mt. Sinai by Emperor Justinian where Moses is reported to have removed his sandals upon sight of the Burning Bush. John had entered the monastery around the age of sixteen, but spent the next four decades of his life as a hermit outside of the monastery. Like countless monks before him, John meditated upon the lives of the saints, prayed and fasted, and accepted visitations from monks in search of spiritual direction. Around the close of the sixth century, against his will, John was elected abbot of St. Catherine's, where he remained for the rest of his earthly life.

It was while serving as abbot that John composed one of the most beloved Christian spirituals of all time—*The Ladder of Divine Ascent*. Apart from the Bible, there is perhaps no other book in the Christian East that has been as read and admired as this one. Written for monks, *The Ladder* spoke powerfully of the Christian life as an upward journey on the ladder toward heaven that was scaled one step at a time by monks on earth. Although several Christian authors had previously written about the Christian life as a ladder, John added new insight and depth, earning him the surname Climacus—*the ladder* in Greek. John Climacus divided *The Ladder* into thirty sections, symbolic of the years of Jesus' life. Each step represented one step closer toward God. From the first three steps of breaking away from the world all the way toward the last four steps of union with God, John spoke eloquently, and sometimes very cryptically, about what it meant to be a holy person. But there was never any doubt about the overall theme of the book. As John wrote with regard to the first of the thirty steps:

> In this world when an emperor summons us to obedience, we leave everything aside and answer the call at once without delays or hanging back or excuses. We had better be careful then not to refuse, through laziness or inertia, the call to the heavenly life in the service of the King of kings, the Lord of lords, the God of gods. Let us not find ourselves unable to defend ourselves at the great tribunal of judgment. . . . [1]

The Question of Holiness

The Ladder by John Climacus could be described as a book written in response to the question of how fallen men and women, though imbued with the Spirit, can still lead a "heavenly life" pleasing to the Almighty. Such a question is relevant to more than hermits and head-strong fanatics. As John wrote in response to a common person's question, "How can we who are married and living amid public cares aspire to the monastic life?"[2] God's "kingdom" is not far from any of us. In this life there will be toil and pain, but there is a divine ladder reaching down into each of our hearts that we can climb, step by step, if we are only "determined" to ascend to God.

1. John Climacus, *The Ladder of Divine Assent* (Ramsey, NJ: Paulist Press, 1982), 78.
2. Climacus, *The Ladder*, 78.

By the time of the writing of *The Ladder* in the late sixth century, there were rival interpretations of what it meant for a Christian to be holy. Christians, in fact, had been contemplating this question since the first century, and John Climacus's book *The Ladder* was simply one articulation of what it meant to be holy amid a welter of rival interpretations. Historian of monasticism Columba Stewart writes that "the period of [monasticism's] greatest expansion was the sixth century,"[3] a time of powerful and prominent holy men and holy women across the Christian world. Although there were substantial differences between the Christian East and West regarding holiness and monasticism (see Figure 6.1 below), there was consensus that holiness was not only one of the greatest calls of the Christian life, but that the pursuit of holiness was best achieved either alone or among a community of monastics—but not among laypeople, since they were too often encumbered by the cares of the world. In this chapter, we will explore the following question: what does it mean to be holy?

A Short History of the Holy Life

The early church, working with categories already well in existence from the ancient world, understood a holy person to be a spiritual athlete who overcame the desires of the flesh by disciplining his or her body. The word *ascetic* derived from the Greek term meaning "training" or "exercise," and the holiest persons in the church were described as ascetics because of their impressive deprivations of human desires and inclinations. Like sports stars depriving themselves of bodily comforts in order to mold their bodies into athletic machines, ascetics were spiritual athletes deeply admired for their spiritual and physical rigors. Christian ascetics not only renounced

---

3. Columba Stewart, "Monasticism," in *The Early Christian World*, vol. 1, ed. Philip Esler (London and New York: Routledge, 2000), 348.

sexual activity and normal eating habits but they also withdrew from towns and villages in pursuit of intimacy with God in solitary places. Such ascetics created a new movement within Christianity called monasticism.

Figure 6.1. Terms Related to Early Monasticism		
Term	**Definition**	**Greek Root**
Monasticism	The quest for union with God through prayer, penance, deprivation, and separation from the world	"alone" or "solitary"
Monk / monastic	One who practices monasticism	"alone" or "solitary"
Ascetic	One who abstains from, indeed, eschews the desires of the flesh	"training" or "exercise"
Eremetical	Monk who lives alone	"desert"
Anchorite	Monk who lives away from society	"withdrawal"
Coenobitic	Monk who lives in a monastic community	"common life"
Abbot and archimandrite	Leader of a monastery	"father" and "highest ruler of a monastery"
Lavra or laura	Settlement of monks living in semi-individual cells	"narrow lane"

Monasticism came to prominence in the Christian world through the publication of a biography of Antony of Egypt, a Coptic ascetic whom Bishop Athanasius of Alexandria wrote about shortly after Antony's death in 356 at the incredible age of 105. Though monasticism had existed as early as the third century, and its religious roots ran deep in the ancient pre-Christian world, Antony became the most famous of monks because of Athanasius's book. Antony came from a wealthy Egyptian family but renounced his possessions in the second half of the third century after hearing the following public reading from the Gospels: "If you wish to be perfect, go, sell your possessions, and give the money to the poor, and you will have treasure in heaven; then come, follow me" (Matt. 19:21). In immediate obedience to the words uttered by Jesus two centuries before, Antony sold his possessions and inaugurated his life as a wandering ascetic in pursuit of Christ. Eating only small amounts of water and bread each day for decades on end, he slept sparingly, prayed continuously, and engaged Satan in spiritual combat. In a world where such behavior was regarded as the pinnacle of sanctity, Antony inevitably attracted countless followers who also wanted to practice a life of holiness apart from society.

In the ancient world, the desert was a place where evil spirits dwelled. It was a place to be avoided. In Egypt, in particular, where life had been lived along the Nile for time immemorial, to live in the desert was countercultural and self-imposed martyrdom. It was to enter death. By venturing into the desert, monks understood themselves to be marching into a spiritual battlefield—much like Jesus did when he encountered Satan in the desert after his baptism: preceded, of course, by the overpowering temptations that the Israelites endured when wandering in the wilderness centuries before. Surprisingly perhaps, there was no shortage of monks and nuns willing to divest themselves of the world in order to live a life of austerity in pursuit of union with God. As Athanasius phrased it in his biography on Antony, "the desert [became] colonized by monks."[4]

Although there is a tendency among some modern Christians to regard monastic separation from the world as socially irresponsible or selfish, ancient Christians believed that monastics separated from society, in part, to serve as intercessors for laypeople. Monks atoned for the sins of laypeople by engaging the spirits on the outskirts of town, much like the scapegoat during the Day of Atonement was "sent way into the wilderness to [the pagan god] Azalel" (Lev.

---

4. Athanasius, *Life of St. Antony*, ch. 14.

16:10). The prayer of the monastics waged war on the frontier of the desert. These monastics served as spiritual warriors who not only protected towns from dark forces but also who ensured the community's salvation. Monks also symbolically lived out the spiritual austerity required of the Christian life at a time when the Christians were growing too accustomed to the comforts of the world. As Orthodox theologian Timothy Ware writes,

> The monks by their withdrawal from society into the desert fulfilled a prophetic and eschatological ministry in the life of the Church. They reminded Christians that the kingdom of God is not of this world.[5]

In addition to their prophetic ministry, monks were well known in the ancient world to be conduits of divine healing. In a world "grazed thin by death,"[6] suffering and sick men and women were just as likely to hunt down holy monks as they were trained physicians for bodily cures. Though living solitary lives away from the world, monks were constantly sought after by townspeople to answer prayers, heal sicknesses, and cast out demons. As John Climacus wrote in *The Ladder*:

> Who [living in the towns and villages] has worked wonders, raised the dead, expelled demons? No one. Such deeds are done by monks. It is their reward. People in secular life cannot do these things, for, if they could, what then would be the point of ascetic practice and the solitary life?[7]

In the ancient world, to renounce the world was to become a friend of God, empowered by the Lord to do miraculous deeds. This gift was given not least because of the valiant sacrifices, including renunciation of sexual activity, of monks and nuns.

---

5. Timothy Ware, *The Orthodox Church*, 2nd ed. (London: Penguin, 1997), 37.
6. Quoted in Peter Brown, *The Body and Society: Men, Women, and Sexual Renunciation in Early Christianity* (New York: Columbia University Press, 1988), 6.
7. Climacus, *The Ladder*, 83.

By the fourth century, Christian monasticism was becoming an established religious institution. There were various forms. Some monks were hermits who lived alone in caves, cemeteries, huts, trees, and even on poles. David the Dendrite, a Syrian monk who died in the mid-sixth century, is an example of a hermit who lived alone. For three years in Thessaloniki, Greece, he lived by himself in the branches of an almond tree until an angel ordered him to dismount. Another form of monasticism included cells of monks who resided in close quarters but who still wanted to pursue the rigors of holy living on their own. This type of coenobitic or "communal" monasticism is often associated with the fourth-century Egyptian monk Pachomius, a man who strictly regulated the spiritual life of monks under his care. Another form of monasticism was a sort of middle path between the extremes of hermitage and communal living. This so-called semi-eremitic life included small bands of monks who lived in close proximity under the guidance of a spiritual director. The fourth-century monk Evagrius of Pontus, who lived in what is now Turkey, is an example of a semi-eremitic holy man. This so-called Desert Father wrote many important works on the spiritual life, and was one of the earliest compilers of monastic sayings.

Wherever practiced, monasticism shared many commonalities. As one historian points out, the "normative practices [of monasticism] were celibacy, liturgical prayer at certain hours of the day and night, memorization of biblical texts for the sake of personal prayer, fasting (both kind of food and amount), manual labour, and consultation with others experienced in life."[8] Despite a common monastic pattern, however, each region represented a unique culture. In the section below, we will discuss some of the different styles of monasticism practiced in the sixth century.

---

8. Stewart, "Monasticism," in *The Early Christian World*, 1:346.

Wulfolaic the Lombard in France (Sixth Century)

Of all the different ways that holy men distinguished themselves in the ancient world, few are more intriguing than the dendrites (tree-dwelling saints) and the stylites (pole-dwelling saints). Surprisingly perhaps, pole sitting or column dwelling was an established practice among Christians in Syria. The first of the pole-sitters was Simeon Stylites (*stylites* is a Greek word meaning "column"). Not finding life in a monastery spartan enough, Simeon longed to be physically closer to Christ, and so constructed a small perch about three feet in diameter at the top of a pole in which he lived for four decades. Though living alone, he was sustained by food brought by admirers from across the Christian world. He was sought after by clerics, laypeople, and even the royal court. The more eccentric he became, the greater his fame spread. By the time of his death in 459, his pillar measured about sixty feet in height.

Simeon's method of attaining union with God by living on a pole was too brilliant to let fall into disuse. He had many imitators, including the fifth-century Syrian Daniel Stylite, who lived on a pillar outside of Constantinople for more than three decades. There was also the Greek saint Alypius Stylite, who is reported to have been 118 years old when he died in the year 640. By this time, there were numerous pole-sitters dwelling in tiny perches no bigger than a telephone booth in pursuit of God.

In the sixth century in Western Europe, a would-be stylite named Wulfolaic emulated Simeon in a heroic battle against the pagans at Carignan—near the modern border of France and the Netherlands. In order to sway the townspeople away from the worship of their goddess Diana and toward the Christian God, Wulfolaic lived on a pillar adjacent to the shrine as if in a spiritual stand-off with the pagan deity. It is not clear who won the battle. Although Wulfolaic eventually persuaded the people through forceful preaching and not a little mockery to tear down the pagan shrine, he was bested by the weather. Northern France is not Syria, and the damp and frigid air was too much to bear for a man so scantily clad. As Wulfolaic later said to Bishop Gregory of Tours:

> when winter came, I was in such wise pinched with the icy cold that often the severe frost made the nails drop from my toes, while frozen water hung from my beard like melted wax of candles.[9]

Barefoot and beleaguered, Wulfolaic's clerical superiors, the bishops, bade him dismount his pole and enter a monastery like a proper Western monk. To his chagrin, the bishops destroyed his holy pillar, and he was forced to dwell among a community of monks less barefaced than himself. Western Europe was no place for pole sitting.

Simeon Stylites the Younger in Syria (521–597)

Despite Western Europe's cold reception of pillar living, the venerable stylite tradition remained steadfast in Syria, where the air was dryer and warmer, and where bishops did not have the moxie to strong-arm holy pole-sitters to descend their stairways to heaven. The sixth-century Syrian Simeon "the Younger" learned of this strict form of pillar living from his mentor John Stylite. Orphaned as a boy, Simeon was taught by John the rigors of pole living, and the two lived side-by-side on adjacent poles for years. Simeon himself was a spiritual prodigy, living by himself on a pole before he had even lost his childhood teeth. While his mentor was able to hold Simeon's austerity in check while alive, John's death left Simeon free to experiment with the extremes of column living.

9. Gregory of Tours, "History of the Franks 8.15," in Richard Fletcher, *The Barbarian Conversion: From Paganism to Christianity* (Berkeley and Los Angeles: University of California Press, 1997), 274.

Deprived of his spiritual guide, Simeon moved from pole to pole like a hermit crab searching for a shell greater than the former. He eventually settled for a pillar near Antioch. Having attracted countless visitors in search of miracles and spiritual direction, Simeon's outdoor living room became the grounds of a monastery and basilica, the ruins of which exist to this day. There Simeon lived on his holy column for almost seventy years. Like Simeon the Elder, Simeon the Younger was believed to possess great authority due to his austere pursuit of God. During the Christological disputes of the era, Simeon acted as a theological arbiter among the rival interpretations of Christ's natures, maintaining a square commitment to what came to be regarded as Chalcedonian orthodoxy in the Byzantine Empire.

Benedict of Nursia in Italy (c. 480–543/547)

While Simeon was searching for a pole, Benedict of Nursia was traversing the Italian countryside looking for a new place to found a community of monks. Although monasticism had been alive and well in the West for centuries, Benedict gave international unity and regulation to the practice in its Western forms. Born in northern Italy in the second half of the fifth century, Benedict cut his teeth on monastic living by retreating to a remote cave, where he dwelled for several years as a recluse. He eventually founded and led several monasteries in central and southern Italy, but was unpopular among monks because of his strictness. In around the year 529, Benedict moved to the very remote hilltop of Monte Cassino in southern Italy, where he founded an extremely influential monastery. There he wrote a guidebook for holy living that incorporated the best insights from monks living generations before.

Benedict's *Rule* bound monks to their abbots. It also regulated every aspect of their lives. From what they could eat to how much they could sleep and to how many hours they labored each day, the *Rule* gave the blueprint for holy living in the West for more than a millennium (and there are, of course, still many monasteries regulated by the document). So-called Benedictine monasteries were immensely successful and easily adaptable to new contexts; and it is impossible to discuss the development of Western medieval Christianity apart from the influence that Benedictine monasteries played.

We may describe the sanctity toward which Benedict's *Rule* directed its adherents as one wholly committed to the Latin expression of *orare et labore* (to pray and to labor). Benedictine holiness was concerned with uniting prayer and manual labor for the glory of God. Benedict was not overly impressed with the ascetism of holy men and women in the East, and instead prescribed a life that was stern yet sensible. Far more important for Benedict was a monk's obedience to his abbot—that was true piety. Whereas Eastern monks tended to be more independent and mobile, Benedictine spirituality underscored the importance of *stabilitas*—living in the same monastery for life under the authority of the *abbas* or spiritual "father" of the monastery—the abbot. The monk was to "follow the Rule as his master," without deviating from it.[10] The cardinal virtues of obedience, humility, and silence were essential to the ordering of the monk's life in a community setting, and there was little patience for those who did not cultivate such virtues.

Radegund the Frank in France (c. 520–587)

During the time that Benedict's *Rule* was being written in Italy, there was any number of female monastics living austere lives in pursuit

10. *The Rule of St. Benedict*, trans. Anthony Meisel and M. L. del Mastro (New York: Doubleday, 1975), 51.

of union with Christ. In fact, ascetic women like Radegund were becoming more and more common in the sixth century. Radegund was a Frankish (or Germanic) barren queen who watched, powerlessly, as her husband, King Clothar, moved from one concubine to another until he finally sired a son who would inherit his throne. She would have preferred to have been a virgin, but society did not allow this option for a princess like herself. It was said that, while her husband slept, she would vacate her bed out of penance for being forced to have sex, "put on a hair cloak and pray on the cold ground near the privy [or outhouse]."[11] As a sort of captive to her husband's desires and to the dictates of contemporary society, Radegund tempered the undesirables of marriage with the founding of monasteries (and hospitals). She was a Roman *matrona*—a woman benefactor. In the middle of the sixth century, after more than a dozen years of fruitless marriage to the king, she finally received permission to enter a convent as a deaconess (since she could not be a nun due to marriage). By 561, she had established a convent in Poitiers (in France) called the Abbey of the Holy Cross and had gathered a number of women around her in need of spiritual instruction.

Now unmolested from the unholy obligations of marriage, Radegund was revered for her bodily deprivations and for her benevolence toward others. According to her biographers, Radegund pursued rigorous devotional practices in pursuit of God. She adopted a meager diet of vegetables and water. Not only did she wear wooly clothes that brushed uncomfortably against her skin at all times, but she once "bound her body with iron circlets and chains" as penitence during Lent. She was also reported to have branded herself with a heated brass plate cross in an effort to feel the pain of the cross on

---

11. Ruth Karras, *Sexuality in Medieval Europe: Doing unto Others* (London and New York: Routledge, 2012), 48.

her body.[12] In all these mortifications, she was heralded as a holy woman of God. Like many others during her lifetime, Radegund venerated the relics of famous saints and spent hours in prayer and contemplation. She died in the year 587 as a woman of great piety.

Columba of Ireland (521–597)

The sixth century witnessed widespread growth of Christianity in Ireland, much as it had in Germany. Although the Irish church had been active for several generations, monastic communities were popping up all across the so-called island of Hibernia. These monasteries were typically coenobitic, populated by monastics wearing long white tunics who ate a spare diet and coupled their rigorous prayer lives with confession and manual labor. Among many other distinguished monks, Columba was a central figure who captured the spirit of the Irish holy person at a time when Ireland as a whole was introduced to monasticism. This era of the Irish church was appropriately called the Age of the Saints.

Columba, otherwise known as Colum Cille, was an Irish prince who founded several monasteries, including the famous monastery of Iona in Scotland. He received a fine Christian education, possibly after converting to Christianity from childhood paganism. In his forties, Columba renounced his homeland and embraced what has been called "white martyrdom," a life of sacrifice, prayer, and pilgrimage outside of one's homeland—a sort of self-imposed banishment for the sake of Christ. White martyrdom was a distinct feature of Irish (and Welsh) Christianity. It was a pilgrimage

---

12. Marilyn Dunn, *The Emergence of Monasticism: From the Desert Fathers to the Early Middle Ages* (Oxford: Blackwell, 2000), 109.

committed to "lifelong exile,"[13] typically with no possibility of returning home.

White martyrdom was so called because it did not involve the shedding of blood. The Irish drew the concept of white martyrdom from Abraham's journey from the land of the Chaldeans to Canaan as well as from the many pilgrimages biblical characters made in obedience to God. White martyrdom was based on Jesus' life, which was summed up as being one where Jesus had "nowhere to lay his head" (Matt. 8:20); as well as Jesus' words that the one who "loves father or mother more than me is not worthy of me" (10:37). White martyrdom was contrasted with other forms of martyrdom, as seen, for instance, in the following Irish text from the seventh century:

> Now there are three kinds of martyrdom which are accounted as a Cross to a man, white martyrdom, green martyrdom, and red martyrdom. White martyrdom consists in a man's abandoning everything he loves for God's sake. . . . Green martyrdom consists in this, that by means of fasting and labour he frees himself from his evil desires, or suffers toil in penance and repentance. Red martyrdom consists in the endurance of a Cross or death for Christ's sake.[14]

After the cessation of prosecution of Christians, at least in the Roman world, monasticism replaced martyrdom as the highest calling of the Christian life. While martyrdom through blood was no longer a possibility, monastics like the Irish embraced a white martyrdom for Christ.

---

13. Malcolm Lambert, *Christians and Pagans: The Conversion of Britain from Alban to Bede* (New Haven and London: Yale University Press), no page number but between footnotes 32 and 33 and about half way through.
14. Ware, *The Orthodox Church*, 15.

Figure 6.2. Types of Martyrdom in the Ancient World	
Name	Description
Red Martyrdom	Suffering that leads to the shedding of blood—typically death
White Martyrdom	Self-imposed exile from homeland
Green Martyrdom	Living in fasting and penance

According to the biographies of Columba—part of a larger type of literature called hagiography, which, like Athanasius's biography of Antony, took poetic license in their celebrations of the lives of famous saints—Columba had the gift of prophecy and healing, and was very learned. Countless miracles were attributed to him, and his ability to see in the future and interact with the spiritual world "flowed from his role as a holy man with access to knowledge denied to ordinary mortals."[15] The "pattern of sanctity"[16] that Columba established was emulated by many other Irish monks, whose white martyrdom led them across the British Isles and even into Continental Europe.

Conclusion: Holy Living as Austere, Ascetic, and Sometimes Bizarre

In the sixth century, Christians understood holiness in various ways. As we have seen, the Christian East tended to produce hermits and semi-hermits that were more independent and more radical; in the West, monastics tended to be in closer quarters and under more scrutinized authority; many Western holy people also practiced mortification. In Egypt, desert living was standard practice; in Syria, it was pole and tree dwellers who were highly regarded. In Italy,

15. Lambert, *Christians and Pagans*, between footnote 36 and 37.
16. Adomnan of Iona, *Life of St Columba* (London: Penguin, 1995), no footnote but in the introduction.

monasticism emphasized obedience to an abbot and manual labor; in Ireland, holiness was linked to white martyrdom and scholarship.

Despite these regional variances, there was a consensus by the sixth century that holiness was best attained through austere labors, renunciation of material goods and familial bonds, and sometimes bizarre behavior. On the narrow path toward heaven, there was no time to lose, and nothing material worth taking. Holy men and women interpreted the biblical commands to hate family, battle with the forces of darkness, liquidate our possessions, and purge those bodily impediments that distract us from the kingdom of heaven quite literally. For them, the Bible demanded immediate obedience, and their bodies were altars of sacrifice bringing about salvation and sanctification. Far from today, which often locates sanctity in wealth, health, and popularity, in the sixth century it was believed that holiness emanated from men and women willing to deprive themselves of all earthly attachments in order to gain union with God—and with such deprivations and austerities, the gifts of healing, discernment, and foreknowledge supernaturally followed like rays of heat from the sun.

7

What's Islam?

It was the year 691. The head of the Church of the East, called the catholicos, was a man named Hnanisho I. His name meant "mercy of Jesus" in Syriac, and he had been leading the East Syrian Christians during a very troubling time in their history. For the past several decades, Islamic rule had overtaken much of the Middle East, and it was not exactly clear what the relationship was between the Church of the East and the new Islamic government. For more than two decades in the early seventh century, for instance, there was no catholicos of the Church of the East because the Islamic government refused to approve any of the church's candidates.

Upon the arrival in Kufa, Iraq, of the caliph of the Muslim Umayyad Dynasty 'Abd al-Malik ibn Marwan in 691, Catholicos Hnanisho formally welcomed him, offering him the usual warm greetings and presents expected of dignitaries at that time. The caliph, curious about what the catholicos knew about Islam, asked a lighthearted question, "What do you think, catholicos, of the religion of the Arabs?"

The caliph was not prepared for the answer. The catholicos promptly replied, "It is a religion established by the sword and not a faith confirmed by miracles, as the Christian faith and the old Law of Moses."[1] Deeply offended, the caliph immediately ordered the removal of the catholicos's tongue. Fortunately for the catholicos, he had influential friends who interceded with the caliph, lessening his punishment from the loss of his tongue to the subsequent loss of his throne. Hnanisho was never allowed to enter the presence of the caliph again, and his brazen remarks gave his enemies an opportunity to remove him from office. The next couple of years for Hnanisho were traumatic. His Christian rival took the office of the catholicosate through bribery, imprisoned him, exiled him, and finally had him thrown off a mountain and left for dead. Found by shepherds at the base of the mountain to have astonishingly escaped death, he was restored to health before eventually being restored as catholicos.

The Question of Islam

The story of Catholicos Hnanisho throws light on a significant time in the church's history. From the point of view of Christians in the East, the Arab Islamic empire was growing at an alarming rate since its emergence in the first half of the seventh century. As Byzantine scholar Judith Herrin writes, "In a single decade (632/42), the Arabs had occupied Syria, Palestine and the richest province of Egypt, including the Christian Holy Places of Jerusalem and Bethlehem."[2]

It took some time for Christians to make sense of the religious and political realities transpiring. Although 'Abd al-Malik's question to Hnanisho in 691 concerning what he thought "about the religion of the Arabs" elicited a negative response, other Christians at this time might have answered differently. In this chapter, we will investigate

---

1. Quoted in Robert Hoyland, *Seeing Islam as Others Saw It: A Survey and Evaluation of Christian, Jewish and Zoroastrian Writings on Early Islam* (Princeton: The Darwin Press, 1997), 203.
2. Judith Herrin, *Byzantium: The Surprising Life of a Medieval Empire* (Princeton and Oxford: Princeton University Press, 2007), 86.

various seventh-century Christian responses to the following
question: what is Islam?

A Short History of Arab Occupation of the Christian East

According to Muslim accounts of Jerusalem's capture, the second
leader of the Rashidun Caliphate, Umar, a friend to the recently
deceased prophet Muhammad and Islamic ruler from 634 to 644,
refused the pleas of the Byzantine patriarch of Jerusalem to offer
prayers in the Church of the Holy Sepulchre. Umar recognized that
Arab Muslims would expropriate the historic church as a mosque had
he prayed there, so he adjourned to the Temple Mount where he
commissioned the construction of a mosque. On that hill today, years
after Umar's mosque has been built and destroyed, stands arguably
the most recognizable symbol of Jerusalem—the Dome of the
Rock—whose ornate golden inscriptions from the Qur'an shout out
to the nearby Church of the Holy Sepulchre, after which it was
designed, and all the Christian inhabitants of city that: "There is no
god but God alone," and that this God, Allah, "did not beget [a son
such as Jesus]."[3] The symbolism spoke louder than words: Islam was
now supplanting Christianity in the city where Jesus was crucified,
buried, and resurrected.

Jerusalem proved just the beginning of Arab Muslim conquest
of the Christian world. As alluded to above, in the same year that
the Arabs took Jerusalem, the Rashidun Caliphate captured Antioch,
where the name *Christian* originated, and where the church
commissioned countless missionaries like the apostle Paul. In 640,
Muslims captured the city of Edessa. This was the center of Syriac
Christianity. Two years later the Armenian city of Dvin fell, the same

---

3. Sidney Griffith, *The Church in the Shadow of the Mosque: Christians and Muslims in the World of
Islam* (Princeton: Princeton University Press, 2008), 33.

year Alexandria was conquered. And by 645 the capital of the Church of the East, Seleucia-Ctesiphon, was overtaken. In short, within a dozen years of the death of Muhammad, every major branch of Christianity in the Middle East was under some form of Islamic rule, including the historic Christian patriarchates of Antioch, Alexandria, and Jerusalem. How would the church respond?

As discussed in Chapter 5, there were three major Christian bodies in the Middle East at this time: (1) the Eastern Orthodox Church, which was the state religion of the Byzantine Empire, and whose most prominent bishops codified the doctrine of the Ecumenical Councils; (2) the Oriental Orthodox Church, representing those churches in the Byzantine Empire whose bishops (and therefore dioceses) fell out of favor with Byzantium upon the conclusion of the Council of Chalcedon in 451, whose "members" generally lived in Egypt, Armenia, Roman Syria, Ethiopia, and Nubia; and (3) the Church of the East, stationed outside of the Byzantine Empire in modern-day Iraq, Iran. and southeastern Turkey. The nature of the division among these three bodies was their contrary understandings of the natures of Christ, which were compounded by ethnic, nationalistic, political, and linguistic differences.

In the seventh century, at which time Arab Muslims began conquering much of the Middle East, each of these three bodies was poised to respond to Muslim occupation in different ways. Byzantine Christians had the most to lose since their religion was directly related to the welfare of the Byzantine Empire. It is not surprising, therefore, that they were most opposed to Muslim rule. The Church of the East, by contrast, would seemingly have found Arab Muslim rule superior to Zoroastrian Sassanian (Persian) rule since the latter had been hostile to Christians under their jurisdiction, especially in the fourth century. Finally, although the Oriental Orthodox Christians generally despised the Byzantines and were pleased to see their clutch of power loosened, they regarded their new Muslim overlords disdainfully.

Contrary to stereotypes in the media today, Arab Muslim rule did not seriously threaten Christians living in the seventh century. As medieval historian Robert Schick explains, "the [archaeological and literary] evidence for the implementation of extensive anti-Christian policies in the Early Islamic period is slight."[4] Rather than demanding conversion to Islam, Arabs preferred to tax non-Arabs as a way to finance their wars against them. It was only later that Islamic rule created an environment in which it was socially and politically more expedient for Christians to convert to Islam than to remain in the church. Because of the unique context of each of the three main Christian bodies in the Middle East in the seventh century, below we will discuss their varied responses to Islam according to their theological branches.

The Eastern Orthodox Church

"The first encounter of Islam with Orthodox [Byzantine] Christianity," writes Orthodox historian John Meyendorff, "took place on the battlefield."[5] Of all the Christian bodies in the Middle East in the seventh century, Byzantine Christians faced the most severe disruption during the rapid expansion of Arab Islam. The Arabs and the Byzantines were in a zero-sum match. The larger the Arab empires grew, the smaller the Byzantine Empire became. The decision of the Arab Umayyad Dynasty to move its headquarters from Saudi Arabia to Syria in 661 was made, in part, to chip away at

---

4. Robert Schick, *The Christian Communities of Palestine from Byzantine to Islamic Rule: A Historical and Archaeological Study* (Princeton: The Darwin Press, 1995), 179.
5. John Meyendorff, "Byzantine Views of Islam," in *Arab-Byzantine Relations in Early Islamic Times*, ed. Michael Bonner (Aldershot and Burlington: Ashgate, 2004), 218.

the Byzantine Empire, which it did until finally overtaking the capital prize of Constantinople in 1453.

The hostility between Byzantine Christians and Arab Muslims is clearly evident in our earliest written documents. Writing in the first half of the seventh century, the Byzantine monk John Moschus bewailed "the godless Saracens"—the word *Saracen* (see Figure 7.1) was a common one for Muslims at that time—who "entered the holy city of Christ our Lord, Jerusalem, with the permission of God and in punishment for our negligence." There they built "the cursed thing" that "they call a mosque."[6] The mosque John was referring to was the dome reportedly commissioned by Umar after he entered Jerusalem in 637. As was common at this time, many Christians understood the conquest of Arab Islam as a form of divine punishment—similar to the way Israelites were punished in the Hebrew Bible for disobedience.

Figure 7.1. Seventh-Century Christian Terms for Muslims	
Term	**Origin**
Saracens	Related to Sarah, Abraham's wife. Some ancient Christians believed Arabs used the term to conceal their descent from Hagar in order to legitimize their ancestry
Hagarenes	Related to the concubine of Abraham, Hagar, an Egyptian slave who mothered Ishmael, commonly believed to be the progenitor of Arabs
Ishmaelites	Related to the first son of Abraham, Ishmael, under the conviction that Arabs descended from Ishmael

John's most famous disciple was a Byzantine monk who eventually became patriarch of Jerusalem. His name was Sophronius, and the two had made many journeys together across the Christian East. We catch a glimpse of Sophronius's disdain for Islam while writing a letter to the patriarch of Constantinople in the year 634. Among other matters discussed, Sophronius appended a list of heresies in

6. Quoted in Hoyland, *Seeing Islam as Others Saw*, 63.

the letter meriting condemnation. In what would be his first among many references to Islam over the next several years, Sophronius prayed that the Christian emperors would soon

> break the pride of all the barbarians, and especially of the Saracens who on account of our sins, have now risen up against us unexpectedly and ravage all with cruel and feral design, with impious and godless audacity.[7]

By the end of the year, Jerusalem was surrounded by Arab soldiers. Unable to give his Christmas homily from the city of Jesus' birth in nearby Bethlehem due to raids, Sophronius tempered his joyous sermon with biting contempt of the Muslims:

> Unwillingly, indeed, contrary to our wishes, we are required to stay at home, not bound closely by bodily bonds, but bound by fear of the Saracens. . . . If we were to live as is dear and pleasing to God, we would rejoice over the fall of the Saracen enemy and observe their near ruin and witness their final demise.[8]

Unfortunately for Sophronius, that day never came. When Caliph Umar captured Jerusalem around the year 637 and summarily hired a Christian man to begin construction of a mosque, Patriarch Sophronius had the man excommunicated for helping build a "place which Christ has cursed."[9] Like John Moschus, Sophronius interpreted the Arab Islamic conquest of Jerusalem as a form of divine punishment "because of our innumerable sins and serious misdemeanours."[10]

In a sermon given on the Feast of Epiphany around the year 636, Sophronius resorted to apocalyptic language to catalog the list of

7. Quoted in Hoyland, *Seeing Islam as Others Saw*, 69.
8. Hoyland, *Seeing Islam as Others Saw It*, 70–71.
9. Ibid., 63.
10. Ibid., 70.

woes the church was experiencing at the hands of the Muslims. As a lengthy excerpt from his sermon reveals:

> But the present circumstances are forcing me to think differently about our way of life, for why are [so many] wars being fought among us? Why do barbarian raids abound? Why are the troops of the Saracens attacking us? . . . Why are the birds of the sky devouring human bodies? Why have churches been pulled down? Why is the cross mocked? Why is Christ, who is the dispenser of all good things and the provider of this joyousness of ours, blasphemed by pagan mouths so that he justly cries out to us: "Because of you my name is blasphemed among the pagans." . . . That is why the vengeful and God-hating Saracens, the abomination of desolation clearly foretold to us by the prophets, overrun the places which are not allowed to them, plunder cities, devastate fields, burn down villages, set on fire the holy churches, [and] overturn the sacred monasteries. . . . Moreover, they are raised up more and more against us and increase their blasphemy of Christ and the church, and utter wicked blasphemies against God. These God-fighters boast of prevailing over all, assiduously and unrestrainably imitating their leaders, who is the devil, and emulating his vanity because of which he has been expelled from heaven and been assigned to the gloomy shades.[11]

For Sophronius, as well as for the other seventh-century Byzantine writers whose writings have survived, the Arab Muslim conquest over the Holy Land could was best described by evoking the apocalyptic and biblical literature of yesteryear. Due to the sins of the Christian community, God was punishing Christians with a "God-hating" foe too feral and ferocious to tame. As Sophronius's Byzantine friend and fellow-monk Maximus the Confessor wrote about the Muslims, Christian "civilization [was now] itself being ravaged by wild and untamed beasts whose form alone is human."[12] Only God could save the Christian world from this political foe.

11. Ibid., 72–73.
12. Ibid., 78.

In the meantime, Byzantine Christians did not shrink back from engaging Arab Muslims in theological dispute. Another seventh-century Byzantine monk, named Anastasios of Sinai, regarded the religious beliefs of Muslims as the "false notions of the Arabs." Writing at the end of the seventh century, his book titled "The Guide" was critical of Islam:

> Because, prior to any discussion at all, we must condemn however many false notions about us the opponent has, as when we set out to converse with Arabs we have first to condemn anyone who says, "Two gods," or anyone who says, "God has carnally begotten a son," etc.[13]

Interestingly, Anastasios's examples of false accusations that Muslims made against Christians were all found in the Qur'an, underscoring how knowledgeable some Christians were about Islam even during the century when Islam emerged. Whatever the case and however much seventh-century Byzantine Christians knew about the religion of the Arabs, they regarded the Arab Muslims as harbingers of destruction whose theological views distorted Christian truth.

The Church of the East

The Church of the East faced an entirely different context than did the Byzantine Christians. Long accustomed to living under pagan rule, the Church of the East had taken shape in the crucible of the Sassanian Dynasty of the Persian Empire. The Sassanians had come to power in 226 CE. They immediately began punishing those not conforming to Zoroastrianism, the state religion. Tens of thousands of Christians were killed in the fourth century alone, and the Sassanian shahs accused Christians under their authority of collusion with Christians in the Byzantine Empire due to the centuries-long rivalry between Rome and Persia. Although persecution had

13. Quoted in Griffith, *The Church in the Shadow of the Mosque*, 28–29.

generally ceased by the time the Arab Muslims took control of Persia in the 630s, the Church of the East still faced bitter disputes with their enemies—the Oriental Orthodox Christians, many of whom lived in the same towns as members of the Church of the East.

The earliest writings from authors connected to the Church of the East "accept[ed] the imposition of Arab rule relatively passively."[14] Some of our first documentary evidence from the seventh century comes from Ishoyahb III, the catholicos of the Church of the East from 650 to 658. He wrote the following letter to a bishop in the Persian Gulf in the 640s:

> As for the Arabs, to whom God has at this time given rule over the world, you know well how they act towards us. Not only do they not oppose Christianity but they praise our faith, honour the priests and saints of our Lord, and give aid to the churches and monasteries.[15]

Later on in the letter, Ishoyahb chastised the bishop for the hasty conversion of Christians in his region to Islam:

> Whey then do your *Mrwnaye* [certain inhabitants of the Persian Gulf, perhaps in modern Oman] reject their faith on a pretext of theirs? And this when the *Mrwnaye* themselves admit that the Arabs have not compelled them to abandon their faith, but only asked them to give up half of their possessions in order to keep their faith. Yet they forsook their faith, which is forever, and retained the half of their wealth, which is for a short time.[16]

There are two things to note from this letter. First, Ishoyahb presupposed that the Christians under Islamic control were not forced to apostatize. In line with other historical documents at this time, Arab Muslims considered Christians protected people, called *dhimmis*,

---

14. Stephen Gero, "Only a Change of Masters? The Christians of Iran and the Muslim Conquest," in *The Expansion of the Early Islamic State*, ed. Fred Donner (Aldershot and Burlington: Ashgate, 2008), 129.

15. Hoyland, *Seeing Islam as Others Saw It*, 181.

16. Ibid.

who were not to be compelled to convert. As the second chapter of the Qur'an says, "There is no compulsion in religion."[17] Second, the dhimmitude of Christians was connected to their paying of a special tax called *jizyah*. As time went on, Christians in the Middle East increasingly converted to Islam, in part, to avoid paying this tax—which was substituted for military service for Muslims (but not for non-Muslims). Surprising, given that contemporary Muslim reports of Ishoyahb III indicate that he was later imprisoned by the Muslim emir for not paying a bribe to him and that Christian churches were destroyed in the meantime, Ishoyahb described the arrival of Islam as superior to that of their former rulers.[18]

Catholicos Ishoyahb's depiction of Arab Muslim conquests over the Church of the East parallels that offered by another East Syrian Christian monk named John bar Penkaye. In an historical book that he dedicated to his abbot around the year 690, John wrote occasionally about the Muslims. Though not above labeling them "a barbarian people" and advancing other prejudicial views, John was not hostile to Arab Muslim reign:

> Before calling [the Muslims], (God) had prepared them beforehand to hold Christians in honour; thus they also had a special commandment from God concerning our monastic station, that they should hold it in honour.[19]

According to John, God sent the Arab Muslims to destroy the Sassanians, but the former did not harass the Christians. "Of each person," John wrote, the Muslims "required only tribute, allowing him to retain in whatever faith he wished."[20] John's only complaint

---

17. *The Qur'an* 2:256, trans. M. A. S. Abdel Haleem (Oxford: Oxford University Press, 2010), 29.
18. For more see, Gero, "Only a Change of Masters?" in *The Expansion of the Early Islamic State*, 126.
19. Hoyland, *Seeing Islam as Others Saw It*, 197.
20. Ibid., 196.

with Muslim lordship was that Muslims did not make enough of a distinction between Christians and pagans. Yet he was also under the belief that the Muslim conquest was indicative of the end times, and he concluded his late seventh-century book "on an apocalyptic note,"[21] dwelling on the destruction of the Arab conquests and of the accompanying natural disasters.

The Oriental Orthodox Church

The Oriental Orthodox Christians probably had the least to lose when the Arab Muslims took over political control of the Middle East. That's because they had been prosecuted by the Byzantine Christians for falling out of favor with conciliar laws, that is, with doctrines adjudicated at the Seven Ecumenical Councils. Nonetheless, their responses to the Arab conquests were not positive, and it was the Oriental Orthodox Christians who first detailed the conquest of the Arab Muslims in apocalyptic literature. Writing in the second half of the seventh century, the Armenian historian and bishop Sebeos connected the appearance of the Arab Muslims with the prophecies of Daniel. Specifically, Sebeos likened the Arab Muslims to the fourth beast of Daniel 7. In his own words, "this fourth kingdom, which rises from the south [east], is the kingdom of Ishmael."[22]

---

21. Ibid., 199.
22. Walter Kaegi, "Initial Byzantine Reactions to the Arab Conquest," in *The Expansion of the Early Islamic State*, 120.

Figure 7.2. Sebeos's Interpretation of the Four Beasts in Daniel 7		
Verse	Beast	Symbol
4	First	Greeks
5	Second	Sassanians
6	Third	Gog and Magog
7	Fourth	Ishmaelites

Probably our most detailed interpretation of the expansion of Islam in the seventh century from the Oriental Orthodox Christians was written around the year 690. *Pseudo-Methodius* is a Syriac document ascribed to Bishop Methodius of Olympus who was martyred in the early fourth century. The apocalypse divided the history of the world into seven millennia, from the Fall of Adam and Eve to the Second Coming of Christ. The author of the book interpreted the Arab conquest as the fulfillment of Old and New Testament prophecy. Looking back into events foretold in the Hebrew Bible, the author of *Pseudo-Methodius* interpreted the battle between "the Children of Ishmael, son of Hagar" and the Romans as a sign of the last times—of life in the seventh millennium. The author interpreted the Arab Muslim as a "wild ass of a man, with his hand against everyone" (Gen. 16:12). As wild donkeys, the sons of Ishmael were destined to wreak havoc on the Romans in the same way the Romans once ravaged and pillaged "the Hebrews and the Persians." As the document states about the "Children of Ishmael":

> It was not because God loves them that he allowed them to enter the kingdom of the Christians, but because of the wickedness and sin which is performed at the hands of the Christians, the like of which has not been performed in any of the former generations.[23]

23. "The Apocalypse of Pseudo-Methodius," trans. Sebastian Brock, in *The Seventh Century in the West-Syrian Chronicles*, ed. Andrew Palmer (Liverpool: Liverpool University Press, 1993), 230–32.

The author of *Pseudo-Methodius* attributed the merciless plunder of the Christians at the hand of the Muslims to Christian deviant sexual practices and prostitution, about which the apostle Paul forewarned in Rom. 1:24–27. God was apparently punishing Christianity for sexual sins. Everything would be impacted by the Arab Muslim conquest—men and women, young and old, fish and animals, land and sea. The persecution would test the resolve of the church, and many Christians would "deny the true Faith . . . along with the holy Cross and the awesome Mysteries."[24]

At the end of the seventh week of endless devastation, and in accordance with New Testament prophecy, "the king of the Greeks"—which we assume to be the Byzantine emperor—was destined to conquer the Muslims, pour out his fury on apostate Christians, and usher in a golden age of peace when "churches will be renovated, towns will be rebuilt, [and] priests will be freed from tax."[25] But this peace will be short-lived:

> The moment the Son of Perdition appears, the king of the Greeks shall go up and stand on Golgotha and the holy Cross shall be placed on that spot where it had been fixed when it bore Christ. The king of the Greeks shall place his crown on the top of the holy Cross, stretch out his two hands towards heaven, and hand over the kingdom to God the Father. And the holy Cross upon which Christ was crucified will be raised up to heaven, together with the royal crown.[26]

This action will then reveal the identity of the Son of Perdition, who will take his seat in "God's Temple" in Jerusalem, deceiving everyone until the Lord's "Advent" will lead to his banishment to hell, while Christ's faithful will praise him.[27] All in all, *Pseudo-Methodius* dwelt on the destruction of the Christian world at the hands of Arab

24. "The Apocalypse of Pseudo-Methodius," 235.
25. Ibid., 238.
26. Ibid., 240.
27. Ibid., 242.

Muslims, who were predestined by God to be used as unholy vessels of wrath before they would then be destroyed at the Second Coming of Christ.

Conclusion: Islam as a Source of Division among Christianity

The seventh century was one of the most significant centuries in the history of world Christianity. Though unforeseen at the time, the expansion of Islamic empires beginning in the seventh century across the Middle East led to the "continuous, if gradual, diminishment"[28] of Christianity in this region, a process that persists to this day. Despite the long-term effects of Arab Muslim conquest of the Middle East, Christianity was not seriously threatened in the seventh century. It was only Arabs, and those Christians living on the frontiers, who experienced forceful pressure to convert to Islam. At first, Islam was seen primarily as a religion for Arabs—and only later as a religion for all people. In the seventh century, there was not really a financial incentive for non-Arabs to convert to Islam since it was Arabs *who happened to be Muslims*—and not Muslims per se—who received tax breaks. It was only later that Christians began converting to Islam en masse, in part, due to the tax breaks they received as Muslims.

What did Christians think about Islam in the seventh century? The Eastern and Oriental Orthodox Christians viewed Islam negatively, and our earliest writers do not really record anything positive at all about the religion or politics of their new overlords. A book called "The Teaching of Jacob," written around the year 634 (only two years after Muhammad's death), summarizes the written testimony of two traditions. When the Christian Palestinian Jacob asked an old Jewish man, "What can you tell me about the prophet [one of the first-known references to Muhammad in all of world history]

28. Griffith, *The Church in the Shadow of the Mosque*, 14.

who has appeared with the Saracens?" the man replied, "He is false, for the prophets do not come armed with a sword."[29] (It should be remembered that Catholicos Hnanisho, speaking a few decades later, is recorded to have stated the same thing to the Muslim caliph). As far as the Church of the East was concerned, which regarded its Arabs overlords as no worse (but no better) than its Sassanian ones, the Muslims were understood to be protectors of its churches who maintained diplomatic relations with its catholicos.

What each of the three Christian traditions had in common was their belief that the Arab Muslim conquests were a result of divine punishment. As historian Sydney Griffith explains, the

> Christians of all communities unanimously regarded the conquest as a disaster, and when they were not blaming it on their own sinfulness they were citing the sins of their Christian adversaries, whom they regarded as heretics, as the proximate cause of the conquest and of the death and destruction it brought in its wake.[30]

Although there was great diversity in terms of identifying who was guilty and what they were guilty of, the seventh-century church interpreted Islamic expansion over Christianity as punishment from God. Like the psalmists of the Hebrew Bible, Christians put forth blunt questions to God, and many framed the conquest of Arab Muslims in apocalyptic language. The use of this writing medium underscored the intensity of the destruction. With some exceptions, it was not until a century or so later that Christians, such as John of Damascus, began transitioning from the literary genre of apocalypse to apology, indicating that Christians were coming to the realization that Islam did not signify the end of the world but merely the end of their way of life. Islam would live on, alongside Christianity, in an

---

29. Hoyland, *Seeing Islam as Others Saw It*, 57.
30. Griffith, *The Church in the Shadow of the Mosque*, 28.

unsteady interchange that would provoke terrible bloodshed in the centuries to come.

8

Are Icons Idolatrous?

It was the year 726. The Christian West was blanketed with petty kingdoms that battled with one another for political supremacy while the Christian East was evaporating at an alarming rate. Within a matter of decades, Byzantium had lost much of its kingdom to Arab invasions in the Middle East, including three of its most historic Christian centers—Alexandria, Antioch, and Jerusalem. The Muslim Umayyad Dynasty was intent on overtaking Constantinople to prove itself the undisputed ruler of the East. The Christian people of Byzantium fretfully wondered why God would allow their land to be taken by Muslims while the Byzantine emperor pondered how to defend his empire from invasion. Then something unexpected happened.

In the summer of that year, according to Byzantine chronicler Theophanes, there was a tremendous volcanic eruption from the depths of the Aegean Sea. Boiling lava and pumice stones were hurled from the explosion. Ash blackened the sky for days on end. Between the islands of Thera and Therasia, a new island was emerging out of the sea while massive waves and lava rocks rushed upon the shores of the Byzantine Empire. In the mind of those affected by the eruption, the end of the world was nigh. The Byzantine emperor, an upstart

Syrian soldier later named Leo III who was quite familiar with Arab Muslims, contemplated what this eruption signified. After consulting with his advisors and no doubt being reminded of the so-called Council in Trullo's decisions in 691/2 to limit icon use, he reasoned that God was punishing Byzantium for its idolatrous veneration of icons in much the same way that the Old Testament Israelites were punished by God for worshiping idols. From this line of thinking, it was not a far stretch to imagine that God was thus allowing the Muslims to gain victory after victory over the Christian East because of its clear rejection of iconography. After all, the Umayyad caliph, Yazid II, had ordered the destruction of Christian art just a few years before, and thus Leo set in motion one of the greatest campaigns against religious icons in the history of Christianity.[1]

The Question of Icons

The Iconoclastic Controversy, which the Byzantines called *iconomachy*—"image struggle"—was a theological civil war that was fought in the Byzantine Empire from the 720s to the 840s. It was a war that involved monks and nuns, emperors and empresses, bishops and laypeople. Over time there were casualties on all sides, becoming, as one scholar has deemed the struggle, "one of the major conflicts in the history of the Christian Church."[2] Although political events brought the issue to a head in the eighth century, the Iconoclastic Controversy had at its root a basic question about the appropriateness of religious art for Christian use (which was also part of a larger question about Christ's human and divine natures). We may pose the

1. Byzantine scholar Leslie Brubaker has challenged conventional scholarship concerning Leo III and iconoclasm. See, Leslie Brubaker and John Haldon, *Byzantium in the Iconoclastic Era, c. 680-850: A History* (Cambridge: Cambridge University Press, 2011); and Leslie Brubaker, *Inventing Byzantine Iconoclasm* (London: Bristol Classical Press, 2012).

2. Georges Florovsky, "Origen, Eusebius and the Iconoclastic Controversy," *Church History* (1950) 19: 77–96.

question as follows: what role do images, particularly icons, play in religious devotion; or more straightforwardly, are icons idolatrous? As was the case with other crucial questions in the history of Christianity, several church councils were convened during the eighth century to discuss this urgent question across Europe—each council arriving at a different conclusion. Even though the question of icon use was centered in Constantinople, the Christian West was thoroughly involved in this dispute, and came to contrasting positions regarding the usefulness of icons for Christian devotion.

A Short History of Icons

The word *icon* comes from a Greek term meaning "likeness," "image," or "picture." This was the word used in the Greek Old Testament to describe humanity being made in God's image. In this chapter, icons refer to images of Christ and saints typically painted (in tempura or encaustic) on panels of wood for veneration in public or private spaces in the Christian East. By "venerating" an icon, Christians would kiss, bow to, light a candle before, or burn incense to the person pictured in the icon as a form of respect and as a way of requesting intercessory prayer. Or described more directly, as the Seventh Ecumenical Council defined veneration, it "was a manifestation of honour."[3] Some of the earliest icons known to the church were attributed to Luke the Evangelist in the first century. Ancient Christians believed that Luke "wrote" several icons of the Virgin Mary. One of the most famous of these icons was reportedly transferred to Constantinople from the Holy Land in the 400s. Lovingly adored in the capital of the Byzantine Empire for a century, it was called the Virgin Hodegetria icon (coming from the Greek words meaning "she who shows the way"). Unfortunately, the

---

3. Ambrosios Giakalis, *Images of the Divine: The Theology of Icons at the Seventh Ecumenical Council* (Leiden, New York, and Koln: E. J. Brill, 1994), 125.

original has been lost since the Turkish conquest of Constantinople in 1453, but duplicates have been preserved. As its name suggests, the icon depicted Mary gesturing her right hand toward the infant Christ, signifying that he was the focus of worship—the light of the world who alone brings salvation.

Over time, a rich theology of icons developed in the Christian East. More than mere pictures of dead saints, icons were heavenly doorways imbued with supernatural powers. "To look through the window of the icon," wrote one Eastern historian, was "to look straight into the celestial world."[4] Understood as heavenly portals, icons "straddle[d] the gap between life and afterlife."[5] Icons operated as if the person imaged was really present (much like the Eucharistic bread and wine conveyed Christ's body and blood), and there are countless stories of the people portrayed in icons conversing with their adorers and answering their prayers. Icons, after all, were pictures of men and women of great spiritual power who brokered their holy influence in behalf of their adorers. The powerful saints imaged in icons were given honor in exchange for protection of individuals, families, legions, and cities alike, and there were no shortage of stories celebrating how different icons saved entire cities from destruction. In the sixth century, by which time icon use had reached new heights, we have several examples of images believed to have been made supernaturally (*acheiropoietoi* in Greek, "not made by [human] hands"). These icons were reported to have healing properties. The most famous of such icons was the mandylion, believed to have been made supernaturally when Christ wiped his face with a cloth and sent it to King Abgar V of Edessa in the first century.

4. Ernst Benz, *The Eastern Orthodox Church: Its Thought and Life* (Garden City, NY: Anchor, 1963), 6.
5. C. Stephen Jaeger, *Enchantment: On Charisma and the Sublime in the Arts of the West* (Philadelphia: University of Pennsylvania Press, 2012), 99.

Unlike Western art, icons were more like windows into heaven than they were items of appreciation. Whereas Western art tended to revel in creativity and originality, in the East "the making of icons [was] a sacred craft . . . based on a tradition that [was] carefully preserved and passed on from one generation of monks to the next."[6] Monks prepared themselves for the holy act of icon painting by fasting, repenting, and consecrating all of the materials. It was a liturgical act. The arrangement of icons in churches followed strict guidelines. Most popular were icons of Christ and of his mother, with other saints portrayed accordingly. In Orthodox Churches, it was customary for believers to first pay respect to the icons at the iconostasis (a wall of icons separating the sanctuary in the back from the nave in front) in a strict order (beginning with Christ) and then proceeding to the analogion (lectern) to pay respect to the icon of the saint of that particular feast day. At homes, icons were venerated with deep devotion and piety.

Muslim Opposition to Icons

In the Christian East, where icon use has always been more prevalent than in the West, Christians venerated icons for centuries without interruption or disturbance. But the practice found resistance beginning around the seventh century among the Jewish population. Icon veneration was also repugnant to Muslims. Even though the Qur'an had little to say about art and Muhammad was believed to have preserved statues of Jesus and of Mary when he "cleansed" the Kaaba in Mecca in the year 630, the religion of Islam cultivated a deep distrust of religious art.

Islam eventually developed an elaborate system of calligraphy contrasting with the figural art used by Eastern Christians.[7]

6. Benz, *The Eastern Orthodox Church*, 4.
7. Figural art in Islam was only prohibited in religious contexts, but not in non-religious ones.

Handwriting in Arabic, particularly verses from the Qur'an, provided a sort of spiritual geometry that decorated not only mosques but books, clothing, coins, shields, and sabers. According to the Qur'an, Jesus did not die on the cross, and Muslims found the ubiquity of crosses in North Africa and the Middle East deeply offensive. "As early as 689," Byzantine historian Michael Angold explains, "the [Muslim] governor of Egypt ordered the destruction of crosses, which culminated in a general ban on the public display of the cross."[8] Muslims developed a deep distaste for icons, and Caliph Yazid II prescribed the use of icons among Christians in the early seventh century, a practice followed by other rulers. The Byzantines, "sensitive to Muslim criticisms,"[9] possibly followed a similar procedure beginning in the first half of the eighth century.

The Rise and Fall of Iconoclasm in Byzantium

Due to the alarming expansion of Islam during the seventh and eighth centuries, the Christian East found itself in a precarious position. By this time, North Africa and much of the Middle East was firmly under Islamic governance even though it would take hundreds of years before Muslims significantly outnumbered Christian inhabitants. It appeared that nothing could retard the growth of this new religiously charged political force, and the once-mighty Byzantine Empire was on the verge of extinction unless it could defend its capital of Constantinople. Christians authored many apocalyptic writings at this time, expecting the end of the world and anxiously worrying about the new and powerful religion of Islam. When Leo III became emperor of Byzantium in the year 717, his most pressing concern was figuring out how to protect

8. Michael Angold, *Byzantium: The Bridge from Antiquity to the Middle Ages* (New York: St. Martin's, 2001), 68.
9. Angold, *Byzantium*, 72.

Constantinople from Arab advance. Up till his death in 741, Leo dutifully defended the city against would-be invaders. Hand in hand with his defense of the empire was Leo's iconoclasm, which he saw as vital to Byzantium's protection, but which his detractors, such as contemporary historian Theophanes, regarded as a "baneful doctrine" indicative of an "Arab [Muslim] way of thinking."[10] In the year 730, the patriarch of Constantinople was strong-armed into resigning and Leo appointed a patriarch in his place who would direct his campaign against icons.

Figure 8.1. Terms Related to Icons		
Greek Term	**English Meaning**	**Description**
Icon	"likeness," "image," or "picture"	Representation of Christ, the saints, or an angel (never of God the Father or God the Spirit)
Iconoclast	"breaker of images" or "smasher of images"	A person opposed to icon use (but not opposed to crosses)
Iconodule or iconophile	"venerator of images" or "lover of images"	A person in support of icon use
Iconomachy	"image struggle"	Usually called the Iconoclastic Controversy, this was a dispute over the use of icons from the late 720s to 843 (the Second Council of Nicea was in 787), eventually ending in favor of iconodules

Leo's highhanded legislation against icons found general support among Byzantine soldiers, but not among monks and laypeople. Among monastic opponents of iconoclasm, none was more vocal than a man living outside of the Byzantine Empire. John of Damascus was an Arabic-speaking Syrian whose full name was Yuhannah ibn

---

10. Quoted in Giakalis, *Images of the Divine*, 5.

Mansur ibn Sarjun. He descended from a prestigious line of Arab Christian administrators. Writing in Greek from within Mar Saba Monastery near Jerusalem, John was raised under the authority of the Muslim Umayyad Caliphate. He possibly worked in the government before adopting the religious life as a monk. In response to the iconoclasm of Byzantium, John wrote three separate apologies for the use of holy images—to this day, perhaps the most cogent defenses of Christian images ever composed—probably during the late 720s, 730s, and even 740s. It has been noted that John's residence in Muslim territory—outside of Byzantine control—is what preserved his life in the midst of his candid critique of not only Byzantine policy but the emperor himself.

John's defense of icons varied in each of his three treatises, but we may boil down his arguments as follows. On the one hand, John regarded an attack on images as an assault against Jesus' incarnation. Although the Old Testament prohibited the adoration of images since it often led to idolatry, the incarnation of Jesus Christ sanctified matter. As such, it led Christians of the New Testament to commemorate God's indwelling of human flesh in a material form—such as an icon. Indeed, it was impossible for Christians to think other than in images, which then brought about spiritual contemplation. On the other hand, John carefully drew a distinction between the terms "veneration" (often translated from the Greek word *proskynesis*) and "worship" (in Greek, *latreia*). While veneration refers to the respect and honor that we give to creatures by bowing down to them, worship is adoration that is given only to the Creator. Veneration or honor is proper for icons, but worship or adoration is proper for God alone. As John famously wrote in his first treatise:

> I do not worship matter; I worship the Creator of matter who became matter for my sake, who willed to take His abode in matter; who

worked out my salvation through matter. Never will I cease honoring the matter which wrought my salvation! I honor it, but not as God.[11]

Despite John of Damascus's intellectually robust defense of icon veneration, the iconoclastic campaign persisted for several more decades in the Byzantine Empire. After John's death, Leo's son, Constantine V, convened a council in 754 condemning icon veneration:

> Because the catholic church of us Christians stands in the middle between Judaism and paganism, she walks the new path of piety and worship . . . without acknowledging the bloody sacrifices . . . of Judaism; despising also the entire practice of making and worshipping idols, of which abominable art paganism is the leader and inventor.[12]

The iconoclasts marshaled several lines of argument against the use of icons. Icon use was opposed to holy tradition (and thus a novelty), rooted in poor theology, and opposed to Scripture. Iconoclasts cited the Second Commandment, which forbade making graven images and bowing down to them (Exod. 20:4–5). Other biblical passages undercutting images included the Pauline corpus (e.g., Rom. 1:23, 25; 2 Cor. 5:7). Those who opposed icons also appealed to other passages from the Bible emphasizing that "God is spirit, and those who worship him must worship him in spirit and truth" (John 4:24; cf. 1:18; 5:37; 20:29). Besides scriptural proofs, the iconoclasts maintained that icons of Christ (whose person was always at the heart of the controversy) could not fully capture the mystery of Christ's human *and* divine natures simultaneously, and were thus presenting heretical theology. The pictures of the saints on earth,

---

11. John of Damascus, *On the Divine Images: Three Apologies against Those Who Attack the Divine Images* (Crestwood, NY: St. Vladimir's Seminary Press, 1980), 23.

12. Daniel Sahas, ed. and trans., *Icon and Logos: Sources in Eighth-Century Iconoclasm* (Toronto: University of Toronto Press, 1986), 110–11, quoted in Judith Herrin, *Byzantium: The Surprising Life of a Medieval Empire* (Princeton and London: Princeton University Press, 2008), 110.

which were always incomplete, were an insult to their memories and their heavenly presence with Christ. For Constantine V, writes theologian Leonid Ouspensky, "a true icon must be of the same nature as the person it represents; it must be consubstantial with its model."[13] For iconoclasts, only the Eucharist was regarded as a lawful icon since, when consecrated, it adequately represented Christ's human and divine natures in the bread and wine. Under the iconoclasts, the Eucharist and the cross were given prominence, though relics per se do not appear to have been attacked.

Under Emperor Constantine, icons were removed from churches and iconodules were removed from offices of power. Violence against iconodules also reached new heights. According to historical records, hundreds of monks, the most dogged opponents to iconoclasm, were imprisoned. One of the most famous imprisoned monks was Stephen the Younger. In the early 760s he rose to prominence as one of the chief opponents of iconoclasm, and also personified a growing rift between monks (who were largely iconodules) and soldiers (who were largely iconoclasts). After being exiled, he was imprisoned for almost a year before being condemned to death around the year 765, at which time soldiers then proceeded to drag his mangled corpse through the streets of Constantinople. Despite some of Constantine's building projects, including the famous Hagia Eirene Church in the heart of Constantinople, which notably contained a giant cross in the apse rather than colorful icons as at the adjacent Hagia Sophia Church, the literary records that survived paint a picture of an iconoclastic monarch like none before or after him. At the same time, it is also important to note that Constantine was a popular emperor, who conducted his reign with the general support of the populace and the military.

13. Leonid Ouspensky, *Theology of the Icon*, vol. 1, trans. Anthony Gythiel (Crestwood, NY: St. Vladimir's Seminary Press, 1992), 122.

The Restoration of Icons in Byzantium

The short reign of Constantine V's son from 775 to 780 created the political circumstances for the official (yet temporary) ending of iconoclasm in Byzantium. Constantine VI assumed rule of the Byzantine Empire at the age of nine and so required the co-regency of his mother Irene until he had come of age. But once gaining power, Irene was reluctant to let it go; she later had her son blinded in the same room she gave birth to him, from which wounds he shortly died. In cunning skill, Irene, a fervent iconodule, lessened taxation of monasteries and convened what was called the last of the Seven Ecumenical Councils. Despite strong initial resistance that led to its suspension and then venue change, the council met in Nicea (the location of the first Ecumenical Council) in 787, and proceeded to rescind the iconoclasm of the past several decades. In the fourth of eight sessions, the council argued for the legitimacy of icon use based on Scripture, tradition, and reason, while in the next session it was recorded that all iconoclastic books were to be destroyed (thus leaving us with precious little literary remains from the iconoclasts).

One of the key arguments of the council members of Second Nicea was, in the words read by Epiphanius the Deacon, that "the honour of the icon is conveyed to the prototype." The example then given was that of an icon of a king.

> When one looks at the icon of a king, he sees the king in it. Thus, he who bows to the icon bows to the king in it, for it is his form and his characteristics that are on the icon. And as he who reviles the icon of a king is justifiably subject to punishment for having actually dishonoured the king—even though the icon is nothing but wood and paints mixed and blended together with wax—so does he who dishonours the figure of any of these [saints] transfer the insult to him whose figure is [on the icon].[14]

---

14. Quoted in Sahas, *Icon and Logos*, 101.

Unbeknownst to contemporaries, Second Nicea would share more than just a namesake with First Nicea. For just as the First Council of Nicea ended decisively one way, its pronouncements were quickly ignored by later emperors. Within a few decades of the Seventh Ecumenical Council's clear victory against iconoclasm, a new emperor of Armenian descent, named Leo V, reinstated legislation against icons soon after the beginning of his reign in the year 813. Faced with great outside threats, Leo adopted the practice of his predecessors, especially Constantine V, by associating military victory with iconoclasm. Leo convened a council in 815 that re-imposed a ban on images.

It was a few years after this council met that the most influential monastic opponent of iconoclasm was active. His name was Theodore the Studite, who was the abbot (or leader) of the famous Studios Monastery in Constantinople, a monastery well known for its opposition to iconoclasm. After continued conflict with the imperial court which naturally led to his exile, Theodore passionately wrote one of the best defenses of icon use since the time of John of Damascus. Like John a generation earlier, Theodore argued that a rejection of icons was a denial of the incarnation of Jesus—of his taking on of flesh in order to redeem the world. If Jesus had only been born of God the Father, Theodore would have repudiated icon use since God the Father does not have a body and therefore cannot be imaged. But since Jesus was born of a human woman,

> He naturally has an image which corresponds to that of His mother. If He could not be represented by art, this would mean that He was not born of a representable mother, but that He was born only of the Father, and that He was not incarnate. But this contradicts the whole divine economy of salvation.[15]

---

15. Quoted in Ouspensky, *Theology of the Icon*, 1:153.

Due to his imperial subterfuge, Theodore was exiled a number of times and also beaten, all hastening his death in 826.

Theodore's opposition to iconoclasm was a great boon to the cause of the iconodules, yet there were no major changes to imperial policies. Indeed, the practice of iconoclasm was kept alive by the supposition that icon use could turn God's favor against Byzantium. What changed matters was the co-regency of yet another Byzantine empress with her son, this one named Theodora (her son's name was Michael III). With the help of the imperial court, Empress Theodora restored icon veneration. This coincided with a new annual festival, called the Triumph of Orthodoxy. Theodora ordered the destruction of all iconoclastic documents. The year was 843, more than five decades after Second Nicea had overwhelmingly affirmed the veneration of icons for both private and public use. In one of the hymns at the festival, the important role that icons played in the economy of salvation is sung:

> No one could describe the Word of the Father;
> But when he took flesh from you, O Theotokos [Mary, the Mother of
>   God],
> He consented to be described,
> And restored the fallen image to its former state by uniting it to the
>   divine beauty.
> We confess and proclaim our salvation in word and images.[16]

Since this time, there has never been a real threat to images and icon veneration in the Christian East, but the violent history of this controversy has deeply shaped Orthodox piety.

---

16. Leonid Ouspensky, "The Meaning and Content of the Icon," in *Eastern Orthodox Theology: A Reader*, 2nd ed. (Grand Rapids, MI: Baker, 2003), 34.

The Western Response to the Iconoclastic Controversy

The centuries-long dispute between iconoclasts and iconodules found an inexact parallel in the Christian West. The papacy, going all the way back to the beginning of the Iconoclastic Controversy in the 720s, had always opposed iconoclasm, and it spoke openly of its disapproval of iconoclastic measures. In 731, Pope Gregory III convened a council of Western bishops, which thoroughly criticized iconoclasm and the machinations of Emperor Leo III. In fact, many Greek monks fled Byzantium for the safety of Rome, strengthening Western monasticism. The dispute between the papacy and the Byzantine court was compounded by additional taxes heaped on Rome and by Leo III's confiscation of papal patrimonies and transference to the patriarchate of Constantinople in the 730s. Since that time, the relationship between the pope and the emperor had cooled, so the papal see was thus quite pleased to hear of Second Nicea's repeal of more than a century of iconoclastic practices in the year 787. Although Rome rejected the hasty promotion of the patriarch of Constantinople, Tarasius, from layperson to patriarch and bemoaned the confiscation of its patrimonies several decades earlier, Pope Hadrian supported Second Nicea based on three lines of thought: first, Christ's incarnation meant that Christians should honor matter; second, icons were useful for the purpose of teaching; and third, holy tradition affirmed the veneration of icons.[17]

Despite papal support of Second Nicea, the Carolingian Christians at the court of King Charlemagne, the great ruler of the Franks, responded negatively. As medieval historian Thomas Noble points out, the Carolingian reaction to Second Nicea "showed the Franks [that is, the Carolingians] just how wide a chasm separated them from

---

17. Andrew Louth, *Greek East and Latin West: The Church AD 681-1071* (Crestwood, NY: St. Vladimir's Seminary Press, 2007), 85.

papal Rome."[18] It would seem that the conflict between iconoclasts and iconodules in the East was playing itself out in the West between the Carolingian and papal courts. In 792, the Carolingian Christians sent a lengthy critique of Second Nicea to Pope Hadrian, who responded with a section-by-section correction of the document—much, we may presume, like an annoyed teacher corrects the homework of a pupil. Around the same time, the Carolingian scholar Theodulf of Orleans began work on what has come to be known as the Caroline Books, and in 794, Charlemagne convened a council in Frankfurt to address a host of issues, including the matter of icon use.

Figure 8.2. Terms Related to Charlemagne

Charlemagne (also known as Charles the Great—*Carolus Magnus* in Latin) was the most powerful secular ruler in the Christian West during the Middle Ages. From 768 until his death in 814, he ruled over the Franks, a Germanic people that eventually came to rule over much of Western Europe. In the year 800, he was crowned by the pope as the Holy Roman Emperor. Charlemagne assembled an impressive team of Christian scholars during his reign that greatly strengthened the intellectual tradition of the Christian West. It was during his lifetime and due to his influence that the pope began looking away from the Byzantine Empire in the East for aid and partnerships and toward Christian kings in the West.

The Caroline Books, more than a hundred chapters in total, was long and circuitous in thought. We may break down the arguments of the Carolingians into the following general points. First, the Carolingians questioned the authority of the council to meet. Not only did the Carolingians look down on the hasty promotion of Tarasius from layperson to patriarch of Constantinople but they rejected the council's declaration that it was an "ecumenical" council on the grounds that no Carolingian bishops were invited and that Tarasius was too theologically inept to provide adequate leadership

---

18. Thomas Noble, *Images, Iconoclasm, and the Carolingians* (Philadelphia: University of Pennsylvania Press, 2009), 168.

to the council. Second, the Carolingians believed that Second Nicea's approval of icon veneration was a base and novel superstition, lacking support from either Scripture or tradition. As the preface to the Caroline Books states:

> we reject all verbal novelties and stupid inventions, and not only do we not receive them but we truly hate such filth as that synod which was held in the region of Bithynia [Second Nicea] on account of the most imprudent tradition of adoring images.[19]

Third, the Carolingian document criticized the various biblical passages that Second Nicea used in defense of icon veneration. As a general rule of thumb, the Carolingians complained that the Byzantines interpreted the Bible too literally, which inevitably promoted a "lack of all mystery,"[20] rather than interpreting the Bible symbolically (as the church had done for centuries). Reasoning from the Book of Hebrews, the Carolingians interpreted images as shadows lacking substance. Images, as shadows, were fine for decoration or even instruction, but they were not suitable for adoration. In short, the Carolingians desacralized art.

The relationship between the papal court and the Carolingian court in the West was stretched thin during this time but was patched up upon the succession of a new pope in the year 795. This new pope would, five years later, awkwardly coronate Charlemagne as Holy Roman Emperor, signifying that the pope would look no longer toward Byzantium for aid but to the Frankish kings of Western Europe. A shift in the stage of world Christianity was taking place, when the Western Church would take on a more central role.

19. Quoted in Noble, *Images, Iconoclasm, and the Carolingians*, 185.
20. Ibid., 189.

Conclusion: Icons Allowed

The Iconoclastic Controversy of the eighth and early ninth centuries demonstrated not only the perils of too close a relationship between the church and state but it also indicated just how divided the Christian Church had become. Although the Feast of Orthodoxy was a joyous liturgical celebration commemorated annually on the first Sunday of Great Lent in Eastern churches as a victory for iconodules, a shadow hung over it. Eastern and Western Christian bodies came to regard one another with suspicion until they simultaneously excommunicated one another in the year 1054. While the Christian East, where the heart of the Iconoclastic Controversy took place, declared triumphantly that icon use was not only acceptable but even spiritually enriching, the Christian West took a much more cautious approach toward images. There, like a dormant volcano, iconoclasm in the West would erupt during the Protestant Reformations (not surprisingly, in Germany, where protest against images had been centered at the Carolingian court). In this way, we see that the legitimacy of religious images was a question that eventually brought a unified affirmation in the eighth and ninth centuries in the Christian East, but eventually led to the Christian West's most painful and long-lasting division during the sixteenth century.

9

Who Has Authority over Newly Christianized Nations?

It was the year 865. Boris I, the khan or ruler of the Bulgarian Empire, was making plans for his subjects to convert from paganism to Christianity in order to enhance his growing kingdom. Although he was exploring a possible religious and political alignment with either the Frankish (Germanic) Catholics or Latin (Roman) Christians in the West, Boris was initially forced to become a client of the Orthodox or Greek Christians in the East. In 865, Boris was officially baptized into the Greek Orthodox Church, and he adopted the Christian name of Michael out of deference to his Christian sponsor Michael III, the Byzantine emperor. Like others at the time, the Byzantine or Greek Christians made no distinction between church and state, and wasted no time converting the Bulgarians and instructing them in Greek culture. Boris, however, was not pleased to be a subordinate to Byzantium. He wanted an autonomous Bulgaria—and an autonomous Bulgarian church.

Though still a client of the Byzantine Empire, Khan Boris's desire for independence led him to "shop around"[1] among the three political-religious market places active at that time: Old Rome (that is, Rome, with the pope as the head), New Rome (Constantinople, with the Byzantine emperor and the patriarch of Constantinople working collaboratively), and Second Rome (the symbolic capital of the East Frankish kingdom in Aachen, Germany, headed by Charlemagne's grandsons). Sending letters of inquiry to each of these "Romes" to determine which one came with the least amount of strings attached, Boris soon found his kingdom flooded with Roman Catholic, Greek Orthodox, and Frankish Catholic missionaries. This was a recipe for an ecclesial disaster. As medieval historian John Thompson writes, although these bodies "had not yet formally split, there had been [ongoing] tensions between them, with disputes over both missionary methods and spheres of influence."[2] Boris, strategically delaying announcing with which of these different Christians strands he wanted to align, wrote to the pope in 866, asking: "what should we do?"[3]

The Question of Church Jurisdiction

Probably more than anybody realized at the time, the question that Boris raised in 866 isolated one of the most important issues in ninth-century Christendom: With Europe fast becoming the continent where Christianity would see its greatest amount of growth in the following centuries, which Christian kingdoms in Europe would evangelize and exercise authority over the Slavic people of central Europe was of vital importance. As medieval historian Richard Fletcher explains, "The Slavonic peoples of central Europe, initially the Moravians and the Bulgarians, were confronted, and not for

---

1. Richard Fletcher, *The Barbarian Conversions: From Paganism to Christianity* (Berkeley and Los Angeles: University of California Press, 1997), 350.
2. John Thompson, *The Western Church in the Middle Ages* (London: Arnold, 1998), 15.
3. James Hopkins, *The Bulgarian Orthodox Church: A Socio-Historical Analysis of the Evolving Relationship between Church, Nation, and State in Bulgaria* (Boulder, CO: East European Monographs, 2009), 18.

the last time, with a question which has been fundamental to their sense of identity. Which way does central Europe face, eastwards or westwards?"[4] From about the ninth century onward, pagan political states residing in what is now Bulgaria, Croatia, Czech Republic, Hungary, Poland, Romania, and Slovakia began turning en masse to Christianity, but it was not clear which of the three existing centers of Christianity in Europe would lead the mission and, consequently, gain worthy political allies in a hotly contested part of the world that would influence world events for centuries to come. In this chapter, we will explore the different responses to Boris's important and practical question by focusing on ninth-century central Europe, particularly on the Christianization of the Moravians and the Bulgarians.

Figure 9.1. A Short History of the Slavs

Who were the Slavs? According to Richard Fletcher, the early history of the Slavs "is extremely obscure. Their ancestors have been located by archaeologists in the cultures of the Dnieper system to the north of Kiev [in modern Ukraine]. From these origins migration took them in three directions: westward into Poland and Bohemia; southward across the Danube into the Balkans and Greece; and north-eastward into Russia. This slow drift of peoples seems to have been at its gradual busiest between about 550 and 700. It brought the western and southern Slavs into a frequently painful proximity with Christian Europe and therefore into the dim glow shed by the meager sources which survive from those literate communities."[5]

A Short History of the Three Major Religious Centers of Europe

In the ninth century, the first of the three centers of European Christianity was the East Roman or Byzantine Christians. Headquartered in Constantinople (now Istanbul, Turkey) since the early fourth century, the Byzantine Empire was the eastern half of the Roman Empire. The official language of the empire was Greek,

---

4. Fletcher, *The Barbarian Conversions*, 332.
5. Ibid.

and the empire claimed possession of much of Eastern Europe, Italy, North Africa, and the Middle East. After the Arab Muslim conquests of the seventh century, its territory dwindled considerably. All of the Seven Ecumenical Councils were convened and enforced by the Byzantine Empire, becoming the basis of what is now called the Eastern Orthodox Church. Although it was technically just one of many prominent patriarchates, the patriarchate of Constantinople came to be the symbolic head of the Byzantine Empire. This was especially the case as the patriarchates of Alexandria, Antioch, and Jerusalem came under Islamic governance (though they continued to operate), and the bishopric of Rome was deemed heretical by the patriarchate of Constantinople in 867 for changing the Nicene Creed.

The second major religious center in Europe was the Latin-based Christians in southern Europe. This body later came to be called the Roman Catholic Church, with the pope as the religious head of that institution and Rome as its symbolic head. The pope was the bishop of Rome, but a longstanding custom had regarded the bishopric of Rome—what we later call the papacy—as "the first among equals," *primes inter pares* in Latin. The bishop of Rome was technically under the political jurisdiction of the East Roman or Byzantine Empire, headquartered in Constantinople. However, in the eighth and ninth centuries, the Roman bishop became estranged from the Byzantine Empire, turning instead to the kingdom of the Franks for protection and political affiliation.

The last major center in Europe in the early ninth century was what we may call the kingdom of the Franks or the Carolingian Empire. This Germanic kingdom had come into prominence in the eighth century, and it became incredibly powerful over the course of the long reign of Charlemagne or Charles "the Great," who ruled from 768 to 814. He was crowned the Holy Roman Emperor in the year 800 by the pope as an awkward indication that the papacy now looked toward the Germans in the northwest rather than to the Greeks in the east for religious and political union. The Franks were staunch Catholics, aggressively evangelistic, and not keen to play second fiddle to either the Latins or the Greeks.

During the ninth century, the bishops of these three loosely affiliated centers competed with one another for ecclesiastical jurisdiction like jockeys vying for position in a horse race. The root of contention was linguistic (they each spoke different languages), cultural (though sharing a common theological core, they were culturally quite distinct), and territorial (they were each competing for new political alliances and unwilling to give up ground). This was the case even though the Romans and Germans shared the same Catholic faith. Each of these centers recognized the fundamental importance of aligning with emerging kingdoms, and they each actively sought to form relationships with them, convert them, and acquire them as vassals or "tributaries." At a time when church and state were one, "cultural imperialism" occurred whenever powerful Christian states converted neighboring people groups by making political alliances with them, typically as subordinates. In this way, "The sponsoring of missionary work can thus hardly be separated from politics."[6] Evangelism and conversion were just as much political enterprises as they were religious ones.

---

6. P. M. Barford, *The Early Slavs: Culture and Society in Early Medieval Eastern Europe* (Ithaca, NY: Cornell University Press, 2001), 211.

Figure 9.2. Three Major Centers of Christianity in the Early Ninth Century			
People Group	Rome	Language-Base	Form of Christianity
Byzantines / Greeks	New Rome	Greek	(Eastern) Orthodox
Romans / Latins / Italians	Old Rome	Latin	Catholic
Carolingians / (East) Franks / Germans	Second Rome	Germanic	Catholic

Who Has Authority over the Moravians?

The migration of the Slavs into Eastern Europe, and their subsequent adoption of Christianity, reconfigured the nature of the church in Europe. The Slavic people originated in the northeastern part of Europe and consisted of various tribes such as Bulgars, Croats, Moravians, Poles, Serbs, Slovenes, and Rus. These tribal groups had migrated southward after the invasions of the Avars and Huns from centuries past. The Moravians settled along the Morava River separating the eastern part of the Czech Republic from the western part of Slovakia. There they established a kingdom in the ninth century called Great Moravia, likely between East Francia in the west and Bulgaria in the east (in Bohemia, Moravia, Slovakia, and parts of Hungary).

Figure 9.3. Different Groups of Slavs[7]	
Classification	Languages
East Slavs	Ukrainian, Belarusian, and Russian
South Slavs	Bosnian, Bulgarian, Croatian, Macedonian, Montenegrin, Serbian, Slovenian
West Slavs	Polish, Czech, Slovak

7. Barford, *The Early Slavs*, 15.

Of the three political-religious centers mentioned above, it was the Latins and the Franks / Germans who first evangelized the Slavic Moravians. In the seventh century, Pope Martin I initiated the process of conversion of the Slavs in the Balkans, and it was natural for Frankish bishops to oversee the mission to the Balkans given their location. The Great Moravian prince Mojmir had been baptized in around the year 822, with mass baptism of his people occurring a decade later. The bishopric (also called a diocese) of Passau held ecclesial jurisdiction over the state. The Christianization of the Moravians by the Franks indicated that the former were subject to the latter. As elsewhere in the Catholic Church, church services were conducted in Latin in Moravia. When Mojmir's nephew, Rastislav, became prince of Great Moravia in 846, he expelled the Germanic clergy despite the fact that the East Franks had helped secure his throne. Rastislav had grown increasingly wary of the Franks as their relationship warmed with nearby Bulgaria. As Orthodox historian J. M. Hussey explains, "Moravia lay dangerously vulnerable between these two powers,"[8] and it was incumbent upon Moravia to form allies that could defend its borders. In addition to his fear of an alliance between East Francia and Bulgaria, Rastislav harbored a deep desire to establish a native Slavic church in Moravia—one that was free of Germanic interference and not conducted in the language of Latin, a tongue which none of the ruler's people spoke. Recognizing his need for Slavic-speaking and Slavic-friendly Christian missionaries, Rastislav turned to Byzantium. Writing to Byzantine emperor Michael III in 862, the Moravian ruler wrote, "Since our people rejected idolatry and came under Christian law, we have not had a teacher capable of explaining this faith to us in our own tongue, so that other countries, seeing this, might imitate us."[9] Though a

---

8. J. M. Hussey, *The Orthodox Church in the Byzantine Empire* (Oxford: Oxford University Press, 2010), 95.

modest political state, Rastislav envisioned Great Moravia as a paragon of Slavic knowledge and culture. Before it could shine out among the other Slavic states, however, it would need learned scholars to establish its reputation.

Fortunately for Rastislav, Emperor Michael III knew exactly the men for the task. In consultation with Bishop Photius of Constantinople, they chose Photius's friend Constantine (later named Cyril) and his older brother Methodius. Greek brothers from Thessaloniki, these two men were experienced diplomats and missionaries, highly praised for their intellectual abilities and fluent in several languages, including Slavic, a language they learned as children among the Slavic communities in and around Thessaloniki. It's likely that the Byzantine emperor tacitly acknowledged the jurisdiction of the Germanic Christians over the Moravians, for it does not appear, argues historian Zdenek Dittrich, that he "seriously considered"[10] having Constantine or Methodius ordained as a priest or a bishop. Whatever the case, Constantine agreed to the missionary expedition on the condition that he could translate the Bible into the Slavic language and evangelize the Moravians in their own language. Toward this end, Constantine, Methodius, and their colleagues devised a new alphabet to render the Slavic language before they left for Moravia. It later came to be called the Glagolitic script, also known as Old Church Slavonic, which was based on the south Macedonian dialect familiar to the brothers. Whether directly revealed by God, as the biographies of both Constantine and Methodius proudly proclaimed, or created by the linguistically gifted brothers and their colleagues, the Glagolitic script deeply fused Slavic identity with Christianity in the decades and centuries to come.

9. Anthony-Emil Tachiaos, *Cyril and Methodius of Thessalonica: The Acculturation of the Slavs* (Crestwood, NY: St. Vladimir's Seminary Press, 2001), 57.
10. Zdenek Dittrich, *Christianity in Great Moravia* (Groningen: J. B. Wolters, 1982), 100.

Constantine and Methodius arrived in Great Moravia in the year 863. With the full support of the ruler Rastislav, the brothers taught the new alphabet to selected Moravians, who learned it with alacrity (though the Macedonian dialect of the brothers was not the dialect spoken by the Moravians). Never lacking in productivity, Constantine and Methodius eventually translated the entire Bible, the church liturgy, and several other religious and legal writings into Old Church Slavonic. Rather than using Latin during Mass, which was the unbending custom of the Catholic Church, the brothers urged the usage of Slavic. A Slavic church was taking shape.

It did not take long, however, before Constantine and Methodius encountered resistance among the Germanic clergy. These clergy had been supported by Louis the German, Charlemagne's grandson and king of the Franks. The cause of the resistance was essentially threefold. First and foremost, the Germanic clergy viewed the brothers as ecclesial interlopers. The brothers had no right to intrude on Germanic ecclesial territory—whether invited by the Moravian prince or not. Second, it was a common Western Catholic belief at the time that there were only three sacred languages in which church services could be conducted: Hebrew, Greek, and Latin. Because Constantine and Methodius encouraged the use of Slavic in church services, the Germanic clergy charged them with heresy. Finally, the Germanic clergy quibbled with the theology of the brothers. By this time, there had been a growing rift between the Catholics and Eastern Orthodox concerning whether the Holy Spirit proceeded from the Father alone (the belief of the Orthodox and the wording found in the original Nicene Creed) or from the Father "and the Son" (in Latin, *filioque*—the belief of the Catholics). The presence of Byzantine missionaries like Constantine and Methodius resurfaced this dispute in Catholic lands, inciting a storm of controversy.

Despite the serious accusations hurled against them, Constantine and Methodius diligently trained native Moravian men with the intention of them becoming the leaders of the church. Such a practice would establish a truly Slavic church in Great Moravia, one of the original aims of the Byzantine mission. But there was a problem. Only bishops could ordain men to the diaconate or priesthood, and neither Constantine nor Methodius was a bishop. Nor would it have proven worthwhile to ask the Germanic bishops to ordain the local candidates. Constantine and Methodius, therefore, left Moravia for Venice, possibly expecting that an Italian bishop would be willing ordain the Moravian candidates. They were sorely mistaken. Far from supporting the work of the brothers, the Venetian clergy charged Constantine and Methodius with heresy! As Constantine's ninth-century biography intones on an ominous note,

> No sooner had he [and his brother] arrived in Venice than Latin bishops and priests and monks all descended upon [them] in a body, like crows upon a hawk, and stirred up the heresy of Trilingualism.[11]

The "heresy of Trilingualism" was the contemporary Catholic belief that God had only prescribed for worship the three languages that Pontius Pilate inscribed on a superscription affixed to Jesus' cross in the first century. Though the brothers ably defended themselves against the heresy, arguing that God had given various languages through which to receive glory, including Slavic, the clerics at the deliberations were fiercely opposed to them. Such was the uproar caused by the brothers that the pope became informed, who invited Constantine and Methodius to Rome in order to end the controversy.

The brothers arrived in Rome in the winter of 867/868. The newly installed pope received Constantine and Methodius cordially, especially after the brothers presented him with the recently

---

11. Tachiaos, *Cyril and Methodius of Thessalonica*, 82.

discovered relics of a first-century pope (who was exiled during a time of prosecution) named Clement, which the brothers had previously found in Crimea. In Rome, the pope ordained Methodius to the priesthood, fully approved of Slavic as a language to be legally used in church services, and had other Slavic Moravian disciples of theirs ordained as priests and others consecrated as lectors (a lesser office in the Catholic Church). Constantine died peacefully in Rome in 869 as a monk (his name was changed to Cyril after taking monastic vows), the same year that the pope received a request from the ruler of a small Slavic state called Pannonia for Methodius to come instruct the churches under his jurisdiction. The pope gave permission to the ruler's request but also sent a letter to other Slavic rulers that Methodius was being sent to them all "by God and by the first apostle Peter, keeper of the keys of the kingdom of heaven."[12] The pope's language in this letter evoked the famous passage from the Gospel of Matthew where Jesus gave the "keys of the kingdom of heaven" to Peter as a transfer of authority. The pope was underscoring that Methodius's pastoral office, now as a bishop, ultimately derived its authority from the pope—and thus from Christ himself.

Pannonia was a former Roman province in modern Hungary. Like Great Moravia, it was a Slavic Christian state with aspirations of establishing an independent Slavic-based church. Yet it was technically under the ecclesial jurisdiction of the archdiocese of Salzburg.

Although matters appeared to be moving in Methodius's favor, a change in rulers in Moravia turned over the hour glass of his influence. In the year 870, a new ruler in Great Moravia displaced Rastislav with the help of the Franks, and thus the path was forged for a greater presence of Germanic clerics in that country. These

---

12. Tachiaos, *Cyril and Methodius of Thessalonica*, 93.

Frankish clergy were extremely territorial—and they had an axe to grind with Methodius. In spite of the pope's decision to elevate Methodius to the office of bishop and appoint him over the Slavs, the Germanic clergy convened a synod to condemn him. At the so-called Council of Salzburg, the Germans found Methodius guilty of ecclesial interference and sentenced him to prison. For more than two years he was miserably treated in a German monastery. It was only two years later, in 873, that the new pope heard of this fiasco and ordered the release of Methodius, who summarily returned to Moravia to continue his work. Although the pope appointed Methodius as archbishop of Sirmium (present-day Sremska Mitrovica, Serbia), the Franks continually harassed him and hamstrung his ministry. For the next dozen years, Methodius attempted to stabilize the fledgling Slavic church with limited success.

The Frankish clergy were relieved to hear of Methodius's death in 885. Although Constantine and Methodius had made great inroads into Slavic culture by translating the Bible, the liturgy, and many other religious and legal documents into Old Church Slavonic, their reputation was being sullied and their progress in Moravia disavowed. The papacy, now backing down from its former support of Methodius as archbishop, returned ecclesial jurisdiction to the Frankish bishops and prohibited the use of Old Church Slavonic in the church liturgy. Worst of all, many of the disciples of Constantine and Methodius who were still residing in Moravia were handed over to the Germanic authorities, "who sold some of them at the slave market in Venice and imprisoned the rest . . . , many of [whom] died of hardship."[13] Thus ended the decades-long battle in Moravia among the three Christian centers for jurisdiction. Ecclesial authority fell to

---

13. Tachiaos, *Cyril and Methodius of Thessalonica*, 108.

the Latin Christians, and the seeds of Constantine and Methodius's labor would only blossom in nearby kingdoms.

Who Has Authority over the Bulgarians?

The same religious and political machinations we saw occurring in Great Moravia occurred in nearby Bulgaria. It's not a coincidence that Louis the German was sending missionaries into Bulgaria the same time his missionaries were being expelled from Great Moravia in favor of Byzantine ones. East Francia was an imperialistic and expansionistic kingdom that had grown to considerable power over the years by simultaneously drawing smaller states into its orbit and enforcing Catholic Christianity on its satellite states. Louis the German was hoping to do the same in Bulgaria. But Bulgaria's khan or leader, Boris I, was an adroit politician, and it was his genius to play the Romans, Franks, and Byzantines against one another to the benefit of his rising empire. As historian of Bulgaria James Hopkins comments, "the khan created an auction for the ecclesiastical jurisdiction of Bulgaria where the winner would be the one offering the best incentive."[14]

The Bulgar peoples had settled in present-day Bulgaria in the seventh century, forming the so-called First Bulgarian Empire. The Bulgars were originally a Turkic people who had intermarried with Slavs after settling in the Balkans. Not uncommon at the time, the Bulgars, though the dominant people group, adopted much of the culture of the Slavs and became a sort of hybrid Slavic nation. But the differences between the Bulgars and the Slavs had to be overcome in order for Bulgaria to expand its influence. In this way, the preservation of the Bulgarian state depended on the happy union of the Bulgars and Slavs, on the one hand, and the religious–political

---

14. Hopkins, *The Bulgarian Orthodox Church*, 20.

alliance with the Frankish, Latin or Byzantine Christians, on the other. The best way to ensure this happy union was to enforce the same language and the same religion.

Khan Boris inaugurated his search for a Christian alliance with the Franks. Although the Bulgarians knew that they had to align with the Christians, they were also mindful that their empire could become "a small cog in a larger ecclesiastical and political wheel."[15] This is the context in which the newest khan, Boris, found himself upon accession to the throne in 852. He eventually made a pact with the Franks in 862, which required his conversion to Catholic Christianity.

Yet fearful of a Frankish-Bulgarian coalition, the Byzantine Empire blocked this joint venture, assembling an army of Greeks, Croats, Serbs, and Slavs to rout the Bulgarians. Realizing defeat, Boris acknowledged his tributary status to the Byzantine emperor, Michael III, and agreed to come under the religious authority of the patriarch of Constantinople. Boris returned to his capital in Pliska with a newly baptized Bulgarian court accompanied by Byzantine missionaries eager to convert the pagan nation. The Bulgarian court, however, was not at all pleased with this development, and Boris had to violently squash a rebellion in order to retain his throne. Despite heavy losses from among the nobility, the Byzantine mission was successful. It created a distinctly "Bulgarian" nation in which Bulgars and Slavs spoke the same language and shared the same faith.[16]

With Bulgaria's conversion to Orthodox Christianity, Boris felt the grip of the Byzantine Empire tightening around his own smaller kingdom. Boris, just like rulers of Great Moravia and Pannonia, wanted autonomy to appoint his own clergy and create his own

---

15. Hopkins, *The Bulgarian Orthodox Church*, 15.
16. R. J. Crampton, *A Short History of Modern Bulgaria* (Cambridge: Cambridge University Press, 1991), 3.

diocese. Gaining no traction with the patriarch of Constantinople—a very prominent figure named Photius—Boris held a meeting with Louis the German in 862. At the meeting Boris requested a political alliance with the Franks, and Frankish Catholic missionaries then entered Bulgaria to convert the people to Frankish Christianity. Hedging his bets, Boris also sent a delegation to Pope Nicholas I in 866 to inquire about a religious alliance with Rome that would lead to an autonomous Bulgarian church, which led to the launch of a papal mission to Bulgaria. Boris wanted to leave no stone unturned when it came to establishing an autonomous Bulgarian church.

The papal mission arrived in Bulgaria in early 867. Headed by Bishop Formosus of Porto, the papal mission flexed its ecclesial muscles by sending the Frankish bishop of Passau out of Bulgaria, signaling that the Bulgarian mission was now directly under the authority of the Roman bishop. Boris likewise expelled all Byzantine clergy from his kingdom, "replacing the Greek with Latin liturgy and re-baptising all the people into the Latin Church."[17] Bulgaria was becoming the setting of a four-team tug of war match among Byzantines/Greeks, Bulgarians, Latins, and Franks.

The papal mission to Bulgaria in 867 brought the pope's responses to all 106 of Boris's tedious questions about how its alignment with Rome would change daily life for Bulgarians. Boris was particularly eager to read the pope's response to his question about whether Bulgaria could become an autonomous church:

> We cannot say anything definitive on this issue before our legates, whom we send to you, have returned and reported to us what a multitude and unanimity of Christians there is among you.[18]

---

17. Hopkins, *The Bulgarian Orthodox Church*, 27.
18. Nicholas I, Epistle 99, chapter 72. http://legacy.fordham.edu/halsall/basis/866nicholas-bulgar.asp.

The pope was not at all willing to grant autonomy to the Bulgarian church before he could get a lay of the land. Even then, it's likely that the pope had no intention of granting Bulgaria an archdiocese after he received a report from his legates. The papacy, a veteran political machine, had likely sent a bishop on the papal mission to Bulgaria in anticipation of Boris's next move—requesting Formosus to become archbishop of Bulgaria, thus making the church in Bulgaria autonomous (technically, autocephalous or "self-governing"). According to canon law, however, bishops were not allowed to transfer bishoprics, so the pope defeated the Bulgarian khan on a technicality. Boris was not humored. Not only was he getting nowhere with the pope but he was getting no indication from the Franks that they would grant him an archdiocese, so he concluded that it his best bet was to stick with the Byzantines.

Boris's next move was well played. The Byzantine Empire was fully aware of Boris's church shopping, and concluded that it was better to grant Bulgaria an archbishopric—and thereby keep Bulgaria as an ally—than it was to face a possible Bulgarian-Frankish alliance. In the winter of 869/870, the Eighth Ecumenical Council was convened in Constantinople and, among other agenda items, it granted Boris's request for the Bulgarians to come under the ecclesial jurisdiction of the patriarchate of Constantinople. Once granted, Boris summarily expelled the Frankish and Roman clergy from Bulgaria. It's not surprising that the Roman Catholic Church rejected this council, and that by the end of the ninth century, the pope would excommunicate the patriarch of Constantinople.

Boris welcomed the Orthodox disciples of Constantine and Methodius (who survived the trauma experienced in Great Moravia) to initiate "a wide-ranging programme of education and scholarship."[19] The use of the Slavonic language in liturgical services allowed Boris to simultaneously accept Orthodox Christianity yet halt the Byzantine-Greek influence over the church. The disciples of Constantine and Methodius began translating religious texts into Old Church Slavonic, at which time that they adapted the Glagolitic alphabet with the Greek one, creating what has come to be called the Cyrillic alphabet (named, of course, after Cyril, who, as mentioned earlier, was known as Constantine for most of his life). Boris sent his son Simeon to Byzantium to be trained as a priest, likely in the hopes that he would one day become the patriarch of Bulgaria. By 893, the state of Bulgaria had made Slavonic not only the official language of the church but also of the state. The Bulgarian church was autonomous, gaining a patriarchate in the year 927 and thus not under the authority of any outside or foreign patriarchate. Boris's strategic chess match with the most powerful Christian centers in Europe was over—and he had won.

Conclusion: Central Europe as an Ecclesial Battleground between East and West

Though not realized at the time, the question that the Bulgarian khan raised in 866 about ecclesial jurisdiction went to the heart of ninth-century central European Christianity. To whom would the emerging Slavic states belong? In many ways, these central European states became "missionary battleground[s]" among the three major Christian centers at the time. Taking Bulgaria as a test case among Slavic states, historian James Hopkins argues that "the dispute over Bulgaria was to mark a turning point in the east-west ecclesiastical conflict . . . , with calamitous consequences for Christendom as a whole."[20] In the next decades, the east and the west would officially part ways, with central Europe becoming more than an ecclesial battlefield. With the growing number of independent kingdoms in

19. Dimitrov, "Bulgarian Christianity," in *The Blackwell Companion to Eastern Christianity*, 51.
20. Hopkins, *The Bulgarian Orthodox Church*, 26.

central Europe becoming Christian in order to enhance their statuses and safeguard their borders among the three Christian "Romes," the temptation to gain new alliances at the expense of old ones was too strong to overcome. In this way, the Byzantine, Germanic, and Latin Christians chose the pathway of competition rather than cooperation, creating all sorts of remarkable religious and political alliances among European nations in the decades and centuries to come.

10

Are These the End Times?

It was the year 1000. A Benedictine monk at the Abbey of St. Vaast in northern France was carefully transcribing on the margins of an Easter table an event of no little significance: "In the one-thousandth year of the Incarnation of the Lord . . . on Good Friday the 29th of March, while Christians were celebrating the sacrosanct mystery of [Christ's] Passion and Redemption, there was a great earthquake." Continuing on, the monk explained that the earthquake "was not like one as often occurs . . . but rather the whole magnitude of earth shook everywhere with a general and vast tremor, so that that which had been promised before by the mouth of Truth might be made manifest to everyone. With these and other signs that had been predicted having been competed by divine operation, hence our hope is made more certain in the sight of all regarding those that remain to be completed in due order."[1]

For this monk in northern France, the earthquake he experienced was the beginning of the last age—a period of time that ushered in the final chapter of world history. In the years to come, the Abbey

---

1. Quoted in David Van Meter, "Apocalyptic Moments and the Eschatological Rhetoric of Reform in the Early Eleventh Century: The Case of the Visionary of St. Vaast," in *The Apocalyptic Year 1000: Religious Expectation and Social Change, 950-1050*, ed. Richard Landes et al. (Oxford: Oxford University Press, 2003), 316.

of St. Vaast was a hotbed of end-times activity. A dozen years after the unknown monk recorded the details of the earthquake in the year 1000, another monk at the abbey was caught up in religious ecstasy. In the second of his visions of the end times, his abbot reported in a letter that an angel from heaven warned him that "today it was revealed to you how in a short while will be the end of the world."[2] The question before us in this chapter is: are these the end times?

The Question of the Last Days

The monks at St. Vaast inhabited a world "of apocalyptic anxiety."[3] In a world acutely aware of how the natural world paralleled or signaled spiritual events, the variety of natural phenomena at this time sparked the wonder of several contemporary writers. Writing about events in the year 1000, a Benedictine monk from Belgium recorded not only how a "great earthquake" seized the region but also how "a burning torch . . . fell to the earth from a fissure in the heavens," igniting a tail of light that looked "like a dragon." Less than ten years later, another chronicler noticed how "drops of blood" fell on people like rain as they congregated for Palm Sunday.[4]

Although we certainly cannot verify all of the intriguing events claimed by medieval writers, and we dare not speculate on their significance, science has confirmed several natural phenomena of note occurring around the turn of the first millennium. Astronomist and physicist Bradley Shafer asserts that "celestial spectacles occurred frequently around the year 1000," including complete and partial lunar eclipses, aurorae, a supernova, and a planetary conjunction on New Year's Day of the year 1001, when "the Sun, Moon, and all of the planets except Saturn were within 30° of each other."[5] In this

---

2. Meter, "Apocalyptic Moments," in *The Apocalyptic Year*, 339.
3. Ibid., 316.
4. Quoted in Meter, "Apocalyptic Moments," in *The Apocalyptic Year*, 340–41.

chapter, we will explore to what degree natural phenomena like these incited Christians to ask whether the turn of the first millennium was the harbinger of the end times. Because of different calendars used by Christians and differences in calculating dates, our time period in this chapter concentrates on the last three decades of the tenth century (roughly, 970–999) and the first three decades of the eleventh century (roughly, 1000–1033).

Figure 10.1. European Dating Methods

The year 1000 does not always mean what we think it does. In Western Europe, it was common to use the founding of Rome—*ab urbe condita* or A.U.C.—to date events. (The founding of Rome was dated to the year 753 BCE.) Other writers used the regnal years of Roman emperors to mark dates.

But in the year 525 CE, a Christian monk named Dionysius devised a new system of dating using the birth of Christ as the starting point—in Latin *anno domini* or AD, "the year of the Lord." This new system was only slowly adopted in the West. In the early eighth century, the English monk Bede used it in his book *Ecclesiastical History of the English Peoples*, and the Carolingians adopted it several decades later, leading to its widespread use thereafter. In the Christian East, however, the AD system was not adopted. Instead, the Byzantine Empire marked its dates with the supposed "beginning of creation"—*apo ktiseows kosmou* in Greek, or *anno mundi* or AM in Latin. Hence, in the Christian East in the year 1000 CE, it was actually the year 6508 AM, based on the reckoning that the year of creation was 6508 BCE or 5508 years before Christ's birth.

The use of BC, *before Christ* in English, or *ante Christum* in Latin, was only invented in the seventeenth century. To make matters even more confusing, it has been common since the late twentieth century for Western scholars to abandon AD and BC in favor of more religiously neutral dating terms—thus BCE, *before the Common Era*, and CE, the *Common Era*. These dates, however, are identical with the BC and AD systems.

A Short History of Living in the Last Days

There has never been a time period when Christians did not speculate whether they were living in the last days. As medieval historian of apocalypticism Bernard McGinn writes, "Christianity was born apocalyptic and has remained so."[6] The New Testament authors left

---

5. Bradley Shafer, "The Astronomical Situation around the year 1000," in *The Apocalyptic Year*, 333.
6. Bernard McGinn, *Visions of the End: Apocalyptic Traditions in the Middle Ages* (New York: Columbia University Press, 1979), 11.

vague clues about the end times that each generation of Christians has attempted to piece together like a puzzle in consultation with contemporary calamities. Let us consider how the following passages might rouse curiosity among Christians living during impoverished times, natural disasters, strange phenomena, new heretical teachings, distant wars, and medical epidemics:

> So also, when you see all these things, you know that he is near, at the very gates. Truly I tell you, this generation will not pass away until all these things have taken place. (Matt. 24:33–34)

> For this we declare to you by the word of the Lord, that we who are alive, who are left until the coming of the Lord, will by no means precede those who have died. For the Lord himself, with a cry of command, with the archangel's call and with the sound of God's trumpet, will descend from heaven, and the dead in Christ will rise first. Then we who are alive, who are left, will be caught up in the clouds together with them to meet the Lord in the air; and so we will be with the Lord forever. (1 Thess. 4:15–17)

> I mean, brothers and sisters, the appointed time has grown short; from now on, let even those who have wives be as though they had none, and those who mourn as though they were not mourning, and those who rejoice as though they were not rejoicing, and those who buy as though they had no possessions, and those who deal with the world as though they had no dealings with it. For the present form of this world is passing away. (1 Cor. 7:29–31)

> The Lord is near. (Philipp. 4:5)

> You must understand this, that in the last days distressing times will come. (2 Tim. 3:1)

> First of all you must understand this, that in the last days scoffers will come, scoffing and indulging in their own lusts . . . the day of the Lord will come like a thief, and then the heavens will pass away with a loud noise, and the elements will be dissolved with fire, and the earth and everything that is done on it will be disclosed. (2 Pet. 3:3, 10)

This list is not exhaustive—and it does not include any excerpts from Revelation, "one of the first biblical texts," medieval historian Ann Matter explains "to be systematically explicated in Latin."[7] From an arsenal of apocalyptic verses, Christians found constant parallels between biblical prophecies and contemporary events. That is to say, among "famines, floods, comets, eclipses, earthquakes, volcanic eruptions, wolves in churches, [and] rains of blood,"[8] it's no wonder that many Christians from generation to generation have concluded that they are living in the last age.

When would the last age arrive, when would Christ return to earth, and what could be expected to happen once he did? Christians did not always agree on how to answer these questions, but there was no shortage of attempts. In the early third century, a Greek-speaking writer named Sextus Julius Africanus wrote a book called *Chronicle*, which calculated the year of the creation of the world to 5500 BCE (see Figure 10.1). In Rome around the same time period, the author Hippolytus followed suit. He reasoned that the world would last 6,000 years, after which time a new millennium would usher in the last days. Many early Christians reached similar conclusions, and it was common for early Christians to expect the last age to arrive in the years 500 or 800/801 CE (depending on one's specific calculations in consultation with biblical books like Daniel and Revelation).

In the fifth century, Jerome and Augustine offered new insights into end-time speculation. Unlike many other interpreters, these two thinkers constructed a symbolic reading of key biblical passages like Rev. 20:2–3 that spoke of "the dragon, that ancient serpent, who is the Devil and Satan" being released on the world after a

---

7. Ann Matter, "Exegesis of the Apocalypse in the Early Middle Ages," in *The Year 1000: Religious and Social Response to the Turning of the First Millennium*, ed. Michael Frassetto (New York: Palgrave Macmillan, 2002), 29.

8. Nancy Marie Brown, *The Abacus and the Cross: The Story of the Pope Who Brought the Light of Science to the Dark Ages* (New York: Basic Books, 2010), 1.

"thousand years" or "*mille anni*" in the Latin Bible—hence the word *millennium* in English to represent one thousand years. These two Latin-speaking scholars refused to conjecture about when Christ would return and did not attribute any importance to dates about the end of the world. As Augustine cautioned in one of his letters to a fellow Christian bishop,

> I do not dare to calculate the time of the coming of the savior that is expected in the end, nor do I think that any prophet has determined ahead of time the number of years before that event, but rather that what the Lord said holds true: *No one can know the times that the Father determined by his own authority* (Acts 1:7).[9]

Upon a further reply to the bishop, Augustine continued to criticize those who speculated about Christ's return: "a person seems to me to be in error not when he knows that he does not know something, but when he thinks that he knows what he does not know?"[10]

Despite's Augustine's historic influence on the interpretive tradition, speculation about the end times did not disappear. Directed to the ruler of Kent in 601, Pope Gregory wrote, "we would have your Highness know that, as we find in Holy Scripture from the words of the Almighty Lord, the end of this present world, and the kingdom of the saints . . . is at hand."[11] A quarter of a century later, around the year 848, Rudolf of Fulda chronicled how a woman named Thiota arrived in Mainz, Germany and predicted the end of the world:

---

9. Augustine, "Letter 197," quoted in Roland Teske, "Augustine on the End of the World: 'Cautious Ignorance,'" in *Augustine and Apocalyptic*, ed. John Doody et al. (Lanham: Lexington Books, 2014), 194.
10. Augustine, "Letter 199," quoted in Teske, "Augustine on the End of the World," in *Augustine and Apocalyptic*, 204.
11. Bede, "Ecclesiastical History of the English Nation 1.32," quoted in Richard Landes, *Heaven on Earth: The Varieties of Millennial Experience* (Oxford: Oxford University Press, 2011), 30.

For she claimed that, as if by divine revelation, she knew the very day of the End of the world and many other matters which are known only to God, and she predicted that the Last Day would fall that very year. Whence many commoners of both sexes, terror-struck, flocked to hear, bringing gifts, and offered themselves up to her with their prayers. And what is still worse, men from the holy orders, setting aside ecclesiastical doctrine, followed her as if she were a master sent from heaven.[12]

Although Rudolf and many other clerics were critical of Thiota's predictions about the end times, it is clear that she was not an isolated example of apocalyptic expectation during the Middle Ages.

Living in the Last Days

It is due to ongoing speculation about the end times among Christians from the first century onward that is the cause of a strong disagreement among medieval scholars. Simply put, since we recognize that there is something inherent in Christianity that entices its practitioners to speculate whether they are living in the end days, the more specific question we have to ask is: does medieval thought around the turn of the first millennium simply represent more of the same type of speculation always present in the church or a heightened sensitivity or fear due to its proximity to the passing of the first millennium? In the section below, we will investigate to what degree several tenth- and eleventh-century writers in the Christian West were especially anxious about the millennial anniversary of Christ's incarnation and passion.

---

12. *Annals of Fulda*, trans. Timothy Reuter (Manchester: University of Manchester Press, 1992), 26, quoted in Landes, *Heaven on Earth*, 37.

Figure 10.2. End-Times Anticipation in the Christian East?

Because Christians in the Byzantine Empire did not date the world from the birth of Christ (AD) but rather from the beginning of creation (AM), we will confine our discussion below to the Christian West. (Remember that in the Byzantine Empire, the year 1000 AD was 5508 AM.) Nonetheless, Byzantine historian Paul Magdalino argues, "The expectation that the world would end in some version of the year 1000 [however calculated] was. . . widely and firmly held" in Byzantium.[13] For more about this, see his edited book, *Byzantium in the Year 1000*.

Adso of Montier-en-Der (c. 910–992)

Adso was abbot of a monastery in northeastern France. His most relevant writing with regard to the end times was composed around the year 950. It was written to the German emperor's sister to address concerns about the Antichrist. As medieval historian Jane Schulenburg writes, Adso composed his writings "in a climate of apocalyptic anxiety." That's because in the middle of the tenth century Western Europe was in a "political crisis" due to the collapse of the Carolingian Empire, and "the Hungarian and Viking invasions were posing a major threat to the security of France."[14]

In his treatise to the queen, Adso offered a two-fold interpretation of the end times. On the one hand, many Antichrists "have already existed," including the wicked Roman emperor Nero and others. On the other, "Even now in our own times,"[15] Adso explained, there were several Antichrists who set themselves up in opposition to the teachings of Christ. The vocation of the Antichrist was to lead astray the people of God and to delude others into thinking of him as a great ruler. When the ultimate Antichrist would be born at an unspecified

---

13. Paul Magdalino, "The Year 1000 in Byzantium," in *Byzantium in the Year 1000*, ed. Paul Magdalino (Leiden and Boston: Brill, 2003), 245.

14. Jane Schulenburg, "Early Medieval Women, Prophecy, and Millennial Expectations," in *The Year 1000*, 241.

15. Adso of Montier-En-Der, "Letter on the Origin and Time of the Antichrist," in *Apocalyptic Spirituality: Treatises and Letters of Lactantius, Adso of Montier-En-Der, Joachim of Fiore, the Franciscans Spirituals, Savonarola*, ed. Bernard McGinn (New York, Ramsey, and Toronto: Paulist Press, 1979), 90.

time, he would "arouse universal persecution against the Christians and all the elect."[16] He would overcome the world by tactics of fear, bribery, and performing amazing signs.

In his letter, Adso warned that the beginning of the end times could not happen until the kingdoms formerly conquered by the "Roman Empire" would rise up anew and conquer Rome. But this could not happen "as long as the Kings of the Franks who now possess the Roman Empire by right shall last," implying that Adso and his contemporaries were not in danger of living in the last days given that the kings of the Franks were Christians and heirs of the Roman Empire. It would only be after the last king of the Franks abdicated that the "end and the consummation of the Roman and Christian Empire" would occur.[17] Even still, the consummation did not include the destruction of the world.

All in all, Adso's treatise to the queen about the end times is ambiguous in terms of answering whether it was believed that his generation was especially beset with apocalyptic anxiety. Although Adso himself argued that the consummation of the ages would be delayed for some time due to the Christian rule of the Frankish empire, "it certainly would not be preposterous to hypothesize that Gerberga's request to Adso was prompted by an apocalyptic unrest that she shared with her subjects."[18] We do know that contemporary sources speak of "a series of natural disasters" occurring around that time, which probably fueled the fire of anxiety among the imperial court.[19] The French monk Abo of Fleury, for instance, wrote of the apocalyptic fear of Christians around the time of the queen's request for Adso to write a treatise about the Antichrist and the end times:

---

16. Adso, "Letter," in *Apocalyptic Spirituality*, 92.
17. Ibid., 93.
18. Daniel Verhelst, "Adso of Montier-en-Der and the Fear of the Year 1000," in *The Apocalyptic Year 1000*, 85.
19. Schulenburg, "Early Medieval Women," in *The Year 1000*, 241.

> When I was a young man I heard a sermon about the End of the world preached before the people in the cathedral of Paris. According to this, as soon as the number of a thousand years was completed, the Antichrist would come and the Last Judgment would follow in a brief time. I opposed this sermon with what force I could from passages in the Gospels, Revelation, and the Book of Daniel. Finally my abbot of blessed memory, Richard, wisely overthrew an error which had grown up about the End of the world after he received letters from the Lotharingians which he bade me answer. The rumor had filled almost the whole world that when the feast of the Annunciation coincided with Good Friday without any doubt the End of the world would occur.[20]

Assuming the accurateness of Abo's account, we might surmise that there were palpable concerns of apocalyptic fear during middle of the tenth century. For instance, there was a real concern at the popular level that the end times would be ushered in on Easter Sunday when Annunciation coincided with Good Friday, an event that actually took place in the year 992. However, monks like Abo and Adso maintained that fears of the last days—despite the approaching of the year 1000, the unusual display of natural phenomena, and contemporary political crises—were not warranted.

Wulfstan of York (d. 1023)

Wulfstan was the archbishop of York from 1002 until his death. A highly regarded preacher and important writer, Wulfstan wrote during an unstable period in England's history. What was taking place? King Aethelred "the Unready" was attempting to overtake the Danish communities in England, which were set up to pillage English towns and coastal regions. From contemporary sources, we hear of regular skirmishes between what we will imprecisely call the English and the Vikings. In the year 1002, for instance, the same year Wulfstan was appointed archbishop of York, King Aethelred

---

20. Abo of Fleury, "Apologetic Work," in McGinn, *Visions of the End*, 89–90.

responded to Viking raids by massacring Danish settlers (later called the St. Brice's Day Massacre), prompting the Danish king to invade and launch a years-long siege against the English. Based on this political crisis in the context of ongoing English speculation about the end times, it's not surprising that the "imminence of the end of the world [was] one of the most important themes . . . for Anglo-Saxon writers in the decades surrounding the year 1000."[21] The English people, it seemed to many, were living in Doomsday.

Figure 10.3. Wulfstan and the Danelaw

The Danelaw was a region in northeastern England that was ruled by the Danes during the Middle Ages. Danish raiders, or Vikings, had begun settling in England since the ninth century, and used their strategic location in England to pillage towns, monasteries, and churches. Wulfstan was the archbishop of York, a town right in the middle of the Danelaw. Among his flock would have been sizeable numbers of Danish residents, who did not generally get along well with the Anglo-Saxons.

In the decades before and after the year 1000, several English authors wrote about the end times. One anonymous homily, written in Old English, predicted the end of the world in the year 971:

> we know [that the end times] . . . is not far distant, for all the signs and portents which our Lord said should occur before doomsday have occurred, except only that the accursed visitant Antichrist has not yet come into the world. It is not long until the time when that must happen for this world must necessarily end in this age that is present . . . In this age then must this world end and most of it has passed, that is, nine hundred and seventy-one years in this year.[22]

In addition, in the year 975, the Anglo-Saxon Chronicle mentioned the appearance of a comet, a famine, and other disturbances. Writing a couple of decades later, the monk Aelfric of Eynsham left many

---

21. Malcolm Godden, "The Millennium, Time, and History for the Anglo-Saxons," in *The Apocalyptic Year 1000*, 155.
22. Quoted in Godden, "The Millennium," in *The Apocalyptic Year 1000*, 157.

works about the last days. In an early writing dating from the last decade of the tenth century, he remarked that "people need good teaching most urgently in this time, which is the ending of the world."[23] In subsequent writings, however, Aelfric recoiled from his earlier ideas. He became opposed to end-times speculation.

Around the turn of the millennium, and building upon the thought of his contemporary Aelfric, Wulfstan launched a series of five sermons about the end times. In the first sermon, Wulfstan asserted, "It seems to us that it is very close to that time, because this world is steadily worsening from day to day."[24] In subsequent sermons, Wulfstan affirmed his anticipation of the end times as a result of the apparent fulfillment of biblical prophecies and of contemporary natural calamities. Writing after the year 1000, Wulfstan noted that

> A thousand years and more have now passed since Christ was among men in human form, and now Satan's bonds are greatly loosened and Antichrist's time is very close, and therefore things are in the world ever the weaker the longer it goes on.[25]

The birth of the Antichrist by the year 1000 notwithstanding, Wulfstan went beyond his contemporary Aelfric by anticipating the imminence of the last days. Writing in the year 1014, Wulfstan warned in his "Sermon to the English":

> Beloved, know what the truth is: this world is in haste and it is nearing the end, and therefore things are in the world ever the worse as time passes, and so it must necessarily get worse before Antichrist's time.[26]

Yet in subsequent years, there is a "gradual playing down of the earlier emphases"[27] of the end times in the thinking of Wulfstan.

23. Ibid., 159.
24. Ibid., 166.
25. Ibid., 171.
26. Ibid., 176.
27. Godden, "The Millennium," in *The Apocalyptic Year 1000*, 172.

While Aelfric was moving in this direction before the year 1000, Wulfstan only gradually loosened his grip on end-times speculation after the turn of the millennium. In place of emphasizing the last days, he slowly turned his attention to the crisis of the Viking invasion and to the collective sins of the English people, whose repentance could halt the coming of the Antichrist. As historian Mary Richards explains, Wulftstan gradually turned to the writing of "laws and sermons as a means of religious and social reform hoping to restore the English to God's favor."[28] By doing so, Wulfstan believed that he could best prepare for the postponement of the coming of the Antichrist.

Ralph Glaber (d. 1050)

Of all the end-time writers in this era, Ralph Glaber was the most noteworthy. A French monk well attuned to the political and religious events of his day, Glaber wrote prolifically about living in the last age. As he explained in the preface to his most prodigious work, the five-volume *Histories*, written in the 1030s, there were "many events which occurred with unusual frequency about the millennium of the Incarnation of Christ our Saviour."[29] Such events included volcanic eruptions, wars, political intrigue, cases of heresy, monastic feuds, demonic encounters, miracles, clerical ungodliness, dreams and visions, and various other natural disasters foreboding the last age.

One of the more intriguing events that Glaber describes is found in the second volume of his work, which narrates the history of the West Franks before the turn of the first millennium. Writing about a case of heresy in Ravenna, Glaber chronicled the story of a learned

---

28. Mary Reynolds, "Wulfstan and the Millennium," in *The Year 1000*, 46.
29. Rodulfus Glaber, *The Five Books of the Histories*, ed. Neithard Bulst (Oxford: Oxford University Press, 1989), 3.

man named Vilgardus who, "stupidly inflated with pride" because of his great learning, made himself vulnerable to demonic attack. In the forms of the greatest classical Latin authors, several demons appeared to Vilgardus, infecting him with heresy, which he then spread across Italy, Sardinia, and Spain until his followers "were exterminated by the orthodox." "All this," Glaber stated in his conclusion to the second book, "accords with the prophecy of St John, who said that the Devil would be freed after a thousand years [see Rev. 20:2–3]."[30] According to millennial scholar Richard Landes, Glaber's statement here "is . . . perhaps the single most anti-Augustinian passage in the historiography of the early Middle Ages."[31] What is so opposed to Augustinian thought about this? Contrary to what Augustine advised, which was a figurative reading of the Apocalypse, Glaber interpreted Revelation 20 literally. Among the natural calamities and bizarre events of his day, he saw the unleashing of the devil after the end of the first millennium literally taking place. Such was not, however, technically "the end of the world," but rather the sign of the last age—a period of unknown duration.

There were many other interesting events in subsequent books that Glaber discussed in anticipation of living in the last age. For instance, he noted in the year 987 that there was an appearance of Halley's Comet, a natural phenomenon that "clearly portends some wondrous and awe-inspiring event in the world shortly after."[32] Later, in the beginning of the fourth book, Glaber explained that even though there were "many prodigies [or signs] which had broken upon the world before, after, and around the millennium of the Lord Christ," there were just as many occurring "at the approach of the millennium of the Lord's Passion."[33] This statement gets to the heart of a common

30. Glaber, *Histories*, 2:93.
31. Richard Landes, "The Fear of an Apocalyptic Year 1000: Augustinian Historiography, Medieval and Modern," in *The Apocalyptic year 1000*, 255.
32. Glaber, *Histories*, 3:111.

misconception. Although some medieval Christians interpreted the millennium as beginning in the year of Christ's incarnation (which, for them, would occur around the year 1000), just as many medieval writers interpreted the millennium as commencing in the year of Christ's passion (for them, roughly occurring around the year 1033). As the first millennium passed in the year 1000 and Doomsday had not appeared, several writers began interpreting natural disasters as harbingers of the last age, which would be ushered in around the year 1033, that is, a thousand years after Christ's death.

Glaber's contemporary Ademar of Chabannes, for instance, spoke in the early eleventh century of "signs in the heavens, severe dry spells, very much rain, many plagues, severe famines and numerous failures of the sun and the moon," including a heavenly sign of Christ affixed to a cross in the sky, "weeping a great river of tears."[34] For many Christians in the early eleventh century, natural disasters were appearing at an alarming rate. The monk of Ademar of Chabannes, in anticipation of the coming millennial terror, made haste to the Holy Land. Like many other Christians at the time, Ademar went on pilgrimage to Jerusalem in order to have his sins forgiven or, if lucky enough, die in the Holy Land and receive burial among the great saints of old. In his fourth book in the *Histories*, Glaber told the story of one man named Lethbaud who was blessed to receive the sacrament of Last Rites in Jerusalem one evening after entering the Church of the Holy Sepulchre.[35] It is believed that, like Lethbaud, Glaber's contemporary Ademar died while on pilgrimage in Jerusalem.

Like Ademar, Ralph Glaber interpreted the natural calamities and political crises of the early eleventh century as indications that the

---

33. Glaber, *Histories*, 4:171.
34. Daniel Callahan, "The Tau Cross in the Writings of Ademar of Chabannes," in *The Year 1000*, 63.
35. Glaber, *Histories*, 4:201.

arrival of the millennium would usher in the last age—though, again, not necessarily the end of the world. Glaber even suggested that the cause of the "unheard-of" numbers of pilgrims to Jerusalem was in preparation for a battle to take place between the Antichrist and God's people.[36] He also mentioned the formation of peace councils for "re-establishing peace and consolidating the holy faith"[37] in anticipation of the millennial turn. At any rate, unlike Adso and Wulfstan, who emphasized the millennial anniversary of Christ's incarnation, Glaber (and Ademar) accentuated the millennial anniversary of Christ's passion or death. Glaber, of course, proceeded to live roughly two decades after the supposed millennial anniversary of Christ's passion in the year 1033, which is another indication that he believed the new millennium would only usher in the last age but not the end of the world.

Conclusion: Heightened but not Complete Apocalyptic Anxiety

Scholars often disagree when interpreting primary sources, and there is long-standing debate among those who insist that medieval Christians attributed great importance to the passing of the first millennium and others who argue that medieval Christians did not ascribe any importance to the millennial anniversary of Christ's birth (roughly, 1000 CE) or death (roughly, 1033 CE). From our brief survey of tenth- and eleventh-century writers, it appears that the truth lies somewhere in between. There was no universal fear in the late tenth century that the world would end when the clock struck midnight in the year 1000. Nor was there a lack of writers in the tenth and eleventh centuries who conveyed apocalyptic anxiety. Unfortunately, as is often the case with history, we are at the mercy of those very few who recorded contemporary events and speculated

36. Glaber, *Histories*, 4:204.
37. Ibid., 4:194.

about their importance. From the limited number of writings we have from the late tenth and early eleventh centuries about the turn of the millennium, we are forced to exercise caution when making definitive pronouncements one way or the other.

All in all, we must agree with the latest cluster of scholars who think that there were heightened "apocalyptic hopes and fears around the year 1000."[38] Such "apocalyptic hopes and fears," however, are not the same thing as believing that the world was going to blow up in the year 1000, 1033, or immediately thereafter. We must keep in mind that expectation of the millennial anniversary of Christ's incarnation or passion was more about ushering in an ultimate yet uncertain period of world history, but not the end of planet Earth. Whatever the case, the passing of the new millennium did not at all cause a lull in speculation about the end times. From the eleventh century onward, we have countless examples of end-times treatises, sermons, and predictions. The twelfth-century monk Joachim of Fiore, for example, is probably the most well-known end-time speculator in the Middle Ages, but many other authors and preachers predicted the end of the world and believed that they were living in the end times—right up to the twentieth-century Left Behind series. From the Protestant Reformations to the turn of the second millennium, there has been no dearth of Christians heralding the end. And now snugly into the third millennium, it does not appear that there will be any shortage of end-time speculation in the years to come.

38. *The Year 1000: Religious and Social Response to the Turning of the First Millennium*, ed. Michael Frassetto (New York: Palgrave Macmillan, 2002), 2; see also *The Apocalyptic Year 1000*.

11

Should Christians Fight Muslims over the Holy Land?

It was the year 1009. The Fatimid Caliphate, based in Cairo, was a powerful Shia Muslim kingdom that ruled over large parts of North Africa and the Middle East. According to tradition, the Fatimids had descended from the favorite daughter of the prophet Muhammad, Fatimah. Whatever the actual lineage of the caliphate, it was becoming one of the major centers of Islamic power in the medieval world. The sixth caliph of the Fatimids was a man named al-Hakim bi-Amr Allah, better known as al-Hakim. He had succeeded to the throne during the last years of the tenth century. Later regarded as eccentric at best and mentally unstable at worse on account of his notorious cruelties and of declaring himself to be divine, al-Hakim did the unthinkable in the year 1009—he ordered the absolute destruction of the Church of the Holy Sepulchre in Jerusalem, the holiest church in Christendom on whose foundations Jesus Christ had been crucified, buried, and resurrected.

The Christian world was outraged at al-Hakim's behavior. Writing about this event from France, one Christian lamented that "the glorious Sepulcher of the Lord Jesus Christ" had been taken over "by unclean Turks," inciting fear among the people that the end of the world was imminent. Out of "fear for their lives," the French author continued, "many Jews converted to Christianity," and "in many places throughout the world, a rumor spread that frightened and saddened many hearts, that the End of the World approached."[1] Although the French author cautioned "those sounder of mind" not to interpret these events apocalyptically, al-Hakim's actions incited a storm of enormous consequences.

The Question of Fighting for the Holy Land

According to some historians, al-Hakim's razing of the Church of the Holy Sepulchre in the year 1009 partly contributed to the launching of the Crusades.[2] The destruction of the central church of Christendom was not only an affront to Christians everywhere but it also prevented pilgrimages to the Holy Land, a centuries-long practice that was commonly believed by believers to grant pardon of sins—a spiritual journey now made possible by foot due to the recent conversion of the Hungarians (or Magyars) to Christianity. Whatever the exact relationship between al-Hakim's ordering of the destruction of the Church of the Holy Sepulcher and the Crusades, one of the most noteworthy questions Christians asked in the eleventh century was how they should respond to the diminishing presence of Christianity in the Holy Land as well as to the apparent rise in violence at the hands of Muslim powers. In this chapter, we will explore how Christians reacted to the changing religious and political climate of the eleventh century by posing the question of whether

---

1. Martin Bouquet, *Recueil des historiens de la France* (Paris: Victor Palme, 1869-1904), 10:262, quoted in Richard Landes, *Heaven on Earth: The Varieties of Millennial Experience* (Oxford: Oxford University Press, 2011), 30.
2. Avner Falk, *Franks and Saracens: Reality and Fantasy in the Crusades* (London: Karnac Books, 2010), 76.

Christians should fight Muslims over the Holy Land—one of the most controversial questions in all of Christian history

A Short History of Muslim Presence in the Holy Land

We cannot understand the cause of the Crusades in the eleventh century without first comprehending the history of Muslim presence in the Holy Land. As explained in Chapter 7, Islam emerged in seventh-century Arabia. After the death of the Prophet Muhammad in 632, Arab Muslims rapidly expanded their rule over much of North Africa and the Middle East. It was during the Rashidun Caliphate—the leaders or caliphs of which each knew Muhammad personally—that the Holy City of Jerusalem was captured in 638. From then on, all of the Holy Land was under Islamic rule, even though Christians continued to be the dominant population for decades to come. The expansion of Arab Islam came at the expense of Christian Byzantium, a kingdom that saw its territory diminish century after century.

By the tenth century, there were three major Muslim empires, each of which was centralized on another continent. In Europe, and based in Cordoba, the Umayyads ruled over much of Spain, or al-Andalus, from the eighth century onward. In Asia, and based in Baghdad, the Abbasids sparked a Golden Age of Islamic architecture and learning, while the Fatimids, based in Cairo, were Shia Muslims with commanding influence over North Africa, the Holy Land, and the holy cities of Mecca and Medina. Like their Christian counterparts, these Islamic empires did not get along; they were ethnically and religiously diverse; and they were just as likely to fight with each other as they were with Christian kingdoms like the Carolingian and Byzantine Empires.

Though no one could predict it at the time, the lease of each of these three Islamic kingdoms over the medieval world was soon to expire. In their place the Turks would gradually take ownership of Western Asia, North Africa, and the Middle East. In particular, it was a fierce people from Central Asia sweeping across the Asian steppes toward the Holy Land and the Christian East that posed the greatest threat to the current Muslim (and Christian) empires. They are referred to as the Seljuk Turks, named after their founding leader Selçuk, who may have been a Christian before the people who bore his name converted to Islam. Writing about their far-reaching migrations in the early eleventh century, the twelfth-century Christian Armenian writer Matthew of Edessa described the arrival of the Seljuk Turks in the Middle East in apocalyptic language:

> [Around the year 1018,] a fatal dragon with deadly fires rose up and struck those faithful to the holy Trinity. In this period the very foundations of the apostles and prophets were shaken, because winged serpents came forth and were intent on spreading like fire over the lands of the Christian faithful. This was the first appearance of the bloodthirsty beasts. During these times the savage nation of infidels called [Seljuk] Turks gathered together their forces.[3]

Unfortunately for the Christian world, the mental resolve of the Seljuk Turks was just as strong as their battle tactics. One of the most decisive battles to take place in the eleventh century was the Battle of Manzikert in what is now eastern Turkey. The year was 1071. Turkic forces were headed by Sultan Alp Arslan while Emperor Romanus IV Diogenes led Byzantine troops into battle. It was a turning point in world history. "For the first time," and certainly not the last, scholar Claude Cahen writes, "a Byzantine emperor was made prisoner by a Muslim army."[4] Turkic possession over parts of Turkey, Syria, and Palestine led to the disruption of pilgrimage routes

---

3. Matthew of Edessa on the Seljuk Turks," in *The Crusades: A Reader*, ed. S. J. Allen and Emilie Amt (Toronto: University of Toronto Press, 2010), 31–32.

4. Claude Cahen, *The Formation of Turkey: The Seljukid Sultanate of Rum: Eleventh to Fourteenth Century* (Oxford and New York: Routledge, 2014), 5.

among Western Christians, forcing them to acknowledge that the Byzantines were no longer "the protectors of Christendom."[5] The situation was becoming dire. While the Byzantine Empire was beset with internal intrigue, the rise of various Turkic states in the East came to threaten the security of the Christian West—and thus of Christendom itself. What were the Western Christians to do?

> Due to their great victories as they traveled westward, the Seljuk Turks were able to establish the Sultanate of Rum (1077–1307), which led to the Ottoman Empire (1299–1923) and then to the Republic of Turkey (1923–).

Should Western Christians Go to Battle against Muslims in the Holy Land?

It did not take long for the pope to respond to the deteriorating situation in the East. In the year 1074, Pope Gregory VII, a man familiar with violence and power, issued a call to action "to all who are willing to defend the Christian faith." In a series of letters, he exaggerated how

> a pagan race had overcome the Christians and, with horrible cruelty, had devastated everything almost to the walls of Constantinople, and were now governing the conquered lands with tyrannical violence, and that they had slain many thousands of Christians as if they were but sheep.[6]

The biblical response to such atrocities, the pope urged, was not only to "be filled with grief" but also to "lay down our lives to liberate [our brethren]." Citing 1 John 3:16, the pope interpreted a verse speaking about Christ's sacrificial death for humankind as a model for killing Muslims. Using all of the authority he could muster by merit of his God-ordained position as pope, he concluded one of the letters: "we

---

5. Steven Runciman, *A History of the Crusades*, vol. 1, *The First Crusade and the Foundation of the Kingdom of Jerusalem* (Cambridge: Cambridge University Press, 1951), 64.

6. "Gregory VII's Call for Assistance to the Greeks," in *The Crusades*, 34–35.

admonish that you be moved to proper compassion . . . [to] undertake the difficult task of bearing aid to your brethren."[7]

Nothing came of his letters. But it was not because nobody understood what the pope was requesting. As medieval historian Christopher Tyerman writes, one of Gregory VII's "favourite scriptural quotations"[8] was Jer. 48:10, "accursed is the one who keeps back the sword from bloodshed." Gregory had repeatedly sought to enlist nobles in the fight against Muslims across Western Europe, even going so far as to announce "his intention to lead in person an army"[9] against the Turks in the Holy Land in one of his letters. It was Gregory's wish to enlist a *militia sancti Petri*, "an army of St. Peter," to defend Christendom against the Turks. In this way, "Gregory VII significantly developed the theory and practice of holy war and holy warriors."[10] Gregory's successors adopted this stance toward holy war, with unthinkable ramifications over the course of the next several centuries.

The real birth of the Crusades occurred in the year 1095. It was the first week of March in the northern Italian city of Piacenza. A council had been convened by the pope, Urban II, to deal in part with what has been called the Investiture Controversy or Investiture Contest, a dispute revolving around what right, if any, secular rulers exercised in the appointment of bishops and abbots. The immediate context for this dispute was the bitter relationship between Pope Urban II and Holy Roman Emperor Henry IV. The pope was seeking to maintain his authority at a time when secular rulers were gaining increased autonomy and asserting their influence in religious affairs. In attendance at the council were thousands of church officials, hundreds of bishops, imperial ambassadors from Byzantium, and tens

---

7. "Gregory VII's Call," in *The Crusades*, 35.
8. Christopher Tyerman, *God's War: A New History of the Crusades* (London: Penguin, 2006), 47.
9. Ibid., 49.
10. Ibid., 47.

of thousands of laypeople. So large was the gathering that the council had to congregate outside of the city. It was during this council that ambassadors of the Byzantine Emperor, Alexius Comnenus, appealed to the pope for military aid against the Turks. It was good timing. The pope, seeing an opportunity to assert his authority and renew ties with Byzantium, endorsed the request and went on campaign like a politician seeking election. He pursued a grueling speaking schedule across France and Italy.

Urban's most famous campaign speech took place outside of the Clermont cathedral in Burgundy in November of 1096. Known as the Council of Clermont, there were hundreds of clerics and knights present at the meeting. The speech that the pope delivered was recorded by several contemporary writers. Despite disagreements as to the exact wording, there is no question that Pope Urban II launched a mighty call to arms in his speech.

> Although, O sons of God, you have promised more firmly than ever to keep the peace among yourselves and to preserve the rights of the church, there remains still an important work for you to do. Freshly quickened by the divine correction, you must apply the strength of your righteousness to another matter which concerns you as well as God. For your brethren who live in the east are in urgent need of your help, and you must hasten to give them the aid which has often been promised them. . . . On this account I, or rather the Lord, beseech you as Christ's heralds to publish this everywhere and to persuade all people of whatever rank, footsoldiers and knights, poor and rich, to carry aid promptly to those Christians who are present, but it is meant also for those who are absent. Moreover, Christ commands it.
>
> All who die by the way, whether by land or by sea, or in battle against the pagans, shall have immediate remission of sins. This I grant them through the power of God with which I am invested.[11]

11. "Urban II's Call for a Crusade," in *The Crusades*, 39–40.

Though many modern readers have found this speech not only high-handed and dumb-founding but biblically wide of the mark, it was not particularly eyebrow-raising in the eleventh century. One of the chroniclers of the First Crusade, Guibert of Nogent, provides a contemporary illustration of how Urban II's speech sounded. Guibert mused:

> God ordained holy wars in our time, so that the knightly order and the erring mob, who, like their ancient pagan models, were engaged in mutual slaughter, might find a new way of earning salvation. Thus, without having chosen (as is customary) a monastic life, without any religious commitment, they were compelled to give up this world; free to continue their customary pursuits, nevertheless they earned some measure of God's grace by their own efforts. Therefore, we have seen nations, inspired by God, shut the doors of their hearts towards all kinds of needs and feelings, taking up exile beyond the Latin world . . . in order to destroy the enemies of the name of Christ, with an eagerness greater than we have seen anyone show in hurrying to the banquet table, or in celebrating a holiday.[12]

Guibert's observation was profound. The eagerness with which pilgrims and Christ-soldiers traveled thousands of miles on foot in order to defend the Holy Land against Muslims for the sake of their Lord is difficult to understand without acknowledging the spiritual and salvation-earning nature of the trip as well as the violent historical context of Europe.

---

12. Guibert of Nogent, *The Deeds of God through the Franks: A Translation of Guibert de Nogent's Gesta Dei per Francos*, trans. Robert Levine (Woodbridge: The Boydell Press, 1997), 28.

Figure 11.1. Scholarly Interpretations of the Origins of the Crusades[13]	
Interpretive School	Description of Interpretive School
Generalist	Locates origins of crusading in the long development of Christian holy war before 1095
Popularist	Favors the idea that crusading emerged as an expression of popular piety
Traditionalist	Insists on the centrality of Jerusalem and the Holy Land as the reasons why crusading became so important
Pluralist	Concentrates on pious motivation, canon law, and papal authorization

For Western Christians in the eleventh century, Christ and his holy saints had secured a sizeable reserve of credit that was loaned out by the master banker, the pope, to individuals upon conditions of spiritual payment through acts of service and obedience to church leaders. God was wrathful and did not abide sin. Salvation was not achieved simply by faith. The best way to gain spiritual credit was by becoming a monk and thereby devoting oneself entirely to spiritual affairs. For the rest of the human lot, however, a reduction of time in Purgatory was best achieved by penance, pilgrimages, venerating relics, and receiving intercessory prayer from saints. It was not, therefore, at all out of line for Western Christians to believe that fighting for Christ on pilgrimage in the Holy Land would guarantee their salvation and protect them from a vengeful God. By pledging themselves as spiritual knights to their lord the pope, the former were absolved of their sins. It was a plan hatched in heaven and secured by Christ's substitute on earth, the bishop of Rome. As the people crowned Urban's speech, *Deus lo volt!*—"God wills it!"

So, who responded to the pope's command to make pilgrimage-war against the Muslims in the understanding that their sins would

---

13. Christopher Tyerman, *The Crusades: A Very Short History* (Oxford: Oxford University Press, 2004), 145.

be forgiven? Interestingly, none of the four most powerful men in Western society took up the cross. Pope Urban II, too busy rallying the European populace, never traveled to the Holy Land but died in Rome as many of his predecessors had. He never got to live out Gregory VII's dream of commanding Christians against Muslims in battle. Nor did Holy Roman Emperor Henry IV, King Philip of France, or King William Rufus of England assume the cross and lead troops to battle. There were also many others who doubted the pope's plans and did not respond positively to the notion of liberating Jerusalem from Muslims. Nonetheless, there were a large number of aristocrats willing to accrue financial debt or risk loss of land for the cause. War, after all, was the livelihood of nobles—and their leisure. Together with their own knights, who owed fealty or loyalty to them, they made the treacherous voyage to what appeared to them to be the other side of the world.

Figure 11.2. Jerusalem in the Middle Ages

Jerusalem was more than a city on the other side of the world in the minds and hearts of Western Christians. Based on the four-fold method of biblical interpretation developed in the Middle Ages, called the quadriga, eleventh-century writer Guibert of Nogent wrote as follows: "Jerusalem . . . according to *history*, is a particular city; according to *allegory*, it signifies the holy church; according to *tropology*, which is to say, *morality*, it is the mind of any one of the faithful who longs for the vision of eternal peace; according to *anagogy*, it signifies the life of the citizens of heaven, who in Sion see in the face the God of gods."[14]

But it was not just the aristocracy who risked life and limb for the sake of Christ. Although Pope Urban II loomed large in the rallying of the Christian populace, there were others who assembled the masses. One of the more intriguing characters during the First Crusade was a man named Peter the Hermit. According to historical records, Peter had been on pilgrimage in the Holy Land before the

---

14. Jay Rubenstein, "How, or How Much, to Reevaluate Peter the Hermit," in *The Medieval Crusade*, ed. Susan Ridyard (Woodbridge: The Boydell Press, 2004), 65.

Crusades were officially launched. While there, he had witnessed first-hand the devastation of sacred places at the hands of the Muslims. In an oath made to the patriarch of Jerusalem, he vowed to return to the Holy Land with an army to reclaim what was lawfully Christian territory. True to his word, Peter, formerly a monk, exhorted Western Christians to join with him in a battle for Christ against the Muslims. So highly regarded was Peter for his piety that followers plucked the hair from the poor mule on whose rugged back he rode to venerate as holy relics. Peter reportedly walked barefoot and abstained from bread and meat. Unlike the noblemen at this time who also commanded Christian forces into battle, Peter won his audience the old-fashioned way—by holiness. Like Urban II, Peter called for immediate service in behalf of Christ, attracting a motley crew if there ever was one—large numbers of peasants, some nobles, and no shortage of criminals, women, and children. According to one contemporary, Peter was not "satisfied to sow this seed among princes alone, but he longed to inspire the common people and men of the lower classes by his pious exhortations to undertake" the journey for Christ.[15] And so, around Easter of 1096 with a crew "numbering about forty thousand,"[16] sometimes called the Peasants' Crusade, Peter departed on foot across central Europe months ahead of schedule.

Due to the preaching of Peter the Hermit and Pope Urban II, unprecedented numbers of Westerners traveled to the Holy Land. It was just as much an urban as rural phenomenon. Fully acknowledging our limitations when calculating numbers in the ancient world, it has been estimated that around 100,000 Christians journeyed in search of "salvation, cash, land, [and] status."[17] Pilgrim-

15. William of Tyre, *A History of Deeds Done beyond the Sea*, vol. 1, trans. Emily Atwater Babcock (New York: Columbia University Press, 1943), 87.
16. Ibid., 99.

warriors from what are now England, France, Germany, and Italy were most numerous, though other regions were also represented. The French were especially prominent, though all the Western Catholics were called "Franks" indiscriminately by those in the East—*Franci* in Latin, *Frangoi* in Greek, *Franj* in Arabic. Based on the orders given by Urban II, the pilgrim-warriors were to have the cross stamped upon their clothes as a symbol of protection as well as a testimony to others that they were on a spiritual mission. More importantly, the sign of the cross on one's clothing was a conscious attempt to fulfill Christ's words, "If any want to become my followers, let them deny themselves and take up their cross and follow me" (Matt. 16:24). There was every indication that the pilgrim-warriors, now sealed by the cross, were denying themselves and following Christ.

Arrival in the Holy Land and the European Crusader States

The various pilgrim-warrior groups arrived in Constantinople and the Holy Land in different stages in the late 1090s. Regrettably, some of these pilgrim-warriors under the leadership of Peter the Hermit, filled with bloodlust, slaughtered thousands of innocent Jews living in Germany. As Tyerman writes, "All Hebrew accounts of the 1096 massacres of Rhineland Jews by the passing Christian armies emphasized that the butchers wore the sign of the cross."[18] The army assembled by Peter the Hermit had encountered opposition along the way, and they arrived in Constantinople with about 10,000 members less than when they departed. Fortunately for the Crusaders, however, the Muslim forces in the Holy Land were not prepared for the onslaught of pilgrim-warriors. They were simply not united

17. John France, "Patronage and the Crusade's Appeal," in *The First Crusade: Origins and Impact*, ed. Jonathan Philips, (Manchester and New York: Manchester University, 1997), 17.
18. Tyerman, *The Crusades*, 13.

enough to make a consolidated defense against the Franj. They would not make that mistake again.

The armies of pilgrim-warriors—though thousands never made it to the Holy Land due to disease, exhaustion, thirst, starvation, death, or capture—were a force with which to be reckoned. Each major army was headed by capable warriors such as the Norman prince Bohemond and Baldwin of Boulogne. The so-called Princes' Crusade was comprised of about six major armies, and it was later joined by Peter the Hermit's remaining crew. Together, along with some aid from the Byzantine Empire, the Crusaders launched sieges against Nicea, Antioch, and Jerusalem. In all, four feudal states were established: the kingdom of Jerusalem, the principality of Antioch, the county of Edessa, and the county of Tripoli. Together, these Latin feudal states were called the *Outremer*, a French word meaning "overseas." The victory in Jerusalem in the year 1099 was seen as the culmination of the First Crusade. The sanctity of the Church of the Holy Sepulcher was safeguarded even while Muslims and Jews were slaughtered. "Jews were burnt inside their synagogue. Muslims were indiscriminately cut to pieces, decapitated or slowly tortured by fire." So great was the carnage that the city's "narrow streets were clogged with corpses and dismembered body parts," and the Muslims who were forced to remove the bodies were summarily killed once the task was complete.[19] Thoroughly outraged, Muslims set pen to paper in great lament:

> The sword [of the infidel] is cutting and blood is spilt.
> How many Muslims men have become booty?
> And how many Muslim women's inviolability has been plundered?
> How many a mosque have they turned into a church?
> The cross has been set up in the *mihrab* [a niche in mosques indicating
>   the direction toward Mecca]?

19. Tyerman, *God's War*, 158–59.

The blood of the pig is suitable for it.
Qurans have been burned under the guide of incense.
Do you not owe an obligation to God and Islam,
Defending thereby young men and old?
Respond to God: woe on you! Respond![20]

Conclusion: Affirmation of the Crusades

When Pope Urban II issued forth a call for Christians to "fight a penitential war-pilgrimage to recover the Holy Sepulchre," writes medieval historian Jonathan Riley-Smith, "he cannot have known that he was initiating a movement which was to last for seven centuries and was to involve millions of men and women" in many parts of the world and in all walks of life.[21] We have concentrated on the First Crusade because it was the earliest crusade and because it fell within the time period discussed in this chapter, but the question of whether Christians should fight against Muslims over the Holy Land did not disappear at the end of the eleventh century. As time passed and the Crusader States were lost to Muslim forces, the question of whether to fight over the Holy land lingered generation after generation. Scholars continue to debate how many "Crusades" there were, and for how long they marched their way into the Holy Land, but it has been traditional to date the Crusades from the year 1095, the year when Pope Urban II exhorted Christians to fight in the Holy Land, to the year 1291, the year the last Crusader state fell into Muslim hands.

However we decide to enumerate the Crusades, we must not underestimate their historical significance. As Christopher Tyerman asserts, the Crusades were "to transform Christian attitudes and practices for half a millennium."[22] In this way, what occurred in the

20. Hillenbrand, "The Muslim Perspective," in *The Crusades*, 137–138.
21. Jonathan Riley-Smith, "Introduction," in *The First Crusade*, 1.
22. Tyerman, *God's War*, 45.

eleventh century was of profound consequence. Christians, stepping into a tradition of just war for centuries and baptizing violence against enemies in holy rhetoric, regarded their cause as just and that of the Muslims as unjust. So when the question arrived of whether the Western Christians should come to the aid of the Eastern Christians and fight against the Muslims for the sake of Christendom, there was resounding affirmation. The agitation caused by hundreds of years of Muslim occupation of the Holy land had remained latent in the Western Christian heart until it finally bubbled forth in the eleventh century with violent indignation. So potent was the agitation that, pressurized by contemporary factors, it continued for centuries to come.

12

Can Priests Marry?

It was the year 1115. A brilliant young teacher named Peter was making a name for himself. This Frenchman, however, was not easy to get along with. He had made a bad habit of one-upping former teachers in public, and intimidating students who attempted to outshine him. In Paris, where medieval universities were just emerging, he was an instant celebrity. Students were mesmerized by his cunning intellect and witty sense of humor. But as Scripture teaches, pride comes before a fall, and Peter Abelard was about to fall from the mountaintop on which he had proudly been perched.

From his autobiography, "The Calamity of My Misfortunes," written many years later, we learn that 1115 was the year that Peter met the love of his life, the talented Heloise. The niece of a canon in the cathedral of Notre Dame in Paris, Heloise was a young woman with an excellent education and fondness for learning. After spotting her with his arrogant eyes, Peter decided that this was the young woman he wanted to seduce. As he shamelessly wrote:

> I considered all the usual attractions for a lover and decided [Heloise] was the one to bring to my bed, confident that I should have an easy success; for at that time I had youth and exceptional good looks as well

as my great reputation to recommend me, and feared no rebuff from any woman I might choose to honour with my love.[1]

Despite his egotism, Heloise returned Peter's apparent lust with an abiding love. Peter persuaded Heloise's uncle into allowing him to move into their apartment to tutor the young girl, confessing that "if [Heloise's uncle] had entrusted a tender lamb to a ravaging wolf, it would not have surprised me more." As Peter published in his autobiography, the lessons he and Heloise conducted were filled with "more kissing than teaching," and he confided that his "hands strayed oftener to her bosom than to the pages"[2] of the books he was supposed to be teaching her. It did not take many lessons before Heloise became pregnant, and so Peter, the greatest master in Paris—whose academic appointment required celibacy, no less—found himself in a serious predicament. As one historian writes,

> A public marriage would wreck [Peter's] career; the rising tide of monastic reform meant that rules were being tightened up—it was now impossible for a cleric in such a prominent position to have a wife.[3]

After being forced into a private marriage, word got out, jeopardizing Peter's career. Peter then forced Heloise into a convent, angering her uncle so profoundly that he hired hooligans to sneak into Peter's room at night to castrate him. Peter's lack of "chastity,"[4] he confessed, had been his downfall.

1. Peter Abelard, "Historia Calamitatum," in *The Letters of Abelard and Heloise* (New York: Penguin, 1974), 66.
2. Abelard, "Historia Calamitatum," 67–68.
3. James Burge, *Heloise and Abelard: A Twelfth-Century Love Story* (London: Profile Books, 2003), 124.
4. Abelard, "Historia Calamitatum," 65.

The Question of Celibacy

The situation Peter Abelard faced in the 1110s raises a question that increasingly demanded a uniform response in the medieval church. As historian Michael Frassetto writes, the "uncertain attitude toward marriage and sexual relations" among clergy had come to a boiling point in the twelfth century. Although many clerics before the time of Peter Abelard were unofficially allowed to either have wives or mistresses, this practice began to change over the span of Peter's lifetime from the late eleventh through the mid-twelfth centuries. This change, it has been said, provoked "one of the great questions of [the] first millennium to emerge: should the leaders of the faithful, the priests and bishops, be allowed to marry?"[5] In our effort to answer this question, we will first provide an historical overview of clerical celibacy in the West before exploring the responses to this question during several church councils in the twelfth century.

Figure 12.1. Clerics

Clerics, also called *clerks* or *clergy*, were men who had taken religious vows in the church. Such could be monks, deacons, priests, or bishops. In this chapter, we will focus on clerics who were not monks.

A Short History of Clerical Celibacy in the West

According to Michael Frassetto, "The history of the issue of clerical celibacy . . . is a long and complicated one."[6] The source of the complexity can be traced back to the Apostle Paul himself, whose affection for and affirmation of marriage was anything but enthusiastic. As he wrote to the Christians in Corinth, "I wish that all were [celibate] as I myself am" (1 Cor. 7:7). Yet, because of lust, Paul

---

5. Michael Frassetto, "Introduction," in *Medieval Purity and Piety: Essays on Medieval Clerical Celibacy*, ed. Michael Frassetto (New York and London: Garland Publishing, 1998), ix.
6. Frassetto, "Introduction," in *Medieval Purity and Piety*, x.

conceded that "it is better to marry than to be aflame with passion" (7:9). Those who chose the lesser path of passion, Paul warned, were limited in their service to the Lord due to domestic distractions.

The Gospels also gave a less than stellar endorsement of marriage among those devoted to the Lord's work. A straightforward reading of the Gospels suggests that neither John the Baptist nor Jesus were married, sowing the seed of clerical celibacy that would be harvested by canon lawyers of the medieval church. Within the context of Jesus' stern teaching about the possibility of divorce, his dumbfounded disciples concluded that "it is better not to marry" (Matt. 19:10). Acknowledging the difficulty of what he was teaching, Jesus continued,

> Not everyone can accept this teaching, but only those to whom it is given. For there are eunuchs who have been so from birth, and there are eunuchs who have been made eunuchs by others, and there are eunuchs who have made themselves eunuchs for the sake of the kingdom of heaven. Let anyone accept this who can. (19:12)

The early church did not unanimously "accept" this teaching. Nor was it exactly clear what Jesus meant when he said to his disciples that "Those who belong to this age marry and are given in marriage; but those who are considered worthy of a place in that age [to come] are in the resurrection from the dead neither marry nor are given in marriage" (Luke 20:34–35). The early church sifted through these verses but did not reach a consensus. The second-century theologian Clement of Alexandria, for instance, emphasized that Jesus was "not rejecting marriage" in this Lukan passage while Bishop Cyprian of Carthage, writing a couple of generations later, cited these verses to valorize "the virtue of continence" and scorn the "pollution" brought about by marriage.[7]

---

7. *Luke*, ed. Arthur Just, Ancient Christian Commentary on Scripture, vol. 3 (Downers Grove, IL: InterVarsity Press, 2003), 313.

Figure 12.2. Terms Associated with Sexuality in the Middle Ages		
Term	Latin	Meaning
Chastity	*Castitas*	Absence of sexual activity or sexual purity
Castrated	*Castratus*	Having had the testicles removed
Celibacy	*Caelibatus*	Singleness or abstaining from marriage
Continence	*Continentia*	Restraint, especially concerning sexual activity
Eunuch	*Eunuchus*	A male who has been castrated

Clearly, there were differences of opinion within the early church regarding the merits of marriage and continence. Such differences can be traced to the Scriptures themselves, and symbolized in the two theologians quoted above. In general, Latin-speaking Catholics in the West came to regard virginity and continence as the pinnacle of piety. Recognizing that women and men were not given in marriage in paradise, they sought to anticipate such a heavenly reality on earth. As the fourth-century Latin theologian Jerome wrote, "marriage fills the earth; but heaven is filled with virginity,"[8] and "There is as much difference between marriage and virginity as there is between not sinning and doing well."[9] Although Eastern Christians, whether Greek-speakers or not, revered continence, they allowed marriage among clerics before their ordinations to the office of priest. In 314, for instance, the Council of Ancyra, held in what is now Turkey, permitted ordained deacons to marry before their ordinations to the priesthood, creating a model that is followed by Eastern Christian deacons and priests today.

In the West, the fourth century experienced a heightened rejection against clerical marriage. The so-called Council of Elvira in Spain

8. Quoted in Elizabeth Abbott, *A History of Celibacy* (Cambridge, MA: Da Capo Press, 2001), 74.
9. Quoted in Philip Lyndon Reynolds, *Marriage in the Western Church: The Christianization of Marriage during the Patristic and Early Medieval Periods* (Leiden: Brill, 1994), 273.

prohibited clerics "from having [sexual] relations with their wives and to produce children; anyone who does so nonetheless is excluded from the dignity of the clergy."[10] As can be detected, the canon recognized that many clergy were married, and so rather than commending separation or divorce, it simply forbade clerics from having intercourse with their wives upon ordination. Married in name only, conjugal rights among married clergy were outlawed. There were several factors that contributed to this new understanding of celibacy.

First among these was the biblical teaching of the Old Testament. Although priests were allowed to be married in the Old Testament, explained Pope Siricius in the late fourth century, such marriages were only because priests had to descend from the tribe of Levi:

> Those priests who have continued to beget children are wrong . . . when they appeal to the example of the Old Testament priests. These latter were permitted to have children only because the law demanded that only descendants of Levi be admitted to the service of God. Such is no longer the case.[11]

What's more, because Christian priests offered up daily sacrifices at the Eucharistic table, sex was completely prohibited in order not to defile the Mass. Like blood polluting the sacred in the Old Testament, sex contaminated the holy sacrifices of the church. The second factor was that of asceticism, which we explored in detail in Chapter 6. The denial of natural physical desires—whether of sex, sleep, family, or food—sanctified a person in the sight of God and of the community. The act of sex, by contrast, diminished a priest's holiness and sullied his religious office. As one historian explains, "It was from sexual purity that the priesthood was believed to derive its power."[12] The

---

10. Paul Beaudette, "'In the World but not of It': Clerical Celibacy as a Symbol of the Medieval Church," in *Medieval Purity and Piety*, 25.
11. Ibid., 24.

final factor contributing to the rejection of clerical marriage in the West was the legalization of Christianity and the subsequent building of churches in the fourth century, which led to the professionalization of the priestly office and to the "sacralization" of church services.

The campaign for continence among the clergy was increasingly successful. By the Middle Ages, there was a veritable religious caste system in the West that elevated sex-free Christians from those who engaged in the unclean act. As the tenth-century abbot Abo of Fleury wrote,

> there are . . . three orders of the faithful, and if three orders, three grades in the holy and universal church . . . the first is good, the second better, the third best. And, indeed, the first . . . is of the married, the second of the continent or widowed, the third of virgins.[13]

What was the only thing that separated one grade from another in this three-tiered system of sanctity? Sex—and it had to be regulated. It was best to have never been contaminated by sex, good to have ceased having sex, and worst to continue having sex. In a context in which holy people were meant not only to outshine but intercede for the less holy, the culture increasingly demanded the celibacy of its priests, who had managed for centuries to thwart prohibitions against clerical marriage like accountants avoiding tax laws.

But this was beginning to change. "It was in the late eleventh and early twelfth century," explains one historian, "that the law of clerical continence was transformed into the law of clerical celibacy."[14] This change was associated with the late eleventh-century papacy of Gregory VII, who spearheaded what has been termed the Gregorian

12. Mayke de Jong, "*Imitatio Morum*: The Cloister and Clerical Purity in the Carolingian World," in *Medieval Purity and Piety*, 50.
13. Elizabeth Dachowski, *Tertius Est Optimus*: Marriage, Continence, and Virginity in the Politics of Late Tenth- and Early Eleventh-Century Francia," in *Medieval Purity and Piety*, 117.
14. Beaudette, "'In the World but not of It,'" in *Medieval Purity and Piety*, 34.

Reform. Gregory VII, a man wildly in support of the Crusades, struggled during his pontificate with increasingly powerful monarchs who sought to meddle in religious affairs. In an effort to assert his authority, he proceeded to limit interference among monarchs by making clerics more loyal to Rome and by keeping property in the hands of the church rather than in the hands of rulers or individuals. By ordering clerical celibacy, Gregory VII ensured that the sons of priests and bishops could not inherit their father's property—churches included, which were sometimes passed on from father to son. To achieve his reform of the church and to order obedience, Gregory VII even encouraged the laity to not attend the Masses of priests or bishops who were married! Although there were some who balked at Gregory's tactics, the late eleventh and early twelfth centuries cemented the ban on clerical marriage. Meanwhile in the East, a married priesthood was the norm from the beginning, and from "the twelfth century" onward, priests were only "required to practice temporary continence before service at the altar."[15] Sex in the East, it appeared, was not as dirty as it was in the West.

Local Church Councils in London (1102, 1125, 1127, 1129)

The late eleventh and early twelfth centuries witnessed the convening of several church councils in the West to deal, in part, with the issue of sex among the clergy. This papal campaign for sexually pure clerics followed the Norman Conquest of England in 1066 by the efforts of the archbishops of Canterbury, Lanfranc and Anselm. Specifically, Archbishop Anselm convened a council in the fall of 1102, "in which," one contemporary historian wrote, "he forbade English priests to have wives."[16] The enforcement of celibacy among the English clerics was warmly received by some

---

15. Helen Parish, *Clerical Celibacy in the West: c. 1100-1700* (Farnham and Burlington: Ashgate, 2010), 83.

but bitterly opposed by others. The doctrine likely went against the grain of Norman thinking about marriage. Yet, one of those clerics who aligned with clerical celibacy in the twelfth century was the archdeacon of Wells, Thomas Agnellus. In one of his writings he berated priests who shamefully went

> from a whore's bed to the table of the lord, from a place of pollution to a place of sanctification, from shameful contact with women to consecrating the sacrament of the flesh and blood of God. . . . Who could withstand such insults, whose mind is not confounded at such injury? . . . Anyone who is of sane mind blushes to touch material bread, ordinary bread, with sordid hands and a polluted mouth, but the priest, in the impurity of his contamination, does not shudder to chew the bread of angels, the bread that descended from heaven.[17]

Such was a standard argument among those opposed to clerical marriage. The development of the doctrine of the full presence of Christ in the Eucharist, a teaching called *transubstantiation*, was directly related to the development of the doctrine of clerical celibacy. It only makes sense that priests were no longer allowed to touch a woman and then the "flesh and blood of God" if it was also believed that the bread and wine actually became Christ's body and blood in the Eucharist.

The archdeacon of Wells notwithstanding, there were plenty of clerics who criticized this line of thinking—regardless of whether the bread and wine were actually Christ's body and blood. Thomas's younger English contemporary, Henry of Huntington, was one such critic. In his *History of the English People*, he maintained that clerical marriage in England "had not been prohibited before" the archbishop went on his campaign to end the practice. Henry then proceeded

16. Henry of Huntingdon, Historia Anglorum: *The History of the English People*, trans. Diana Greenway (Oxford: Clarendon, 1996), 451.
17. Quoted in Hugh Thomas, *The Secular Clergy in England, 1066–1216* (Oxford: Oxford University Press, 2014), 32.

to tell a scandalous tale of Cardinal John of Crema, the cleric later sent by the pope to enforce clerical celibacy among the English after the First Lateran Council (discussed below). Around the year 1125, Cardinal John of Crema had been present at a council in London in which the following canon had been decreed:

> We forbid any apostolic authority priests, deacons, subdeacons, and canons from living with wives, concubines, or any women. . . . He who breaks this decree should, on confession and conviction, endure the loss of his order.[18]

After the council, however, Cardinal John was reportedly "discovered after vespers with a whore"—"on the very same day he had made the body of Christ" during Mass!"[19] This scandal forced the cardinal out of England in shame, but the campaign against sexually active clergy continued.

Several years later, in about 1127, another council at Westminster was convened to mandate clerical celibacy. This time the stakes were raised higher:

> We utterly forbid priests, deacons, subdeacons and all canons illicit intercourse with women. If any remain attached to concubines (which God forbid) or wives, then they are to be removed. . . By our authority and by God's we further command archdeacons and officials, charged with this duty, to totally root out with energy and care this evil from the church of God. Those negligent in this task or (which God forbid) acquiescing in the evil . . . are to be fittingly corrected by the bishop. . . . The concubines of priests . . . should be expelled . . . [or] arrested.[20]

The king of England, after hearing the decrees of the council, gave his hearty approval, though it's likely that he then undermined the

---

18. John of Worcester, *The Chronicle of John of Worcester*, trans. P. McGurk (Oxford: Clarendon Press, 1998), 165.
19. Henry, Historia Anglorum, 451, 475.
20. John, *The Chronicle*, 171.

decisions by allowing priests to pay him money to maintain their offices and keep their concubines/wives. The same thing occurred two years later at another church council in London.

The tide against clerical marriage, however, was becoming too strong—even in England. Although there remained a powerful minority in favor of clerical marriage, others were suspicious of sex, and would have shared the advice that a twelfth-century English monk named Aelred of Rievaulx gave to his sister concerning the sexual temptations ever lurking in the world around us:

> in food and drink, in sleep, in speech, let [a woman] always be on guard against a threat to her chastity. . . if she has to speak to someone let her always be afraid of hearing something which might cast even the least cloud over the clear skies of her chastity; let her not doubt that she will be abandoned by grace if she utters a single word against purity.[21]

The First (1123) and Second (1139) Lateran Councils in Rome

The First and Second Lateran Councils were landmark councils in the question over clerical marriage. Unlike the local councils in England in the same century, these councils were universal in scope. They were much more influential in terminating the practice of clergy being allowed to marry either before or after ordination. As historian of celibacy Helen Parish writes, "the real turning point in the history of clerical marriage"[22] came between the years of these two councils in the early twelfth century. Historian Jennifer Thibodeaux is more direct: "These [two] councils destroyed clerical marriage."[23]

21. Ruth Karras, *Sexuality in Medieval Europe: Doing unto Others* (London and New York: Routledge, 2012), 62.
22. Parish, *Clerical Celibacy in the West*, 104.
23. Jennifer Thibodeaux, "The Defence of Clerical Marriage: Religious Identity and Masculinity in the Writings of Anglo-Norman Clerics," in *Religious Men and Masculine Identity in the Middle Ages*, ed. P. H. Cullum and Katherine Lewis (Woodbridge: The Boydell Press, 2013), 51.

The fifth canon of the council read as follows:

> We strictly forbid presbyters [that is, priests], deacons, subdeacons, and monks to have concubines or to contract matrimony; and we judge, according to the definition of the sacred canons, that marriages contracted by such persons are to be dissolved and the persons should be brought to penitence.[24]

By now, it was commonly believed that the only appropriate response to clerical marriage was to annul it. It was also at this time in the High Middle Ages that Christians increasingly believed that bishops were married not to a physical wife but to a spiritual one—the bishop's diocese. In the consecration of one bishop in France, the ritual included the following statement upon the bishop being presented with a wedding ring: "With this ring of faith we commend to you the bride of Christ, [this] church."[25] As some contemporary authors mused, a bishop who had an earthly wife in addition to his spiritual bride was adulterous (officially a bigamist) just as a bishop who was sexually united with a woman from his diocese was incestuous. It did not take long for this attitude to impact priests and their parishes. A priest, it was beginning to be understood, was "married" to his parish—end of story.

The Second Lateran Council confirmed the teaching of the First Lateran Council. As the seventh canon of the council read:

> But that law of continence and purity, so pleasing to God, may become more general among persons constituted in sacred orders, we decree that bishops, priests, deacons, subdeacons, canons regular, monks, and professed clerics who, transgressing the holy precept, have dared to contract marriage, shall be separated. For a union of this kind which has been contracted in violation of the ecclesiastical law, we do not regard as matrimony.[26]

24. Beaudette, "'In the World but not of It,'" in *Medieval Purity and Piety*, 23.
25. Megan McLaughlin, "The Bishop of Bridegroom: Marital Imagery and Clerical Celibacy in the Eleventh and Early Twelfth Centuries," in *Medieval Purity and Piety*, 211.

These pronouncements against clerical marriage were not issued simply to keep the office of the priesthood pure. As mentioned above, these regulations were also about the centralization of the papacy at a time when monarchies seriously threatened the pope's authority. By demanding clerical celibacy, priests became more subordinate to bishops and popes than to kings and princes. We should also keep in mind that, in a world where everybody was a Christian, the regulation of sex became the best way to distinguish the clerics from the laity—the truly devout from the ordinary, the sacred people from the mundane. For hundreds of years in the West, the priests looked little different from the people to whom they ministered. Clerics owned property, farmed their land, married, and sired children. The prohibition of sex among clerics, however, became the Gordian knot that unrivaled these undesirables. Without sex, priests could not get married, have children, direct their sons to enter the priesthood, and thereby inherit their property—thus ending priestly dynasties that endured for generations. The so-called Gregorian Reform of the late eleventh and early twelfth centuries were slowly restructuring the makeup of the church. These changes would be profound and incredibly long-lasting.

Conclusion: Clerical Celibacy Mandatory in the West (but Not in the East)

As historian James Brundage asserts, "The war against clerical marriage reached its climax in . . . the twelfth century."[27] In the West, despite its continued practice, leaders of the Catholic Church thoroughly condemned clerics who engaged in sexual intercourse— married or not. If anything, the belief was becoming more

---

26. Beaudette, "'In the World but not of It,'" in *Medieval Purity and Piety*, 24.
27. James Brundage, *Law, Sex, and Christian Society in Medieval Europe* (Chicago: University of Chicago Press, 1987), 220.

widespread that clerics were supposed to be married only to their parishes—to a heavenly bride, we might say, but not to an earthly one. The Catholic stance against married clergy "came to be the accepted policy of the church."[28] The First and Second Lateran Councils made this patently evident. The fact that celibacy was not mentioned in the canons of the Third Lateran Council of 1179 suggests that both papal and popular opinion was winning the day against a sexually active clergy.

Still, sex was a habit too hard to break. Despite clear church teachings against sexual intercourse, many clerics were apparently "aflame with passion" (1 Cor. 7:9), and preferred to marry in secret, marry outside of their parishes, or continue to have sexual intercourse outside of marriage with so-called concubines. In the year 1274, for instance, Bishop Henry III was deposed from his diocese at Liege for siring at least sixty-five illegitimate children. It was even rumored that the old devil had boasted at a public banquet of having fourteen children born to him over the course of the year. For the next several hundred years, it was not uncommon for sons of priests to follow their father's footsteps into the priesthood, some of whom actually became bishops and prominent theologians. In the early 1500s, however, the issue of clerical celibacy reached new heights as a growing number of priests married as a product of the Protestant Reformations. Meanwhile, it continues to be the practice in the East that priestly candidates can marry before ordination—the act of sex not in the least diminishing their capacity to break bread and perform other priestly duties.

28. Frassetto, "Introduction," in *Medieval Purity and Piety*, x.

13

What's the Relationship between Faith and Reason?

It was the year 1210. It also happened to be fall in Paris, but nobody was gathered this day to marvel at the beauties of what would later be called the City of Lights during one of its most delightful seasons. No, this November day peasants and priests alike were huddled in the marketplace of Champeaux to watch ten heretics be put to death. The heretical group about to be burned alive was called the Amalricians. Almaric or Amaury, the founder of this movement, had been a professor at the recently established University of Paris. Before his death in 1207, Almaric had provoked a storm of theological controversy over the relation between faith and reason.

Almaric's disciples, who adopted and spread his theological beliefs despite censure from church and university officials, were now making a death march toward the stake. Unfortunately for the executioner, a thunderstorm was brewing and nonstop rain was making it difficult to sufficiently light the wood. Fortunately for the Amalricians, the wet wood released smoke that likely suffocated them before the flames could engulf them at the stake. Whatever the case, the onlookers braving the strong winds and persistent rains this day were treated, no doubt to their amusement, to a rather unsavory addition to the public spectacle. Almaric, now a three-year old rotting corpse recently exhumed for this special occasion, was hurled into the smoldering flames to be united with his faithful disciples one last time.

The Question of Faith and Reason

The burning at the stake of Almaric and his disciples for heresy was not just a gruesome casualty of thirteenth-century religious politics but also sign of a greater intellectual controversy. In places like Spain and Sicily, Muslim strongholds now gradually being re-conquered by European Christians, centers of translations were forming that would forever change the course of Western civilization. Ancient Greek treatises on the sciences and medicine were hastily being translated from Arabic into Latin, at which time these books were eagerly consumed by professors and students studying at the newly formed universities popping up all across the European continent. Almaric was one such inquisitive professor, whose embrace of the new sciences put him at odds with classic Christian theology. Before long, Almaric was giving lectures to his students on Aristotle—arguing that God was synonymous with creation, that those who love God cannot commit sin, and that neither heaven nor hell exists.

The author of Ecclesiastes once wrote that there's nothing new under the sun, but Almaric embodied the transition from the Age of Faith to the Age of Reason during the Middle Ages. As historian of science James Hannam writes, "The sad story of the Amalricians was to have long-lasting consequences for natural philosophy ... [Almaric] had used reason and logic not to defend Christianity, but to undermine it."[1] The introduction of the philosophical and scientific writings of Greek authors such as Aristotle sent intellectual shockwaves across the Western world, leading students and scholars to shift focus from divine revelation to the natural world—a subtle change at first but one with colossal consequences long-term. This shift of focus from revelation and faith to nature and reason did not go unnoticed or unchallenged in the Middle Ages. Roger Bacon, Bonaventure, and Thomas Aquinas each raised the question of how, if at all, the study of the sciences related to theology. In this chapter, therefore, we will survey various responses to an increasingly important question during the Middle Ages: what's the relation between faith and reason?

A Short History of Faith and Reason

The slowness of Christianity to become the dominant religion in the Roman Empire meant that Christianity necessarily grew up intellectually in the midst of pagan philosophy and learning. This incited two general responses to pagan learning among Christians—cautious assimilation and outright rejection. Among those who cautiously made use of pagan learning were the likes of Justin Martyr, Origen, and Augustine. Israelites argued that Christians, like the Israelites plundering of the Egyptians in the book of Exodus, should fully claim intellectual property from any source as long as it accords with Christian beliefs. Because truth is one, they believed, truth may equally arise out of Christian or non-Christian sources. But not everyone thought this way. Among those who strongly rejected the learning of the pagan world were important figures such as Tertullian, Eusebius, and Basil. As Tertullian rhetorically asked in one of his treatises:

---

1. James Hannam, *The Genesis of Science: How the Christian Middle Ages Launched the Scientific Revolution* (Washington, D.C.: Regnery Publishing, 2011), 71.

> What indeed has Athens to do with Jerusalem? What concord is there between the academy and the Church? What between heretics and Christians? . . . Away with all attempts to produce a mottled Christianity of Stoic, Platonic, and dialectical composition! We want no curious disputation after possessing Christ Jesus, no inquisition after enjoining the gospel! With our faith we desire no further belief![2]

The disagreement about how to regard pagan thought in the early church leaked over into the Middle Ages. Although in the West, Christianity was becoming almost indistinguishable from larger society, the church was still not exactly sure how to make use of the classical, pagan intellectual culture on which it had been built. In the sixth century, Boethius and Cassiodorus were two of the last theologians in the West to keep feet in both Greek and Latin literature and philosophy. Boethius, in particular, kindled an ember of Greek logic and science among posterity by means of both his original and translated works. In the late eighth and ninth centuries, during the so-called Carolingian Renaissance, Charlemagne ordered the creation of cathedral and monastic schools taught by abbots and clerics that sought to standardize Latin—now a dead language—and teach a common curriculum to those in pursuit of holy orders. The sciences were included, but revealed doctrine was of prime importance.

The birth of the university in the twelfth and early thirteenth centuries was one of the turning points of world history. Before that time, students were trained in cathedral and monastic schools, where faith and doctrine took center stage. Collective conformity to the deposit of Christian dogma was its goal. As philosopher Charles Lohr explains, it "was not the individual who taught, but the Church through the clergy."[3] The emergence of universities, however, caused a crack in the intellectual edifice of Western society that has only

---

2. Tertullian, "On Prescription against Heretics" 7, in *The Ante-Nicene Fathers*, vol. 3, ed. Alexander Roberts and James Donaldson (New York: Charles Scribner's Sons, 1896–1903), 246.

widened over time. Rather than privileging faith and revelation, autonomous scholars or "masters" began introducing the method of critical questioning to engage theological discourse. Their only authorities were themselves. Scholars such as Peter Abelard, whom we briefly discussed in Chapter 12, embodied this new learning, with critical and independent thought at its center. His career, pregnant with controversy, witnessed the growing pains of a new age. Peter himself was condemned on two separate occasions for novel theological positions, a foreshadowing of things to come among the new generation of scholars.

Due to the legal status of the universities as medieval corporations, they effectively became autonomous. Of the four faculties or academic divisions at the medieval university—the arts, medicine, law, and theology—each held various rights and privileges, but professors were increasingly given a long leash with regard to what they believed. In the beginning, theology was the core discipline–and gaining the necessary competencies to teach in the theology department required more time and money than in any of the other faculties. Nevertheless, the arts faculty played a foundational role in the university. Unlike medicine, law, and theology, which were all graduate departments, students were required to first excel in the arts by earning a bachelor's and master's degree in that faculty or department before gaining admission to study in the other three faculties. And because mastery of what we now call logic and science had to precede the study of the other disciplines, these undergraduate core requirements became the means by which the graduate disciplines were studied and learned. In short, in the hand of the university, the discipline of theology turned into a labyrinth of

---

3. Charles Lohr, "The Ancient Philosophical Legacy and its Transmission to the Middle Ages," in *A Companion to Philosophy in the Middle Ages*, ed. Jorge Gracia and Timothy Noone (Malden and Oxford: Blackwell, 2003), 15.

rational discourse. Theology was now about questions, and these questions did not have the faintest connection with the practical Christian life. In short, academic theology was worlds away from the simple faith of the average man and woman in the Middle Ages.

Figure 13.1. The University in the Middle Ages

University students in the Middle Ages were always males. These young men entered the university around the age of fourteen upon mastering the Latin language. Latin—a foreign tongue no longer spoken—was the only language of instruction. These adolescents could study anywhere in Europe since Latin was the only language used, and many university students were foreigners who were eagerly taken advantage of by the emerging merchant class of each university town. The basic course of study consisted of grammar, logic, and rhetoric (the so-called *trivium*); and arithmetic, astronomy, geometry, and music (the so-called *quidrivium*). Students earned the bachelor's of arts after several years of study of the *trivium* and the master's of arts after two or three additional years of studying the *quidrivium*. For those few who could afford it, these degrees gained admission into the fields of law, medicine, and theology, which required several additional years of studying and teaching.

The translation of Aristotle's naturalistic works into Latin in the late twelfth and thirteenth centuries provided the ingredients necessary to create an entirely new way to look at the world. Medieval universities took immediate advantage of the translated works of Aristotle and other Greek thinkers, particularly in the area of what is called natural philosophy. Such a discipline included what we today call physics, optics, cosmology, meteorology, astronomy—in short, the hard sciences.

The University of Paris was the first to raise objections to the use of Aristotle's natural philosophy. Bans were issued in 1210 and 1215. The impetus for the bans was Aristotle's naturalistic convictions that conflicted with Christian dogma. Specifically, Aristotle believed that the world was eternal, that only the rational part of the soul was immortal, that there could only be one universe, and that there was little room for miracles or divine intervention. By the middle of the century, however, the campaign against the new philosophy was losing steam. Even though Pope Gregory IX had ordered a commission in 1231 to "eliminate all that is erroneous or that might cause scandal"[4] among Aristotle's works, it's likely that the orders were never followed. Whatever the case, the University of Paris had lifted its ban on students reading Aristotle's works on natural philosophy by 1255, by which time Aristotle, a philosopher dead for more than fifteen hundred years, was unofficially baptized into Christian theology. All of Aristotle's works were now *required* reading for all arts students. What we might call Aristotelian Christianity had been born, and it exercised enormous influence on the development of the Western intellectual tradition. The *trivium* and the *quidrivium*, the standard course in the medieval university, "was gradually either replaced by or adapted to Aristotle's writings."[5] Needless to say, the new curriculum, thoroughly pagan in orientation, posed a real threat to theology.

Roger Bacon (c. 1220–1292)

We will begin our study of three famous masters who struggled with the relation between faith and reason during the thirteenth century with Roger Bacon. An Englishman of considerable wealth, Roger Bacon studied at Paris before later teaching there and at Oxford. He later became a Franciscan, and wrote many treatises on any number of scientific and mathematical subjects. Of all the masters in the Middle Ages, Roger Bacon was one of the first to lecture on Aristotle's works on natural philosophy. Despite the ban on teaching Aristotle, he was already lecturing on Augustine's *Metaphysics*,

---

4. Quoted in David Lindberg, *The Beginnings of Western Science: The European Scientific Tradition in Philosophical, Religious, and Institutional context, Prehistory to A.D. 1450*, 2nd ed. (Chicago and London: The University of Chicago Press, 2007),
5. Alexander Hall, *Thomas Aquinas and John Duns Scotus: Natural Theology in the High Middle Ages* (London: Continuum, 2007), 2.

Physics, On Generation and Corruption, and *On the Soul* by the 1240s at Paris before eventually moving on to teach at Oxford.

Bacon was a philosopher rather than a theologian. He lectured in the arts faculty and was thereby excluded from lecturing on theology. Without at all elbowing Christian theology off the table of intellectual discourse, however, he sought to make full use of the new sciences introduced by Greek thinkers such as Aristotle. According to Bacon, the sciences were instruments to enable a better understanding of theology; they were not ends in themselves:

> I say. . . that one discipline is mistress of the others—namely, theology, for which the others are integral necessities and which cannot achieve its ends without them. And it lays claim to their virtues and subordinates them to its nod and command.[6]

Bacon was a good disciple of Augustine, who had argued centuries earlier that pagan philosophy belonged to Christian theology when it accorded with the truth of revelation.

Bacon devoted much of his attention to the study of the natural world in the service of the church. He was particularly interested in optics and astrology. He provided new theories of vision based on the new sciences available in the thirteenth century, and dedicated a considerable amount of time to mathematics. In one of his writings on mathematics, he carefully argued that mathematics, the foundation of all learning, was still a servant to theology. Rather than conflicting with theology, mathematics served as a stepping stone of intellectual inquiry:

> all the wise men in ancient times labored in mathematics, in order that they might know all things, just as we have seen in the case of men of our own times, and have heard in the case of others who by means of mathematics, of which they had an excellent knowledge, have learned

---

6. Roger Bacon, "Opus Majus" 3.36, in Lindberg, *The Beginnings of Western Science,* 236.

all science. For very illustrious men have been found, like bishop Robert of Lincoln [otherwise known as Robert Grosseteste] and Friar Adam de Morisco, and many others, who by the power of mathematics have leaned to explain the causes of all things, and expound adequately things human *and divine*. Moreover, the sure proof of this matter is found in the writings of those men, as, for example, on impressions such as the rainbow, comets, generation of heat, investigation of localities on the earth and other matters, of which both theology and philosophy make use. Wherefore it is clear that mathematics is absolutely necessary and useful to other sciences.[7]

More than anything else, Roger Bacon was a great advocate for the new sciences, and he eagerly attempted to persuade the pope, the primary addressee of his works, of their efficacy for the benefit of the church.

Bonaventure (1217–1274)

Bonaventure was born Johannes Fidanza in Italy before later becoming a friar in the newly organized Franciscan order. Like Bacon, Bonaventure studied at the University of Paris while the university was changing its core curriculum from the study of the *trivium* and the *quidrivium* to Aristotle's works. This curricular change created a climate of hostility, for it was not apparent how Aristotle's model of classifying all disciplines into the sciences would impact the study of theology—long held to be the queen of the medieval disciplines. Bonaventure later become a master at Paris, and entered into the controversy represented by the faculties of the arts and of theology. For his part, Bonaventure wrote a treatise titled *Retracing the Arts to Theology*. As historian of science Edward Grant explains, this treatise "sought to show that theology is the queen of the

---

7. Roger Bacon, "On the Importance of Studying Mathematics," trans. Robert Burke, in *A Source Book in Medieval Science*, ed. Edward Grant (Cambridge: Harvard University Press, 1974), 94 (italics added).

sciences, because, in the final analysis, all learning and knowledge depend upon divine illumination from Sacred Scripture."[8]

Grounding the entire discussion on divine revelation, Bonaventure started this treatise with a quotation from the book of James: "Every . . . perfect gift . . . is from above, coming down from the Father of lights" (1:17). Based on this passage, Bonaventure argued that all illumination ultimately shines forth from God. Specifically, "the manifold rays which issue from that Fount of light" are divided into four parts:

> the *external* light, or the light of mechanical art; the *lower* light, or the light of sense perception; the *inner* light, or the light of philosophical knowledge; and the *higher* light, or the light of grace and of Sacred Scripture.[9]

By dividing light into these four categories, Bonaventure cleverly set the stage for the rest of his argument.

All sources of knowledge—mechanical, mathematical, philosophical, or theological—come from God's light, but the "higher" light of theology surpasses the others. The first light, that light of mechanical art, refers to those base things that remove human sorrow or add comfort to our lives. It includes things such as farming, hunting, and weaving. Though important in their own right, they are confined to things done primarily in the body, and so do not help us in our quest to find God. The second light, the sense of perception, refers to optics. It is a lower light because it has to do with the material. It is the third light, that of philosophy, that begins to take humankind in that upward journey toward God. This light is found by reasoned study, specifically by study of the curriculum in the arts faculty at the medieval university. But it is the fourth

8. Edward Grant, *The Foundations of Modern Science in the Middle Ages.*
9. Bonaventure, *Retracing the Arts to Theology* 1. http://people.uvawise.edu/philosophy/phil205/ Bonaventure.html.

light, that of divine revelation, that transcends all human thought and reasoning. Bonaventure explained that this light "is not acquired by human research, but comes down by inspiration from the "Father of Lights."[10] As if to make even clearer his elevation of the fourth light, Bonaventure ended his treatise as follows:

> It is evident too how all divisions of knowledge are handmaids of theology, and it is for this reason that theology makes use of illustrations and terms pertaining to every branch of knowledge. . . . And this is the fruit of all sciences.[11]

As the fruit of all sciences, theology or faith was to take precedence over all the other academic disciplines, including reason or philosophy.

Thomas Aquinas (1225–1274)

Thomas Aquinas was one of the most brilliant medieval thinkers. A student of the prolific and insatiably curious Albertus Magnus, Thomas embodied the question of the relation between faith and reason in the Middle Ages. He became a Dominican friar despite the protests of his family and served as a professor of theology at the University of Paris from 1257 to 1259 and then again from 1269 to 1272. While at Paris, Thomas was swept up in the controversy existing between the arts and theology faculties over how far the sciences could take one intellectually without recourse to revelation. Thomas, for his part, stood in noted opposition to those who blindly accepted the new sciences apart from divine revelation. As he once wrote, "I don't see what one's interpretation of the text of Aristotle has to do with the teaching of the faith."[12]

---

10. Bonaventure, *Retracing the Arts to Theology*, 5.
11. Ibid., 26.
12. Vernon Bourke, *St. Thomas Aquinas Commentary on Aristotle's Physics*, trans. R. J. Blackwell et al. (New Haven: Yale University Press, 1963), xxiv.

At the same time, Thomas did not reject Aristotle and the new sciences lock, stock, and barrel. On the contrary, Thomas integrated Aristotle's natural philosophy into theology more profoundly than perhaps anyone before or after, and he wrote no fewer than a million words on the writings and ideas of Aristotle. Thomas found Aristotle a great ally when it came to understanding the world independent of revelation. Highly influenced by the Greek philosopher Aristotle, Thomas even famously offered five demonstrations of God's existence apart from any recourse to the Bible or faith.

One of the most commonly quoted sayings of Thomas is found in the first part of his *Summa Theologiae*, his greatest single writing on theology that was intentionally left unfinished. There he famously wrote that "Grace does not destroy nature but perfects it."[13] Though profound and indicative of how Thomas understood the relation between faith and reason, this concept originated in the writings of Thomas's contemporary Bonaventure, yet was ultimately indebted to Greek thought. At any rate, this terse sentence does fully capture Thomas's views of faith and reason. Faith and reason, Thomas argued, are both given by God and therefore good and proper. Reason, given freely by God to all human beings, enables us to understand the natural world; but faith, given supernaturally by God through the auspices of the church, enables us to better understand not only the natural world but especially the supernatural world. As he wrote in his treatise *Faith, Reason, and Philosophy*, "even though the natural light of the human mind is inadequate to make known what is revealed by faith, nevertheless what is divinely taught to us by faith cannot be contrary to what we are endowed with by nature."[14]

---

13. Thomas, *Summa Theologiae* 1.1.8 ad 2.
14. Quoted in John Freely, *Before Galileo: The Birth of Modern Science in Medieval Europe* (New York and London: Overlook Duckworth, 2012), 115.

Figure 13.2. Thomas Aquinas on the Relation between Faith and Reason		
Faith Alone	Reason Alone	Faith and Reason Together
We can only know particular theological beliefs, such as the Trinity, based on faith.	We can only know specific general truths, such as that all material things are made up of form and matter, based on reason.	We can know some things, such as the existence of God, based on faith and/or reason.

Thomas and His Academic Opponents

Such a synthesis of faith and reason stood in noted contrast to some of Thomas's colleagues in the arts faculty at Paris. One of them, Siger of Brabant, was heavily influenced by the twelfth-century Muslim scholar Averroes, or Ibn Rushd, whose writings on Aristotle had recently been translated into Latin. Thomas and Siger aimed specific academic tracts against each other as part of this larger debate over faith and reason. One of their disputes revolved around whether individual souls exist in all human beings or whether the human intellect is eternally caused by God and therefore not unique to any given human. The latter view, taught by Aristotle and based on reason, directly contradicted Christian teaching (as taught by the Bible and the church fathers)—that the individual soul was eternal. In this argument, Siger sided with Aristotle—and thus with reason—while Thomas sided with the church—and thus with faith. Siger allegedly argued that reason says one thing and faith another. Rather than one perfecting the other, as Thomas taught, the two were both true. Thomas's synthesis of faith and reason—in which both come from God and are therefore not in conflict—was the opinion that won the day, and Siger had to recant those views of his that defied Christian theology. Yet the day was dawning when reason, unattended by revelation, would become the greater truth of reality in the West.

This emphasis on reason over faith existed in seed form in another of Thomas's opponents at Paris, Boethius of Dacia. Like Siger, Boethius argued that philosophy had as its only source reason and the intellect while theology appealed to divine revelation and church authority. Thus, when it came to assessing the age of the earth, reason suggested that the earth was eternal while faith believed that the earth was created by God at a certain point of time. Boethius wrote that

> It belongs to the philosopher to determine every question that can be disputed by reason; for every question that can be disputed by rational argument falls within some part of being. But the philosopher investigates all being—natural, mathematical, *and divine*. Therefore, it belongs to the philosopher to determine every question that can be disputed by rational arguments.[15]

This type of thinking was not popular in the thirteenth century and, in 1277, the bishop of Paris condemned 219 statements from the minds of these new academics that were interpreted to be out of sync with revealed religion. One condemnation was aimed at the statement, not very far off from what Boethius seemed to be getting at, "That the only wise men of the world are philosophers" and "That theological discussions are based on fables."[16] But the condemnations were short-lived. Boethius's sentiment was a foreshadowing of things to come. Theologians were increasingly sidelined in the game of intellectual inquiry; they were free to play around with their "special revelation" on the bench while the professional players, the philosophers, entered the field in their stead. There, it seems, the theologians have been forced to sit ever since.

15. Quoted in Lindberg, *The Beginnings of Western Science*, 245.
16. "The Condemnation of 1277," trans. Edward Grant, in *A Source Book in Medieval Science*, 50.

Conclusion: Reason Becoming Increasingly Independent of Faith

The thirteenth century was the first century in which the disciplines of religion and science were placed so closely together under the umbrella of the same university system. Together, these two disciplines piqued the interest of professors and students more so than any others. As one historian of philosophy notes, "No other issue concerned the medieval more than the relation of faith to reason."[17] In the early part of the thirteenth century, of course, the disciplines were more properly called sacred doctrine and natural philosophy, and the latter was seen as a tool to enable the real work of sacred theology to be done. There was no conflict between the two. One of the more commonly used medieval analogies, in fact, was that philosophy was theology's handmaiden or mistress. As we have seen, this was more or less the view of Roger Bacon, Bonaventure, and Thomas Aquinas.

Over the course of the thirteenth century, however, philosophy began flexing its muscles. It increasingly looked like no "handmaiden." As the judgment of Siger of Brabant and Boethius of Dacia indicated, Western thought was tracking in a different direction. If anything, the tail began to wag the dog. As the historian of scholasticism Ulrich Leinsle bluntly put it, "without philosophy no theology."[18] Because philosophy was not only a prerequisite to the study of theology but also the instrument through which theology was studied, theology became captive to highly rationalistic ways of thinking. Meanwhile, natural philosophy took root in the medieval university system and later developed into modern science, by which time it had become completely unattached to theology and was regarded as a more sensible and intellectually defendable discipline.

17. Jorge Gracia, "Introduction," in *A Companion to Philosophy in the Middle Ages*, 3.
18. Ulrich Leinsle, *Introduction to Scholastic Theology*, trans. Michael Miller (Washington, D.C.: The Catholic University of America, 2010), 121.

14

How Should We Respond to Mass Death?

It was the year 1347. Twelve galleys of merchants from Genoa, Italy, had just pulled into the Messina harbor in northeastern Sicily. This was a regular occurrence, and the harbor masters initially thought nothing of it. But then, to their great dismay, they spied the men aboard the ships. They were walking corpses. In addition to the pile of rotting bodies littered in the galleys, the men who were alive—for the moment, at least—were noticeably stricken with some dreadful disease. As the Franciscan friar who chronicled this event marveled, these seamen "brought with them a plague that they carried down to the very marrow of their bones." No one was safe. The disease apparently spread so effortlessly that it could be contracted just by speaking with an infected person. The harbor masters, greatly disturbed by what they encountered, feverishly attempted to quarantine the fleet.

It was too late. Even as the ships were being tied to the docks, the very fleas that had infected the sailors were getting a joy-ride into the city on the furry backs of their rodent hosts. It did not take long before most of the inhabitants in the city of Messina were suffering the effects of the great disease. "And not only did everyone die who spoke with the victims," Friar Michele da Piazza explained, "but also anyone who bought from them, touched them, or had intercourse with them."[1] At least half in the region of Sicily where the disease first entered was either dead or had fled within six months. Everyone, it seemed, was either spitting up blood, spotting dark swellings on their skin, or racing with fever. "This scene," writes medieval historian Robert Gottfried, was "repeated thousands of times in ports and fishing villages across Eurasia and North Africa."[2] Nobody knew exactly what was going on, but everyone was impacted. The greatest disaster in European history was about to be unleashed on unsuspecting souls from Sicily to Scotland.

The Question of Death

The arrival of the Black Death in the middle of the fourteenth century was one of the most devastating human disasters in history. Although it's true that death lurked over every community in the Middle Ages, the Black Death was qualitatively different. Whole communities were sometimes wiped out over the period of weeks. Doctors were scarce, and even those who attempted to cure patients were no match for this medical onslaught. As one contemporary writer despaired, "There was no help from anywhere."[3] Families were forced to make the dreadful decision of whether to forever abandon their infected spouses and children or else helplessly watch them die in anguish. In this chapter, we will investigate the varied responses to

---

1. Michele da Piazza, "Chronicle," in John Aberth, *The Black Death: The Great Mortality of 1348-50, a Brief History with Documents* (Boston and New York: Bedford/St. Martin's 2005), vii.
2. Robert Gottfried, *The Black Death: Natural and Human Disaster in Medieval Europe* (New York: The Free Press, 1983), xiii.
3. John VI, "History," in Aberth, *The Black Death*, 36.

mass death in the fourteenth century, with an eye toward seeing how Christian Europe reacted to the greatest medical crisis in its history.

A Short History of the Plague

There were regular outbreaks of disease and mass death across the ancient and medieval world. In Europe, three significant outbreaks occurred before the spread of the Black Death in the fourteenth century. The first was the introduction of smallpox into Europe in the late second century CE. It was called the Antonine Plague on account of the Antonine dynasty of Roman emperors ruling during the second century. The famed Greek physician Galen, most active in the late second century, estimated that up to a third of the Italian population died due to smallpox alone. The next major outbreak of disease and disaster was likely the introduction of measles into Europe around the middle of the third century. So severe was this disease at its height that several thousand people reportedly died every day in the city of Rome.

Yet by far the greatest outbreak of infectious disease across Europe was the so-called Plague of Justinian in 541–542. This plague, which was the first recorded example of bubonic plague in Europe, was a foreshadowing, exactly 800 years earlier, of the Black Death. Although Emperor Justinian managed to survive, many of his subjects were less fortunate. Contemporary records make the scarcely conceivable claim that 10,000 people were dying every day in the capital city of Constantinople at the peak of the disease. As the contemporary Byzantine chronicler Procopius explained, "During this time there was a pestilence, by which the whole human race came near to being annihilated . . . it spread over the whole world, always moving forward and traveling at times favorable to it."[4]

---

4. Quoted in Suzanne Austin Alchon, *A Pest in the Land: New World Epidemics in a Global Perspective* (Albuquerque, NM: University of New Mexico Press, 2003), 28.

In addition to these three great outbreaks of infectious disease in Europe, there were cycles of plague and disease that occurred throughout the Middle Ages. In the 1030s, for instance, a chronicle claimed how "a twin plague went through the people" across France. Conditions were so dire that "every person thought that he was to be killed by a sudden death." If a person lived to see morning, it was believed that death would overtake him or her by night. A council was assembled to deal with the crisis, concluding that God had sent the plague on the people on account of their great sins. In order to protect themselves and appease God's wrath, they agreed to remove the relics of a holy person at the altar of the church and offer prayers and devotion to the dead saint. At the news of the unearthing of this holy man, the people "came flying eagerly from nearly all of the country. Bringing with them such gifts as each was able, they gave them to the saint, and they ardently surrounded him with hymns and devout prayers."[5] On account of the intercession of this saint in behalf of the people, God relented and the plague diminished. Such was a common way in the Middle Ages to gain divine approval or deflect divine fury—and such a scene was repeated countless times when disaster struck three centuries later.

It was the fate of the West to experience its worst medical disaster, the Black Death of 1348–1350, at a time when the population had risen considerably since the time of Justinian's plague 800 years prior. In the early Middle Ages, populations were low and life was bleak. Average life expectancies were in the thirties, and there was just as good a chance of a baby not surviving into adulthood as surviving. Around nine out of ten people lived in tiny villages, and European cities as we think of them today were non-existent. Between the

---

5. David Van Meter, "Selected Documents on Eschatological Expectations and Social Change around the Year 1000," in *The Apocalyptic Year 1000: Religious Expectation and Social Change, 950-1050*, ed. Richard Landes et al. (Oxford: Oxford University Press, 2003), 342.

year 1000 and 1200, however, recent technological inventions and warmer temperatures created the conditions necessary for longer life spans, better nutrition, and population growth. The invention of the wheeled plow, the horse collar, and crop rotation led to fertile fields that could grow nutrient-rich crops to feed more people and generate more offspring. In the British Iles, the population increased from about 500,000 in the seventh century to 5 million on the eve of the Black Death, corresponding with an overall population of 20 million in the seventh century and 75 million when the great plague struck.[6] These statistics suggest about a 300% increase in the European population between the tenth and the middle of the thirteenth centuries.[7]

With the rise of a new market economy based on money rather than land, many in this growing population were now living in newly created cities in search of work or trade or study. Universities were forming across Europe, and society as a whole was changing. Trade routes were opening up regularly, the feudal world of the Middle Ages was crumbling, and the desire for new goods greatly increased contact among Europeans, Africans, and Asians. This new contact, good for business but bad for disease, provided an endless chain of victims in the middle of the fourteenth century and beyond.

The Black Death of 1348–1350

The plague of 1348–1350 devastated Europe. Called the "Great Mortality" by some contemporaries but the "Black Death" by historians today, this plague originated in Central Asia in the first half of the fourteenth century and reached Europe through trade and commerce. Under normal circumstances, the plague spread via rat

6. James Hannam, *The Genesis of Science: How the Christian Middle Ages Launched the Scientific Revolution* (Washington, D.C.: Regnery Publishing, 2011), 7.
7. Gottfried, *The Black Death*, 15.

fleas infected with *Yersinia pestis*—*Y. pestis* for short. When the bacilli of infected rat fleas multiplied in their stomachs, fleas felt hungry, stimulating them to seek a meal from their hosts. While feeding, they regurgitated bacteria into their hosts, causing rats to become infected with the disease. This type of plague would normally remain among animals, but once the rat population was decimated, the fleas turned to human hosts for survival, who contracted the disease in a similar way to rodents.

Fig. 14.1. Scientific Classification of *Y. Pestis*	
Domain	Bacteria
Kingdom	Eubacteria
Phylum	Proteobacteria
Class	Gammaproteobacteria
Family	Enterobacteriaceae
Genus	Yersinia
Species	Y. Pestis

It is generally believed that the Black Death was a combination of bubonic, pneumonic, and septicemic plague strains. A person contracted one of these different forms of plague depending on the how the bacterium *Y. pestis* entered the body. The first type, bubonic plague, was the most common and widespread. Though quite deadly, it was the least pernicious. Bubonic plague was contracted through a flea bite. Its incubation period was up to a week, after which time purple blotches and swellings called buboes appeared around the lymph nodes, beginning with the region where the person was bit by the infected flea. The mortality rate was about 50 percent. Pneumonic plague, by contrast, was much more heinous. Its incubation period was only a couple of days, and the fatality rate was more than 95 percent. The *Y. pestis* bacterium, which resided in the bloody sputum that pneumonic plague victims spat up, was transmitted airborne from person to person through these types of respiratory fluids. Once a person was infected, pneumonic plague was passed on without the presence of fleas. Finally, septicemic plague was the rarest but most lethal form of the plague. Virtually none of its victims survived. A rash appeared within hours of the *Y. pestis* bacterium entering one's bloodstream through the fleas, and death struck within a day.

In Europe, these three forms of the plague spread like wildfire in the savannah. It's possible that "the Black Death killed up to 50 percent of the inhabitants of Europe in a little over two years."[8] The percentage of deaths depended on a number of factors; some areas were almost completely annihilated while others, such as modern Poland, were not greatly impacted. Weather patterns and changes of temperature dramatically altered the spread of the plague, as the *Y. pestis* bacterium can thrive, die, or remain dormant depending on its environment. Nevertheless, the whole of Europe suffered setbacks of all kinds—economic, agricultural, medical, vocational, psychological, and, of course, religious. Below we will turn to both medical and theological responses to the great plague that struck with vengeance between 1348 and 1350 across Christian Europe.

Medical Responses

As we learned from the previous chapter, the birth certificate of the sciences was written in the Middle Ages. The translations of previously inaccessible Greek writings on the sciences and medicine into Latin in the late twelfth and thirteenth centuries revolutionized Western thought. The combination of this new learning with the creation of the medieval university in the twelfth and thirteenth

8. Aberth, *The Black Death*, vii.

centuries enabled the educated classes to newly evaluate the natural world, the heavens, and the human body. The appearance of the Black Death in the middle of the fourteenth century coincided with this medical development. Yet still, medicine was in its infancy. The Greek-speaking Galen, whose influence was widespread throughout the Middle Ages, had attributed sickness to an imbalance of one of the four "humors": blood, phlegm, reddish bile, and blackish bile. Patient diagnosis might consist of assessing the imbalances of one of the humors in a person based on gender, the changes of the air, the changing of the seasons, and the properties of the wind.

Not surprisingly, when it came to the Black Death, medicine posited a relationship between disease and the heavens. In his highly famous Latin treatise on surgery, the French physician to the papal court Guy de Chauliac, arguably one of the top surgeons of the day, described the epidemic in detail as well as the medical treatment that saved his life after contracting the dreadful disease. He was the first doctor to make a distinction between bubonic and pneumonic plague, and he attended to no less than three popes throughout his lifetime. Writing about the plague in Avignon, where the papacy was then residing, de Chauliac commented that it spread so effortlessly that one could obtain the sickness "simply by looking" at the infected person. In terms of the sickness's cause, de Chauliac cataloged the views common at the time—that the Jews had poisoned Christian wells, that the "mutilated poor" were responsible, and that the nobles had organized the whole affair. As a man of science, however, he recognized that such stories were old wives' tales. "But whatever the people said," he protested, "the truth is that the cause of this mortality was twofold: one active and universal, one passive and particular."[9]

---

9. Guy de Chauliac, "Bubonic Plague," trans. Michael McVaugh, in *A Source Book in Medieval Science*, ed. Edward Grant (Cambridge: Harvard University Press, 1974), 773.

We will focus only on the active cause, since it was the catalyst for the passive cause. Guy de Chauliac explained:

> The active, universal cause was the disposition of a certain important conjunction of three heavenly bodies, Saturn, Jupiter, and Mars, which had taken place in 1345, the 24th day of March, in the fourteenth degree of Aquarius. For (as I have said in my book on astrology) the more important conjunctions presage marvelous, mighty, and terrible events, such as changes of rulers, the advent of prophets, and great mortalities; and they depend on the [zodiacal] sign and the aspects of the bodies in conjunction. . . . Because the [zodiacal] sign was a human one, it foretold grief for humanity; and because it was a fixed sign, it signified long duration. For [the mortality] began in the East, a little after the conjunction, and was still abroad in the West [in 1350]. It so informed the air and the other elements that, as the magnet moves iron, it moved the thick, heated, poisonous humors; and bringing them together within the body, created [swellings] there. From this derived the continuous fevers and spitting of blood at the outset, when this corrupt matter was strong and disturbed the natural state. Then, as this lost its strength, the natural state was not so troubled, and expelled what it could, mainly in the armpits and groin.[10]

Few doctors today would attribute disease to the zodiac, but such was common practice in the Middle Ages. The illustrious Faculty of Medicine at the University of Paris likewise attributed the Black Death to astrology. It argued that the conjunction of three planets on March 20, 1345 in the zodiacal sign of Aquarius caused the human catastrophe. As Aristotle himself taught centuries before, the planetary conjunctions of Saturn and Jupiter always spelled disaster for human beings, death being paramount. In short, the chemical reaction brought about by the passing of different planetary vapors brought about death in the damp conditions of Paris.[11]

---

10. Chauliac, "Bubonic Plague," in *A Source Book*, 774.
11. Anna Campbell, *The Black Death and Men of Learning* (New York: Columbia University Press, 1931), 40.

Religious Responses

In the Middle Ages, religion was a thread that ran through all of society. Most of the contemporary records of the Black Death from Christian Europe assume God's hand in the great pestilence. More often than not, the disease was attributed to humankind's sin, and God was punishing that sin until God's wrath was satisfied. In this section, we will examine separate responses to the Black Death that highlight how important a role theology played in this drama of the Middle Ages.

The first of these religious responses comes from the Italian lawyer Gabriele de Mussis, who died in the year 1356. In his book, "History of the Plague," he envisioned a dialogue between God and Earth. God was the first speaker in this dialogue, who entreated Earth to unleash her vengeance on the sinful and law-breaking world. This the Earth does. "I, the Earth," she responded, "founded by your Majesty, will open my veins and swallow the numberless criminals in accordance with your commands." So began the Black Death, which "was sent down to infect the whole human race, aiming its cruel darts everywhere."[12] The only recourse was to accept the punishment in penitence and implore the saints and the blessed martyrs of the church for pardon. And for those who could, a pilgrimage to Rome was most beneficial to their cause.

A similar response to the Black Death can be found in the chronicle of the Franciscan friar Michele da Piazza. Saints became a primary refuge of those seeking asylum from the dreadful disease. In Sicily, many men and women devoted themselves to the Virgin Agatha of Catania, a woman tortured to death for her faith during the Decian Persecution of 251 and buried in Catania, Sicily. Others appealed to the Virgin Mary of Santa Maria della Scala, whose image was stolen

---

12. Gabriele de Mussis, "History of the Plague," in Aberth, *The Black Death*, 99.

and brought into the city of Messina as a sort of talisman against death. There, "the women of Messina showered the image with silk cloth and precious jewels,"[13] calling upon the Virgin Mary to save them from their sins.

But for some, it was not enough to simply entreat saints and martyrs for mercy. For them, the saints, let alone the sacraments of the church, were of little value in countering this divine pestilence. God had sent down the Black Death as a punishment, and the most appropriate response was self-penance and self-flagellation—beating oneself with a whip or a stick for the glory of God. All across Europe the so-called Flagellant Movement emerged as a way to harness God's wrath. Writing about a group of flagellants in Germany in the year 1349, Dominican friar Heinrich of Herford chronicled how these people struck their naked bodies so often that "the[ir] scourged skin swelled up black and blue[,] and blood flowed down to their lower members and even spattered the walls nearby." Having watched these flagellants up close, Father Heinrich described in detail "how the iron points [of their whips] became so embedded in the flesh that sometimes one pull, sometimes two, was not enough to extract them."[14]

In between public self-beatings, these flagellants entered churches, took off their shirts, sang hymns, and prostrated themselves at different locations in the sanctuary in the sign of the cross. On the cold floor, cruciform and contrite, they repented of their sins. Then at some point during their prayers, one of the flagellants would arise with a whip and strike the other flagellants, saying: "God grants you remission of all your sins, arise!" Commenting on the sheer devotion and awe of this ceremony, Heinrich confessed that "One would need a heart of stone to be able to watch this without tears."[15] Nevertheless,

13. Michele da Piazza, "Chronicle," Aberth, *The Black Death*, 103.
14. Heinrich of Herford, "Book of Memorable Matters," in Aberth, *The Black Death*, 123.

the clergy disapproved of this movement since it disdained the offices of the church and rejected its authority. Laypeople were not authorized to forgive people's sins, plague or no plague.

Not all of the responses to the Black Death were so extravagant. How were regular parish priests responding to the crisis? For the most part, parish priests died of the plague just as commonly as their parishioners did. They, unlike certain laypeople who might cloister themselves from the public, generally put themselves in harm's way during the weekly exercise of their religious duties. Regardless of consequences, they were expected to perform the sacrament of Last Rites, administered to people on their deathbeds, and perform burial services—both of which ceremonies exposed them to the plague. It's not surprising that some priests, out of self-preservation, abandoned their parishes completely. In 1350, well aware of this trend, the archbishop of Canterbury issued a warning to parish priests that they were not allowed to leave their churches. Apparently, many priests recognized that the death of so many in their parishes meant that they would not receive enough of a tithe each year to sustain themselves financially. So they simply left their churches and began performing private services that could gather a better income. The archbishop reminded the "surviving priests" that "divine intervention spared them . . . so that they can carry out the ministry that was committed to them on behalf of God's people." He also exhorted English bishops "in the bowels of Jesus Christ" to "use whatever censures are sanctioned by the Church"[16] to crack down on rogue priests. The campaign was not successful. The bishop of Rochester, for instance, agreed to allow priests to perform ceremonies outside of their parishes in order to supplement their incomes. And the bishop of Ely, conceding that "it is not seemly for a [clergyman] . . . to beg for

15. Ibid., 124.
16. Simon of Islip, "Unbridled," in Aberth, *The Black Death*, 105.

life's necessities,"[17] granted priests in his diocese extra money. Death, it seemed, was bad for business in the church.

Conclusion: The Black Death as Europe's Watershed Event

The Black Death was "a watershed event in history,"[18] with unimaginable social and religious ramifications. As a contemporary Byzantine emperor, John VI, wrote about the plague, "No words could express the [horror] of the disease."[19] The people suffering from this pandemic responded in any number of ways—from reckless abandonment to saintly devotion to self-penance. No aspect of European society was left untouched, and many historians have argued that the Black Death transitioned medieval Europe into the modern world.

Although we have focused on the plague from 1348 to 1350, it's important to remember that the plague stimulated cyclical outbreaks for centuries to come. These repeated outbreaks were probably the most pernicious aspects of the plague. Though human populations are surprisingly resilient in the face of a single catastrophe, it is incredibly difficult to maintain that resiliency after repeated catastrophes. These outbreaks contributed to low populations across Europe for decades, but they also spurred invention and innovation among Europeans, the likes of which would unite the entire world within two centuries. Meanwhile, muses one historian, "the microbes that had been incubated for millennia by the dense populations of Europe"[20] were soon to prove fatal to the inhabitants soon encountered by the Europeans during the so-called Age of Discovery.

17. "Register of Hamo Hethe," in Aberth, *The Black Death*, 107.
18. Aberth, *The Black Death*, 2.
19. John VI, "History," in Aberth, *The Black Death*, 36.
20. Robin Blackburn, *The Making of New World Slavery: From the Baroque to the Modern, 1492-1800* (New York: Verso, 1997), 132.

15

Who Owns Newly Discovered Territory?

It was the year 1493. Christopher Columbus had just returned from his first voyage to "Asia." In the months to come, the Spanish would be mesmerized by his rapturous tales of the exotic people he encountered and the virgin lands he discovered. Arriving in Spain in the spring of 1493, Columbus secured an audience with King Ferdinand and Queen Isabella in the city of Barcelona. To the eagerly interested Spanish monarchs, he described his discovery of "Cipangu," what we today call Japan—though, in actuality, it was the Bahamas. Columbus conceded that he had not returned with much gold, silver, or other precious commodities, but he was certain that future voyages would unveil the hidden wealth of Asia for the glory of Spain. Though the Spanish Crown would have certainly preferred to have received a more immediately profitable return on its investment, it was delighted with Columbus's tantalizing report, looking gapingly at the rainbow-colored parrots, good-humored monkeys, and head-painted captives Columbus had paraded about. The untapped potential of the land Columbus had discovered would pay off in the end, and Spain was eager to commission future endeavors toward that end. The glorious festivities associated with Columbus's return lasted for days on end in Spain, capped off with Columbus's acceptance of the title "Admiral of the Ocean Sea."

But not everyone was happy. During his return trip to Spain in 1493, a storm had forced Columbus to dock at a Portuguese harbor before entering Spain. Soon thereafter, in a rural area east of Lisbon, Columbus recounted his exploits to the monarch of Portugal, King João II. The king was astonished—and annoyed. Columbus, after all, had lived in Portugal for years, learning the mariner's trade from the best (Portuguese) sailors in the world, and had initially petitioned João II in 1484 to finance his voyage to Asia. Yet, after João II's advisors inspected Columbus's plans, they concluded that they were faulty, and therefore passed on the offer. Easy come, easy go. As the Portuguese committee of experts who examined Columbus's plans concluded, the Genoese-born merchant Columbus had underestimated the globe's circumference. Besides, Portugal was more interested in Africa.

But now things were different. Columbus's trip had been a success, leading the Portuguese Crown to pursue a different tactic. The king of Portugal now began to question the rights of Spain to explore regions previously ceded by the pope to Portugal. Columbus pleaded ignorance, and appealed to his patrons—the mighty king and queen of Spain. At face value, however, it appeared that the Portuguese king was not mistaken. In a series of papal bulls in the late fifteenth century, particularly *Aeterni regis* of 1481, the pope had granted the Portuguese sovereignty over all newly discovered territory south and west of the Canary Islands. An intense, and dangerous, game of world domination was coming to a head. As author Stephen Bown writes, "Before Columbus had even returned to Spain, his voyage threatened to erupt into an international quarrel between two leading maritime nations of the era."[1] Spain and Portugal, neighboring rivals for centuries whose proximity to each other only egged one another on, were positioning themselves for the same prize. But who had legal rights to it? Who owned newly discovered territory?

The Question of Ownership

The clash between Spain and Portugal over newly discovered territory in the late fifteenth century naturally required the assistance of the most influential religious-political authority in Europe—the pope. Pope Alexander VI, the purchaser of his office and the head of the infamous clan of Borgia who had sired countless illegitimate children before holding the holiest office on earth, now found himself the arbiter between two of the greatest nations in Christian Europe. As author James Reston explains, "It was to [this] illegally elected, degenerate pope . . . that Ferdinand and Isabella now appealed in the spring of 1493 to settle the epic question"[2] that had emerged from the two great sea-faring powers. The "epic question" posed to Pope Alexander VI was as straightforward as it was stupefying—at least from a modern perspective: who owned the newly discovered territory, Spain or Portugal? Though he could not have foreseen this at the time, the ramifications of the pope's pronouncement forever altered the course of world history. In this chapter, we will survey the varying responses to the remarkable question of who owned newly discovered territory.

A Short History of European Exploration

It was during the Middle Ages that trade opened up like never before in Africa, Asia, and Europe. (It was not yet known, from a

---

1. Stephen Bown, *1494: How a Family Feud in Medieval Spain divided the World in Half* (New York: Thomas Dunne Books, 2011), 125.
2. James Reston, Jr., *Dogs of God: Columbus, the Inquisition, and the Defeat of the Moors* (New York: Doubleday, 2005), 319–20.

European perspective, that America existed.) The famed "traveler's tale" was growing in popularity across Europe in the thirteenth century. The European encounter with the Mongols, in particular, stimulated the writing of several accounts about life on the other side of the world. In the mid-thirteenth century, for instance, the Italian friar John of Plano Carpini wrote a *Description of the Mongols* in response to his interaction with the Mongol Empire over the course of his papal-approved missionary adventures in China. Most famous of all, however, were the stories of Marco Polo, the son of an Italian merchant. Marco Polo had served in the Mongol court of Kublai Khan in Peking (now Beijing) at the end of the thirteenth century, and he wrote a best-selling narrative called *Travels* about his adventures. Polo's *Travels* were followed by many other European books, including John Mandeville's *Travels*. Combined, these traveler's tales fueled European imaginations, which were only extinguished due to the Black Death in the fourteenth century.

But in the early fifteenth century, at which time Europe as a whole was rising from the ashes of the Black Death, new inventions were being made that would propel the continent forward. Marco Polo's *Travels* was still being printed, and there was not an explorer alive in the fifteenth century who had not read it. One of the most important "tools" in the early fifteenth century was the reintroduction of Ptolemy's *Geography* more than a millennium after it was originally written. Composed in Greek in the second century after Christ, it lay hidden from Western eyes until translated into Latin around 1406. Its reappearance was timely. It enabled explorers to have a better frame of reference for the construction of global maps by using the concepts of longitude and latitude. Though Ptolemy's coordinates were not exact and were often exaggerated—and he believed that the planets revolved around the earth—they were still superior to the calculations of maps previously available to Europeans.

The earliest maritime expeditions of Europeans outside of their continent began modestly. Surprisingly, given that the kingdom only included about a million inhabitants in the fifteenth century, Portugal was the first nation to become master of the seas. Recent advances in cartography and navigation enabled Portugal to sail ahead of much larger, stronger, and wealthier European nations. Their motivators were financial gain, Muslim conquest, and discovery of a faraway and flourishing Christian kingdom, supposedly headed by "Prester John," that was surrounded by Islamic empires.

In 1415, Henry the Navigator, the son of King João I, captured a fortress in what is now Morocco, formerly controlled by Muslim forces. He also established a nautical center on the Portuguese coast, where he "engaged in three related activities: training captains and pilots, sending expeditions down the coast of Africa, and gathering astronomic and oceanographic information that would assist the expeditions."[3] Over the course of the fifteenth century, Portugal launched several maritime explorations, opening up the spice trade and human trafficking with Africa and Asia. Spain, meanwhile, the larger and stronger of the two Iberian Kingdoms but one that was only recently united, also embarked on voyages of discovery, creating a sibling rivalry over who would rule the seas. Ferdinand Magellan, Bartolomeu Dias, Vasco da Gama, Pedro Alvares Cabral, and Christopher Columbus—these would be the men who would contend with uncharted waters, serve as the initial ambassadors of Europe, and change the course of global history. It was a magical era for Europeans, who, for the first time ever, "learned to think of the world as a whole and of all seas as one."[4] But the same cannot be said

---

3. Daniel Headrick, *Power over Peoples: Technology, Environments, and Western Imperialism, 1400 to the Present* (Princeton: Princeton University Press, 2010), 21.

4. John Horace Parry, *The Age of Reconnaissance: Discovery, Exploration, and Settlement, 1450-1650* (Berkeley: University of California Press, 1982).

for the people groups they encountered and exploited for their own ends.

As difficult as it is for readers today to comprehend, Spanish and Portuguese monarchs, who were absolutely essential in the financing and authorization of the voyages led by the famous explorers mentioned above, believed they ruled by fiat of God Almighty. Their right to reign was a God-given authority that demanded credence and deference. There was no forum for negotiation. From their perspective, their launchings of explorations into new lands were fitting extensions of their divinely approved kingdoms, whose role it was to convert the heathen nations to Christ and establish the Holy Catholic faith wherever they landed. There was no thought given to the rights of those they conquered. In principal, these monarchs believed that they were God's representatives on earth, and that any newly discovered territory rightfully belonged to them, particularly given that the people currently occupying their land were pagans—and, incredibly enough from their vantage point, perhaps not even human beings. When Francisco Pizarro and his Spanish crew conquered and destroyed the Incan Empire of South America in the sixteenth century, for instance, they did so under the belief that the sovereignty of their king was universal in scope. As the Spaniards declared to Atahualpa and his men, the monarch they serve "is King of Spain *and of the universal world*."[5]

The Bulls of Alexander VI (1493)

The exciting news that Christopher Columbus had discovered a new world required swiftness of action on the part of Spain. Not at all unfamiliar with the realities of territorial expansion and political negotiations, the Spanish Crown immediately sought to secure papal

---

5. *Reports on the Discovery of Peru*, trans. Clements Robert Markham (London: Hakluyt Society, 1872), 56 (italics added).

sanction of Columbus's newly found territory in order to colonize the land, evangelize the people, and embark on international trade. As mentioned above, it was to their great luck that the current pope, Alexander VI, happened to be from Valencia, now part of the newly unified Spanish Empire. He also had a long history with the Spanish monarchy, having forged the legality of Ferdinand and Isabella's marriage while cardinal. The pope was to be a great boon to the new Spanish monarchy in its quest for world domination and religious unity, beginning with the issuance of several papal bulls in Spain's favor.

Figure 15.1. Papal Bulls

Papal bulls are official decrees issued by the pope. They are so called based on the seal (or *bulla* in Latin) used to guarantee their authenticity. The title of bulls, always initially composed in Latin, are taken from the first couple of words in the document.

The papal bulls that Alexander VI issued in 1493, called the Bulls of Donation, "rank as some of the most significant bulls ever issued, having the greatest historical impact on global events."[6] The first was the most important. Called *Inter Caetera*, the pope granted unprecedented powers upon the Spanish Crown:

> we . . . by the authority of Almighty God conferred upon us in blessed Peter and of the vicarship of Jesus Christ, which we hold on earth, do by tenor of these presents . . . give, grant, and assign to you and your heirs and successors, kings of Castile and Leon, forever, together with all their dominions, cities, camps, places, and villages, and all rights, jurisdictions, and appurtenances, all islands and mainlands found and to be found, discovered and to be discovered towards the west and south, by drawing and establishing a line from the Arctic pole, namely the north, to the Antarctic pole, namely the south, no matter whether the said mainlands and islands are found and to be found in the direction of India or towards any other quarter, the said line to be distant one

6. Bown, *1494*, 145.

hundred leagues towards the west and south from any of the islands commonly known as the Azores and Cape Verde.[7]

What did this bull mean? Essentially, the pope had drawn an imaginary line in the Atlantic Ocean along a north-south axis. All the territory to the west and south of the imaginary line was to go to Spain. Although Spain was not given authority over any discovered land that happened to be ruled by Christians, all newly discovered land ruled by pagans was fair game. Such territory was to fall under direct control of the Spanish Crown—with all of the corresponding profits to be stowed away into Spanish coffers. Any who dared doubt the drawing skills of the pope, or who questioned his authority to make such an audacious pronouncement, was to be excommunicated from the Holy Catholic Church and suffer a lifetime of divine retribution. As the pope concluded the bull:

> Let no one . . . infringe, or with rash boldness contravene, this our recommendation, exhortation, requisition, gift, grant, assignment, constitution, deputation, decree, mandate, prohibition, and will. Should anyone presume to attempt this, be it known to him that he will incur the wrath of Almighty God and of the blessed apostles Peter and Paul.[8]

The authority that was given to Spain was just as much material as it was spiritual. Several years earlier, in 1486, Pope Innocent VIII was constrained to grant the Spanish Crown the right of patronage, or *patronato*, for help in securing the pope's Italian interests. This right of patronage meant that the Spanish Crown could effectively appoint its own bishops without any objection from the pope and eventually be able to collect all money acquired by the church—an astounding entitlement that was to have huge ramifications in the New World. The papal bull *Inter Caetera* made references to the fact that Spain was

---

7. *Inter Caetera*. http://www.nativeweb.org/pages/legal/indig-inter-caetera.html. Accessed on February 6, 2015.
8. Ibid.

granted all this newly discovered lands for the purpose of evangelism and the spread of Christianity. The pagan inhabitants of the new lands were "to embrace the Catholic faith and be trained in good morals"[9] by means of qualified, Spanish-appointed, clerics. Once the bull reached Spain in August of 1493, the king and queen hastily sent a copy of it to Admiral Columbus, who was preparing a galley of seventeen ships to claim the New World for Spain and the Catholic faith. As the personal letter of the monarchs accompanying the bull stated to Columbus:

> The authority has come today, and we send you an authentic copy of it to publish, so that all the world may know that no one can enter into these regions without authorization from us. Take it with you that you may be able to show it in every land.[10]

Despite the clarity of the papal bull in some parts, there were some gray areas. For instance, it appeared that *Inter Caetera* abrogated property rights previously granted to Portugal. The papacy must have recognized this, for a second papal bull called *Eximiae Devotionis* immediately followed *Inter Caetera*, which spelled out a little more clearly what territorial rights Spain now legally exercised in relation to its indignant brother Portugal. As that document stated:

> But inasmuch as at another time the Apostolic See has granted divers privileges, favours, liberties, immunities, exemptions, faculties, letters, and indults to certain kings of Portugal, who also by similar Apostolic grant and donation in their favour, have discovered and taken possession of islands in the regions of Africa, Guinea, and the Gold Mine, and elsewhere, with the desire to empower with our apostolic authority . . . we grant to you and your aforesaid heirs and successors.[11]

---

9. Ibid.
10. Quoted in Reston, *Dogs of God*, 327.
11. *Eximiae Devotionis.* http://clc-library-org-docs.angelfire.com/Eximiae.html. Accessed on February 6, 2015.

It appeared that Spain was getting a better deal than Portugal. The reason may lay in the fact that Pope Alexander VI, the ruler of the so-called Papal States, was involved in a territorial dispute with the Spanish king's brother, and so the pope probably wagered that it was more important to please the monarchy of Spain than that of Portugal.

Whatever the case, another papal bull, also called *Inter Caetera*, was issued that favored Spain over Portugal in the rights over global expansion. This bull was mostly a restatement of the first bull with the same name (essentially a revision of the first one), but it was strongly in Spain's favor. The pope made sure to grant territory to Spain that Columbus wanted to explore during his second voyage to the New World. Finally, in the fall of 1493, the pope issued another bull—this one called *Dudum siquidem*—that amplified the territorial rights of Spain. As the document stated:

> we do in like manner amplify and extend our aforesaid gift, grant, assignment, and letters, with all and singular the clauses contained in the said letters, to all islands and mainlands whatsoever, found and to be found, discovered and to be discovered, that are or may be or may seem to be in the route of navigation or travel toward the west or south, whether they be in western parts, or in the regions of the south and east and of India. We grant to you and your aforesaid heirs and successors full and free power through your own authority, exercised through yourselves or through another or others, freely to take corporal possession of the said islands and countries and to hold them forever, and to defend them against whosoever may oppose.[12]

As before, any person who dared contravene the pope's words was to be immediately excommunicated.

---

12. *Dudum Siquidem*. http://www.reformation.org/dudum-siquidem.html. Accessed on February 13, 2015.

The Treaty of Tordesillas (1494)

Although Spain was a commanding empire not to be trifled with, Portugal was a tremendous maritime power that was not at all amused by the special treatment Spain was receiving. Portugal, as discussed above, was the first nation-empire of Europe to begin overseas exploration, and it was not about to cede all of its overseas interests to its rivaling neighbor. It was most concerned with maintaining its interest in Africa, though, to be sure, it did not want to forfeit any territorial rights in Asia either. And the nation of Portugal could ill afford to go to war with Spain. Negotiations began to take place between Spain and Portugal in the spring of 1494. These negotiations lasted for months before representatives of each empire convened in the town of Tordesillas in northern Spain in the summer to divide the New World more equitably—if that term can plausibly be used—between the two great powers.

The Treaty of Tordesillas, as the document came to be known, was signed and ratified in that summer of 1494. (It was officially confirmed by the pope in the bull *Ea Quae* in 1506.) This treaty was one of the most remarkable and controversial documents of the early modern period, dividing the world, historian Hugh Thomas writes, "in a way that influenced it forever."[13] No consideration was given to the actual inhabitants of the New World, who had lived in the region for millennia. Nor were any other European powers considered to be the rightful landowners. Instead, Portugal was given a greater piece of the global pie. The original line of demarcation drawn by the pope the year before was extended 270 leagues further west of Cape Verde, enabling Portugal to colonize any territory 370 leagues (about 1,200 nautical miles) west of these islands. (This explains why

---

13. Hugh Thomas, *The Slave Trade: The Story of the Atlantic Slave Trade: 1440-1870* (New York: Simon & Schuster, 1997), 89.

Brazil, a nation that pops out much farther east than the rest of South America, speaks Portuguese, while most of the other countries on the continent of Latin America speak Spanish.) As historian of Portugal James Anderson explains, "All islands and continents discovered or to be discovered on the east side of the line went to Portugal, the west side to Spain and to the respective monarchs and their heirs forever."[14] Despite the geographic ambiguity still inherent in the treaty, Spain and Portugal rushed to their new and legally owned territories with even more gusto than their original explorations. The treaty effectively brought Spain and Portugal into a maritime cease fire, enabling each nation to carry on with its own interests in its legally prescribed boundaries. Given that so much land was given to only two nations, it would appear that their neighborly struggles were over.

In the years to come, Spain and Portugal would indeed conquer the world. In September of 1494, Columbus embarked on his second voyage to the New World with 1,200 men and a dozen priests for the glories of Spain. Four years later, Vasco da Gama, backed by Portugal, sailed around the Cape of Good Hope in Africa to India, thereby opening up the immensely profitable spice trade. Then two years later, in 1500, the Portuguese explorer Pedro Alvares Cabral, blown off course by strong winds, spotted Brazil and laid claim to this territory in accordance with the Treaty of Tordesillas. As author James Reston mused, "World history was lurching into a new epoch."[15]

With Spain and Portugal leading the way toward mastery over the seas, these two nations soared to new economic and political heights during the storm-ridden sixteenth century. As historian Nigel Cliff writes, "Soon nations whose names were barely known to Europe

14. James Anderson, *The History of Portugal* (Westport, CT: Greenwood, 2000), 62.
15. Reston, *Dogs of God*, 329.

would discover that they had been parceled out between two European powers they had never even heard of."[16] Spain extracted ungodly amounts of gold and silver from the Americas, while Portugal monopolized the spice trade in Asia. Both Iberian empires, green-eyed and with papal approval, recognized that they could become richer if they began importing African slaves into their new territories to perform the back-breaking labor needed to work the mines and harvest the spices. This they did, bringing the world together in new and lopsided ways that would have long-lasting repercussions—setting an example that the English, French, and Dutch would follow for centuries to come. To be sure, discovery of new lands and imperial conquest were vigorously pursued in the hope of converting the nations to Christianity, and thereby extending God's glorious reign across the globe, but the means through which this occurred were often violent and confrontational.

Conclusion: Spain and Portugal as Masters of Land and Sea

The papal bulls of 1493 and the Treaty of Tordesillas in 1494 can hardly be overestimated. With a few imprints and signatures, the world was forever changed. The papacy, in a manner in which it had grown accustomed, regarded itself as the international arbiter of justice and the chosen agent of God's ownership of the world. It saw little objection in bequeathing a land it scarcely knew existed to two of its most powerful subjects. Regrettably, as Stephen Bown writes, the bulls issued by the pope "provide a justification for the conquest of indigenous America and were the wedge that drove European nations into hundreds of years of warfare."[17] Spain and

---

16. Nigel Cliff, *Holy War: How Vasco da Gama's Epic Voyages Turned the Tide in a Centuries-Old Clash of Civilizations* (New York, HarperCollins: 2011), 152.

17. Bown, *1494*, 145-46.

Portugal became the legal owners of a vast stretch of land, which it exploited for material gains every bit as much as for spiritual ones.

Over the course of the next decades, the Spanish and Portuguese Crowns would accrue incredible entitlements. In 1501, for instance, the papacy granted the Spanish monarchy all tithes levied in the New World in perpetuity, and in 1508 the papacy gave the Spanish Crown the right of patronage, thereby allowing the Spanish monarchs to control all the money acquired by the church in this territory. With these concessions, writes one historian, the Spanish Crown became "absolute master"[18] of the New World. There were now no contenders and no checks on Spanish power. All of Spain's vast subjects—Christian, native, or otherwise—were under her legal authority. "The Age of Empire had begun."[19]

---

18. J. H. Elliot, *Imperial Spain, 1469-1716* (London: Penguin, 1990), 102.
19. Reston, *Dogs of God*, 329.

16

Can Christians Own Slaves?

It was the year 1511. A Dominican friar, now living in the tiny colony of Santo Domingo in the Dominican Republic, had arrived in 1510 along with fourteen other Dominicans. In only a year's time, the friar had seen enough. He was disgusted with the deplorable practices of his fellow Christian Spaniards toward the native Taino peoples of Hispaniola. As he mounted the pulpit that Fourth Sunday of Advent in late December of 1511 in the straw-thatched Cathedral of Santo Domingo, Antonio de Montesinos decided the time had come to unleash God's word on the sinful Spaniards. For the occasion, he had selected in the Gospels the words of one of the most fearless prophets of the entire Judeo-Christian tradition, John the Baptist: *ego vox clamans in deserto*—"I am the voice of one crying in the wilderness." After a few cursory remarks about the season of Advent, de Montesinos lit into the Spaniards with glittering rebuke. Before they knew what hit them, de Montesinos had compared the combined conscience of the Spaniards to a "sterile desert" on a collision course with "damnation" and eternal Hell. Transitioning from the words of John the Baptist to those of Jesus the Messiah, he shouted, "I am the voice of Christ crying in the wilderness of this island . . . this voice will be the strangest, the harshest and hardest, the most terrifying that you ever heard or expected to hear."

By now, the audience was fidgeting and fuming, though de Montesinos showed no signs of ending his invective. "This voice," he continued, "declares that you are in mortal sin, and live and die therein by reason of the cruelty and tyranny that you practice on these innocent people. . . . Are you not bound to love them as you love yourselves? How can you lie in such profound and lethargic slumber? Be sure that in your present state you can no more be saved than the [Muslim] Moors or Turks who do not have and do not want the faith of Jesus Christ."[1] With words like these, the sermon was bound to register offense with the Spanish audience. Governor Diego Columbus, son of the famous Admiral of the Ocean Sea Christopher Columbus—the very man who had founded this colony not twenty years prior—was hot with indignation. So stunned and offended were the Spanish men at the sermon that they could not even finish the service with the customary celebration of the mass. Antonio de Montesinos and his fellow Dominicans left the cathedral in triumph, while the Spanish laymen formed a mob eager to deport de Montesinos back to Spain.

The Question of Slavery

At the center of Antonio de Montesinos's stinging rebuke of the Spaniards in 1511 was the issue of gross maltreatment and enslavement of the native peoples. "Tell me," the Dominican friar bellowed forth from the pulpit, "by what right or justice do you hold these Indians in such cruel and horrible slavery?"[2] The arrival of Europeans into the New World at the end of the fifteenth century

---

1. Quoted by Bartolome de las Casas in *Religion in Latin America: A Documentary History*, ed. Lee Penyak and Walter Petry (Maryknoll, NY: Orbis, 2006), 23–24.
2. Quoted in *Religion in Latin America*, 23.

led to one of the greatest cultural collisions in world history. As historian Hugh Thomas writes, following Antonio de Montesino's condemnation of his fellow Spaniards, "a complicated controversy was beginning about the treatment of the indigenous peoples of America," causing "the most searching questions that any imperial nation can ask of itself" to be discussed.[3] In this chapter, we will explore the different responses to the question of whether—or more properly, in what way—slavery was permitted in the New World, concentrating on sixteenth-century Latin America.

A Short History of Christianity and Slavery

Slavery was part and parcel of society when Christianity emerged in the first century. Jesus lived and died at the height of Roman imperialism, at which time slavery was peaking in the ancient world, and Jesus interacted with both slaves and slaveholders. The New Testament assumes the existence of the institution of slavery and does not offer any sustained criticism of the practice or of slaveholding in general. On the contrary, as historian of slavery Jennifer Glancy notes, "Slaveholding [in the early church] was not considered a sin."[4] Despite Paul's dictum that Christians should all "becomes slaves to one another" out of mutual love (Gal. 5:13), the lack of direct condemnation of institutional slavery made Paul's moral plea ineffective against slaveholding. Slave holders and slaves jointly populated the earliest churches, both of whom played a part in the extension of the Christian message in the earliest centuries after Christ. Although maltreatment of slaves was criticized, it was generally acceptable for a Christian to own slaves. The following

---

3. Hugh Thomas, *The Slave Trade: The Story of the Atlantic Slave Trade, 1440-1870* (New York: Simon & Shuster, 1997), 96.

4. Jennifer Glancy, "Slavery and the Rise of Christianity," in *The Cambridge World History of Slavery*, vol. 1, *The Ancient Mediterranean World*, ed. Keith Bradley and Paul Cartledge (Cambridge: Cambridge University Press, 2011), 462.

passage from the New Testament, part of what is generally called "household codes," summarizes how the earliest generation of Christians understood the duty of slaves vis-à-vis Christianity:

> Let all who are under the yoke of slavery regard their masters as worthy of all honor, so that the name of God and the teaching may not be blasphemed. Those who have believing masters must not be disrespectful to them on the ground that they are members of the church; rather they must serve them all the more, since those who benefit by their service are believers and bellowed. Teach and urge these duties. (1 Tim. 6:1–2; see also Col. 3:22–25 and Eph. 6:5–9; Tit. 2:9–10; 1 Pet. 2:18–20)

"But is there any one thus intended by nature to be a slave?... There is no difficulty in answering this question, on grounds both of reason and of fact. For that some should rule and others be ruled is a thing, not only necessary, but expedient; from the hour of their birth, some are marked out for subjection, others for rule." (Aristotle, *Politics* 1.5)

The medieval church inherited the patriarchy of the ancient world and the ambivalent teachings of the New Testament when it came to slaveholding. Just as Aristotle had argued that there were natural slaves whose barbarian features and temperament made slavery acceptable, so many groups of early Christians did not see a discrepancy between the freedom one received from Christ and the enslaving of other human beings for temporal goods. The Council of Chalcedon (451), for example, ruled that slaves could only enter a monastery after receiving permission from their slave holders, underscoring that slavery was still practiced among Christians—and that the practice was not sinful in and of itself. Despite some notable exceptions, Christians largely accepted slavery as part of society and did not offer significant criticism. As historian Hector Avalos summarizes, "The first millennium of Christianity saw an overwhelming acceptance of slavery by significant theologians, higher clerics, Church councils, and the Pope himself."[5]

The fifteenth century marked a turning point in the history of Christianized slavery due to the maritime explorations of Portugal and Spain in Africa, Asia, and the Americas. In the papal bull *Romanus Pontifex* (1454/55), King Alonso of Portugal was given permission to "reduce . . . to perpetual slavery" Muslims and Africans. The pope's approval of slavery of these foreigners was based on the belief that to "subdue all Saracens [Muslims] and pagans whatsoever, and other enemies of Christ wheresoever placed"[6] was a way to introduce Christianity. With a nod from the pope, the Portuguese Crown began granting licenses to select European slaveholders in the fifteenth century. The Spanish—Portugal's main competition in the race toward maritime mastery—followed suit in the sixteenth century. In turn, the Spanish were emulated by the British, Dutch, and French in the seventeenth century. The papacy largely supported the trafficking of slavery among Christian Europeans since the practice was a form of evangelism. As Avalos notes, "Not only did some popes own slaves, but they repeatedly enunciated policies that allowed Christian monarchs to enslave millions of people."[7]

Early Slavery in the New World: The Encomienda

In the New World, slavery was sanctioned by the highest echelon of European society. It was largely supported by both church officials and laypeople. In Spanish colonies, the system was called *encomienda*. It can be translated as "charge" or "mission," though many today would simply regard it as outright slavery. The practice began under

5. Hector Avalos, *Slavery, Abolitionism, and the Ethics of Biblical Scholarship* (Sheffield: Sheffield Phoenix Press, 2011), 171.
6. Quoted in Avalos, *Slavery, Abolitionism, and the Ethics of Biblical Scholarship*, 186.
7. Avalos, *Slavery, Abolitionism, and the Ethics of Biblical Scholarship*, 198.

Governor Nicolas de Ovando in 1503, who was sent by the Spanish monarchy to deal with the deplorable political conditions then existing in the New World, which historian Lesley Byrd Simpson once described "as something like absolute chaos."[8] Because many of the Spaniards who risked their lives by traveling to the New World were criminals, convicts, and adventure seekers, something was needed to curb their appetite for treasure and pleasure and also to guarantee a decent return on Spanish investment. The encomienda became the instrument through which the Spaniards were to achieve both these ends. On the one hand, the Spaniards were to become Christian ambassadors to the native peoples while, on the other, the native peoples were to work and mine Spain's new territories. This document, signed by the king and queen, ordered Governor de Ovando as follows:

> you will compel and force the said Indians to associate with the [Spanish] Christians of the island and to work on their buildings, and to gather and mine the gold and other metals, and to till the fields and produce food for the Christian inhabitants . . . and you are to have each one paid on the day he works the wages and maintenance which you think he should have . . . and you are to order each cacique [an Arawak term meaning tribal chief] to take charge of a certain number of the said Indians, so that you may make them work wherever necessary. . . . This the Indians shall perform as free people, which they are, and not as slaves. And see to it that they are well treated, those who become Christians better than the others, and do not consent or allow that any person do them any harm or oppress them.[9]

This system was roughly based on the serfdom model practiced in Spain and elsewhere in Europe. Here is how the system worked in the New World: an *encomendero*, a Spanish man "entrusted" with

---

8. Lesley Byrd Simpson, *The Encomienda in New Spain: The Beginning of Spanish Mexico* (Berkeley: The University of California, 1982), 7.
9. Quoted in Simpson, *The Encomienda in New Spain*, 13.

the *encomienda* (essentially a grant of land, technically owned by the Spanish Crown), ruled over a certain number of Native Americans. In the process, the encomendero often made a fortune. In return for obligatory back-breaking labor wherever or however the encomendero demanded, the encomendero paid whatever fee he thought reasonable, agreed to teach the Native Americans the Catholic faith, and provided food and protection. The natives who converted to Christianity were to be treated more kindly than those who retained their pagan ways. In theory, the encomienda system was a form of Christian evangelism in the guise of forced labor. In practice, however, the encomienda system was little more than a forum for Spanish abuse and oppression. As one historian describes this system, it was "irregular, uncontrolled, and highly exploitative."[10] Although the native peoples were not to be regarded as "slaves," they were treated as such and had to decide among obedience to this humiliating system, a risky escape, or suicide. A contemporary description of the system, by an encomendero no less, lamented how a royal official worked the natives over whom he had charge "so hard" that only thirty out of 300 were still alive after only three months of labor. The encomendero's reward after losing 270 Indians to the mines was to receive approval for 300 more natives. "The more he received," the acquaintance of the royal official wrote, "the more he killed, until eventually he himself died and the Devil took his soul."[11]

---

10. Charles Gibson, *Spain in America* (New York, Evanston, and London: Harper & Row, 1966), 50.
11. Bartolomé de las Casas, *A Short Account of the Destruction of the Indies*, trans. Nigel Griffin (London: Penguin, 1992), 30.

Bartolomé de las Casas (1484–1566)

The man who wrote these words was to become the greatest advocate for the rights of the indigenous people of Latin America. His name was Bartolomé de las Casas. He was a Spaniard born in Seville, and had gained his first glimpse of Native Americans as a child on March 31, 1493 when Christopher Columbus paraded about several Taino Indians on his first return voyage to Spain from the Caribbean. While still a young man, las Casas traveled on board the fleet of ships that left with Governor de Ovando in 1502. But it was only about ten or so years later that his conscience was stricken by the teaching of the Dominicans, who had recently arrived on the islands. Though not in attendance at the Cathedral of Santo Domingo when Antonio de Montesinos preached against the abuses of the Spanish toward the Indians during Advent of 1511, he soon received the notes, which eventually proved very meaningful for him. Though ordained a secular priest (see Figure 16.1) in 1510—the first priest so ordained in the Americas—las Casas was also an encomendero, and he did not see any discrepancy between making his living from New World slavery while attempting to convert the native peoples to Christianity until after the Dominicans had redirected his thinking.

Figure 16.1. Priests in the New World

There were two types of priests in Latin America: (1) *Regular priests* lived according to a monastic rule (*regula* in Latin), did not typically administer the sacraments, were celibate, and were under the jurisdiction of their monastic superiors. (2) *Secular (or diocesan) priests* lived according to the world (*saeculum* in Latin) rather than a rule, were accountable to bishops in a diocese, were supposed to be celibate (though some were not), and earned money by collecting tithes and performing duties such as baptisms and marriages. Regular priests were organized into different orders, including Franciscans, Dominicans, Jesuits, Carmelites, Augustinians, and Mercedarians. In the New World, there was constant tension between the regulars and seculars.

Things came to a head for las Casas around 1514. Now living on the island of Cuba, where he was both a secular priest and a wealthy encomendero, he was witnessing first-hand the atrocities committed against the native peoples of the Caribbean. On one occasion, a group of Spaniards, "without the slightest provocation, butchered, before my eyes, some three thousand souls—men, women and children—as they sat there in front of us." "I saw that day," he later confessed in his famous tell-all *A Short Account of the Destruction of the Indies*, "atrocities more terrible than any living man has ever seen nor ever thought to see."[12] Based on these personal experiences, his reading of Scripture, and his conversations with the Dominicans (he was actually barred in 1514 from the sacraments by a Dominican friar for holding slaves), Las Casas decided to give up all of his holdings and slaves and become an advocate for the native peoples in the Americas. When las Casas told his plan to the governor, he was dissuaded from freeing his slaves: "Padre, think of what you are doing. Do not regret your good fortune. It is God who wants to see you rich and prosperous."

But las Casas had already resolved to free his slaves and cast his lot with the Dominicans. Upon returning to Spain in 1516, las Casas was appointed Protector of the Indians by Archbishop Francisco Ximenes de Cisneros of Toledo, a man perhaps most famous for his printing of the first edition of the Greek New Testament. Las Casas went to task quickly and shrewdly, politicking the rest of his life about the illegality of enslaving the American Indians. Due to his efforts, new Spanish laws were formulated in behalf of the natives of the Americas. In 1542, King Charles I issued the so-called New Laws, which were designed to eventually abolish the enslavement of Native Americans in the New World by terminating many encomiendas

12. Las Casas, *A Short Account*, 29.

and not permitting any encomenderos to bequeath their slaves to their relatives, as was common practice. The New Laws replaced the Laws of Burgos, originally decreed by King Ferdinand I in 1512, as a way to curb exploitation of the native peoples. As historian Lawrence Clayton explains, there were five basic precepts enunciated in the New Laws of 1542:

1. The dignity of the Indian as subjects of the crown.

2. The elimination of Indian slavery.

3. Provisions for the extinction of the *encomienda* as a principal form of exploiting the Indian as labor and vassal.

4. Prohibiting further wars of conquest.

5. Strict and detailed laws and decrees for the enforcement of all the above.[13]

Though espousing grand ideals and greatly influenced by las Casas's deep concern for the Indians, these laws were ineffective and unenforceable. In 1556, for instance, the third viceroy of Peru, Marquis de Cañete, wrote to King Ferdinand II of Spain:

> Not all problems can be resolved, especially that regarding the treatment of the Indios at the hands of the *encomenderos*, which is worse than ever. Please realize, Your Majesty, that it will take more than a viceroy to assure that each *vecino* does not rob, mistreat, and work to death these people. And this behavior is so widespread that, however hard I make my heart, it breaks in two to see that which takes place . . . and the Indios are being used up; if God does not intervene, they will suffer the same fate as those of Santo Domingo, where the same things took place.[14]

---

13. Lawrence Clayton, *Bartolomé de las Casas: A Biography* (Cambridge: Cambridge University Press, 2012), 282.
14. Quoted in Massimo Livi-Bacci, *Conquest: The Destruction of the American Indios* (Cambridge: Polity, 2008), 30.

God did not intervene. The natives of Peru died off in droves just like the natives of Hispaniola. In conjunction with maltreatment and death through exhaustion, European diseases annihilated the original inhabitants of the Americas. Writing several years earlier, Alonso de Castro concluded that "the Indios [in Hispaniola] are extinct."[15] It has been estimated that of about 50 million inhabitants of the Americas in 1500, only about 8 million were left alive by 1600.[16] Though greatly alarmed at the continuation of the encomienda and the high death rates of the native peoples, las Casas pressed on in his advocacy work. He was bishop of Chiapas from 1540 to 1550, and devoted much attention to travel, study, and writing in behalf of the Indians, arguing for a complete abolition of the encomienda.

Dispute over Enslavement of Native Americans in Spain (1550)

According to historian Hector Avalos, the "high point of las Casas's dramatic life"[17] occurred when he debated the Spanish theologian Juan Ginés de Sepúlveda over the rights of the Spaniard's to enslave and Christianize the Native Americans "in accordance with [Pope] Alexander's bull" of 1493.[18] If it was not the high point of las Casas's life, it was certainly was that of Sepúlveda's, whose learned background and stellar connections have been overshadowed due to his unpopular theological conviction that the Indians were rightly and lawfully allowed to be enslaved by the Spaniards. The famous junta held in 1550 in Valladolid, Spain between las Casas and Sepúlveda was not the first of its kind. Quite uniquely in world

---

15. Quoted in Massimo Livi-Bacci, *Conquest*, 24.
16. Robin Blackburn, *The Making of New World Slavery: From the Baroque to the Modern, 1492–1800* (New York: Verso, 1997), 132.
17. Avalos, *Slavery, Abolitionism, and the Ethics of Biblical Scholarship*, 202.
18. Eduardo Andújar, "Bartolomé de las Casas and Juan Ginés de Sepúlveda: Moral Theology versus Political Philosophy," in *Hispanic Philosophy in the Age of Discovery*, ed. Kevin White (Washington, D.C.: The Catholic University of America Press, 1997), 69. For more about Alexander's bulls, see the previous chapter.

history, the Spanish Monarch had convened several such debates about the fairness of the Spanish conquest of the Americas, some of which las Casas had taken part.

The debate in Valladolid occurred over the course of a week in August of 1550. Remarkably, King Charles I had ordered all conquests of the New World to cease until a proper decision had been made regarding Spain's right to do so. The first one to speak in the debate (the participants were actually separated and never debated face-to-face, but rather read their pre-prepared remarks to a panel) was Sepúlveda, who had earlier published writings regarding the subject of Spain's conquest of the New World.[19] Whereas las Casas later argued for a Christian ethic that called for love toward the Native Americans, Sepúlveda cited biblical texts affirming love within the context of servitude—such as passages legitimizing Israelite violence in the Old Testament. He also cited many Old Testament passages that condoned violence against pagan nations, especially those practicing human sacrifice and sorcery—allowing Sepúlveda to draw parallels between these pagan nations to be destroyed and contemporary Native American cultures. While it was las Casas's strategy to emphasize the gentleness and meekness of the Indians, Sepúlveda regarded them as depraved and human-sacrificing savages in need of tough love. It was only after civilizing the American Indians, he believed, that they would then be receptive to the Christian message.

Using many biblical sources and especially the concept of natural law, Sepúlveda argued for the justness of enslaving the American Indians due to their inferiority in relation to others such as the Spaniards. Sepúlveda described the Indians in this way:

19. Because no records of the proceedings have been found, the following remarks come from their respective writings relating to the topics of the debate.

In prudence, talent, virtue, and humanity they are as inferior to the Spaniards as children to adults, women to men, as the wild and cruel to the most meek, as the prodigiously intemperate to the continent and temperate, that I have almost said, as monkeys to men.[20]

Envisioning the Spanish conquistador Hernán Cortés, who crushed the Aztec Empire in the valley of Mexico in the 1520s before it was known centuries later that his crusade against the Aztecs was greatly aided by the microbes that his men unsuspectingly carried with them, Sepúlveda mused: "Can there be a greater or stronger testimony how some men surpass others in talent, industry, strength of mind, and valor? Or that such peoples are slaves by nature?"[21] For Sepúlveda, at any rate, the conquest by the Spaniards of the American Indians was the legitimate start to their mission to civilize and Christianize. There was nothing necessarily un-Christian about enslaving inferior people, particularly since this enslavement would eventually lead the slaves toward Christianity.

It was las Casas turn to speak next. Whereas Sepúlveda spoke breezily and for only three hours, "Las Casas responded with a numbing five-day reading, word for word"[22] of a 500-page manuscript he had composed! His arguments were many and multi-faceted, which appeared in other writings. In contrast to Sepúlveda, who had never traveled to the New World and who had spent his life in the halls of the academy, las Casas spoke from the heart. He appealed to Scripture and the classic tradition as they conformed to his personal experiences while living in the colonies. As las Casas summarized in his book called *Defense*:

---

20. Quoted in Lewis Hanke, *All Mankind Is One: A Study of the Disputation between Bartolomé de las Casas and Juan Ginés de Sepúlveda in 1550 on the Intellectual and Religious Capacity of the American Indians* (DeKalb, IL: Northern Illinois University Press, 1974), 84.
21. Quoted in Hanke, *All Mankind Is One*, 85.
22. Clayton, *Bartolomé de las Casas*, 353.

The Indians are our brothers, and Christ has given his life for them. Why, then, do we persecute them with such inhuman savagery when they do not deserve such treatment? . . . [They] will embrace the teaching of the gospel."[23]

Las Casas diligently attempted to prove that the American Indian society was on par with Spanish society, even going so far as to suggest that human sacrifice in American Indian society was an indication of some knowledge of God, for even God had ordered Abraham to sacrifice his son!

Ultimately for las Casas, the Bible was to be read and interpreted in a way that was very different from how Sepúlveda interpreted it. Whereas Sepúlveda interpreted the Old Testament laws as sanctioning divine vengeance against pagan nations, las Casas boldly stated that "not all of God's judgements are examples for us."[24] As he had said in another treaty, "What does the gospel have to do with firearms? What does the herald of the gospel have to do with armed thieves?"[25] For las Casas, the Bible advocated a gentle form of evangelism that was rooted in the equality of humankind rather than in stark class divisions. By evangelizing through violence, las Casas argued, the American Indians would regard Christianity as an evil religion and would do all they could in order to avoid accepting it.

The Rise of African Slavery in the Americas

Despite the meticulous arguments presented by Sepúlveda and las Casas, the Spanish council disagreed with each other and no consensus was reached. Both men left the debate convinced of the accuracy of his statements, and life continued as normal in the New World. Nonetheless, by the time the debate at Valladolid took place,

23. Quoted in Hanke, *All Mankind Is One*, 76.
24. Ibid., 90.
25. Ibid., 90–91.

the encomienda system was gradually fading away (though it would linger for decades more). But its disappearance was much more closely linked with disease than with the debate discussed above—however important it was in New World history. As mentioned above, European disease wiped out large percentages of Native Americans throughout the sixteenth century. Diphtheria, influenza, measles, and smallpox were diseases carried by the immunized Spaniards but fatal to those not formerly exposed to them. With no shortage of needs in the New World but now with so little native workers to speak of, the Europeans had to look elsewhere for their labor force.

Ironically, the very man who was the greatest advocate for the abolition of Indian slavery was one of the men who suggested the enslavement of Africans in the New World. So concerned was las Casas about the welfare of the natives of the New World that he was willing to allow the enslavement of Africans if it meant the end of the encomienda. In 1535, las Casas wrote to King Charles I: "the remedy of the Christians is this, that His Majesty should think it right to send to each one of the islands 500 or 600 blacks or whatever number seems appropriate"[26] to farm and mine the land in place of the Native Americans. It was only two decades later that las Casas recognized the hypocrisy of his thinking and repented for believing that African slavery was less heinous than Native American slavery.

But it was too late. Besides, the Europeans had held African slaves since the fifteenth century, so it was not a completely novel idea. Not only did the enslavement of Africans solve the shortage of labor caused by the death of the Indians but it also raised money for the royal treasuries of Spain and Portugal. Throughout the sixteenth century, in fact, it has been estimated that about 10 percent of the

---

26. Quoted in Thomas, *The Slave Trade*, 98.

populations of Seville, Spain and Lisbon, Portugal were African slaves. And as early as 1510, King Ferdinand I of Spain had ordered fifty slaves, no doubt Africans, to be sent to Hispaniola to work the mines. Ferdinand, occupied with many other pressing matters and well accustomed to dealing brutally with his victims and enemies, "would have spent little time considering the fate of a few hundred black slaves."[27] After Ferdinand's order in 1510, more black slaves were sent from Europe to the Americas each consecutive year, even while natives from the New World were likewise being forced into the encomienda system before they largely died through disease and exhaustion. In 1518, King Charles I of Spain gave permission for African slaves to be imported to the Americas. Thereafter, both he and the Portuguese monarchy granted regular licenses to people of note to participate in human trafficking of African slaves. Not surprisingly, the money that encomenderos had amassed through exploitation of the Native Americans enabled them to purchase seemingly endless numbers of African slaves.

According to one estimate, "about 40,000 slaves were probably shipped from Africa to the Americas" during the second quarter of the sixteenth century alone, with that number consistently increasing throughout the rest of that century (and, of course, the following ones).[28] Large numbers of these African slaves came from Angola and Congo, and were sent to work the sugar mines of Brazil or those in Cuba. Many increasingly went to Colombia, Venezuela, Argentina, or elsewhere in the Caribbean. "The New World Spaniard," one historian grimly notes, "regarded possession of African slaves as a badge of rank."[29] In the highly class-based society of the New World, Europeans—whether "peninsulars" born in the Old World or

27. Thomas, *The Slave Trade*, 93.
28. Ibid., 114.
29. Blackburn, *The Making of New World Slavery*, 143.

"creoles" born in the New World—were at the top of the social rung, with African slaves at the bottom, where they struggled for survival.

Conclusion: Slavery Increasingly Allowed, Especially of Africans

Although the Spanish and Portuguese were the first to take ownership of the New World and begin construction of their vast empires, other European countries were desperate for what they regarded as their fair share of the newly discovered world. Throughout the sixteenth and seventeenth centuries, the British, Dutch, and French, in particular, sought to break up the Spanish and Portuguese monopoly in the New World, claiming new regions in the Americas (and beyond) for themselves. These new lands required extensive farming and mining to make them profitable, work which most Europeans were unwilling to perform—thus leading to the enslavement of countless Native Americans. Once the number of indigenous peoples had been depleted due to European diseases, exhaustion, and maltreatment, the circumstances were forming for "one of the largest systems of slavery in human history" to coalesce: the Atlantic Slave Trade.[30] Between 1500 and 1870, twelve to fifteen million Africans were imported to the Americas for labor. Between one and two million of these Africans died on route to the Americas and were casually discarded into the sea.

Although some strident voices were raised that questioned slavery, they were silenced by the overwhelming acceptance of the practice by leading Europeans in the Old World and most of those in the New World. The Bible, newly printed and available for the masses for the first time in world history, became a weapon used to vigorously preserve the institution of slavery rather than a source to liberate disenfranchised men and women. It was commonly assumed that

30. Ibid., 3.

Noah's curse on his son Ham legitimated enslavement of Africans, which New Testament teachings had not annulled. For roughly three centuries, in other words, the trafficking and enslavement of slaves was an international business largely sanctioned by the Church—whether Catholic or Protestant. It would not be until the nineteenth century that the European conscience was united in its rejection of both the slave trade and slavery, after which time irreparable damage had been perpetuated in the name of God.

17

Is Confucianism Compatible with Christianity?

It was the year 1601. Matteo Ricci, a Catholic priest living in Beijing, was considering with which group of the Chinese he wanted to start a church. A man with cunning intellect and cultural sensitivity, he knew that Christianity had a better chance of taking root in China if it were adopted by those in the top echelon of society. Upon observing the different groups of people in the capital of Beijing, he zoned in on a small group of men granted unusual respect, special privileges, and elevated status. The group of men was called mandarins, and they were the scholar-officials of their generation. Because of their societal and public obligations, the mandarins whom Ricci attempted to convert were required to observe countless Chinese customs associated with Confucianism, the system of thought and practice that developed from Confucius's teachings.

After Ricci's death, the door to the Forbidden City was opened to additional Catholic missionaries. These missionaries immediately took offense to the strategies Ricci had employed. They asked questions like, *Can a Christian bow down to a statue of a non-Christian?*

Can a Christian participate in a non-Christian funeral? Can a (pagan) Chinese term be used to refer to the God of the Bible? It did not take long before these different Catholic orders began arguing vigorously with one another, taking sides as if in battle formation. So heated was this debate that even the pope and emperor of China became deeply involved, provoking a controversy with huge ramifications for the West in general and the Christianization of China in particular.

The Question of Chinese Rites

The debate that erupted in China in the seventeenth century among the Catholic Church is called the Chinese Rites Controversy. As historian of China Robert Entenmann explains, "Chinese Catholic behavior was profoundly affected by the Rites Controversy,"[1] and it left a noticeable scar on Christian and Chinese relations. Although the Chinese Rites Controversy began four centuries ago within a Catholic context, the issues it raised continue to this day in all forms of Christian expression not only in China but throughout Asia. As we seek to understand the issues surrounding this controversy in this chapter, we will concentrate on European and Chinese responses in the seventeenth and eighteenth centuries to the following question: is Confucianism compatible with Christianity?

A Short History of Christianity in China

Christianity entered China by at least the seventh century. We have reliable documents that describe the arrival of East Syrian Christians, who were part of the Church of the East, in 635. The presiding government, the Tang Dynasty, gave imperial support to

---

1. Robert Entemann, "The Problem of Chinese Rites in Eighteenth-Century Sichuan," in *China and Christianity: Burdened Past, Hopeful Future*, ed. Stephen Uhalley and Xiaoxin Wu (Abingdon and New York: Routledge, 2015), 128.

Christianity for more than two hundred years. Churches and monasteries were built and Christian writings were translated into Chinese. The next imperial court, the Song Dynasty, overran the Tang Dynasty in the second half of the tenth century. It did not endorse Christianity. This caused the disappearance of Christianity in China until the Christian-friendly Mongols briefly ruled China during the Yuan Dynasty in the thirteenth and fourteenth centuries.

Catholic Christianity first entered China during the Yuan Dynasty. But when the missionaries arrived, they immediately clashed with the East Syrian Christians who had been ministering in Asia since the first century. The Franciscan John of Montecorvino, the later archbishop of Beijing (called Peking until the later part of the twentieth century), was the first successful Catholic missionary in China. In the early fourteenth century, he established several mission stations, baptized six thousand people, and it was rumored that he even converted Külüg Khan to Catholicism, the third emperor of the Yuan Dynasty. Although Catholicism, together with East Syriac Christianity, experienced decline when the Mongolian-ruled Yuan Dynasty ended in 1368, Catholic Christianity re-established a reputable presence in China toward the end of the Ming Dynasty.

Christianity became a permanent part of the Chinese religious landscape in the sixteenth century. Christianity's success can be attributed to the strategies of a new order of Catholics. The Society of Jesus, whose members are referred to as Jesuits, emerged in the wake of the European Reformations in the first half of the sixteenth century. Burdened to save the lost outside of Europe and fueled by deep spirituality, Pope Paul III gave papal support to the Jesuit order in 1540. Now backed by Rome, the Jesuits unleashed an army of theologically adept missionary-soldiers all across the world, from Asia to the Americas.

The most famous Jesuit missionary to China was Matteo Ricci. Born in Macerata, Italy in 1552 and trained at the Jesuit College in Rome, Ricci was the first European allowed to live in Beijing during the Ming Dynasty. Ricci's missionary practices were highly irregular at that time—and novel. He mastered Chinese and published poetry and other scholarly works in that language. He also adopted the clothing of a Chinese scholar, grew a beard, and adopted local customs. His policy, in this way, was highly accommodationist. Although the Jesuits proselytized Chinese people of all social backgrounds,[2] Ricci's missionary strategy was centered on converting the mandarins, that is, the elite scholar-officials who had passed the state examinations of the imperial court and who therefore enjoyed honor, prestige, and influence, and who could ensure the future success of Christianity among the common people and establish it as a reputable religion among the upper class. As Ricci himself wrote to his superior:

> At this early stage [of Christian presence in China], it is necessary to concentrate on a few rather than a large number and to have among them some graduate scholars and mandarins whose standing can give confidence to those who are frightened by this novelty.[3]

In concentrating attention on the mandarins, Ricci hoped to fully integrate Christianity into Chinese culture.[4] But in order to convert the mandarins, Jesuits like Ricci allowed baptized Asians to participate in state ceremonies and to observe ancient funerary rites that were Confucian in orientation[5] (though the missionaries did not consent

2. See more discussion about the caricatures of Ricci's missionary strategy as a simple top-down approach in Liam Matthew Brockery, *Journey to the East: The Jesuit Mission to China* (Cambridge, MA: Harvard University Press, 2008), 47–48.
3. As cited in Jean-Pierre Charbonnier, *Christians in China: A.D. 600 to 2000* (San Francisco: Ignatius Press, 2007), 205.
4. John Young, *Confucianism and Christianity: The First Encounter* (Hong Kong: Hong Kong University Press, 1983), 27.
5. Brockery, *Journey to the East*, 11.

to other common practices among the mandarins such as concubinage).[6]

Figure 17.1. Short Biography of Confucius

Confucius, or Master Kong, was born in the northeastern part of China in the year 551 BCE during the same time the defeated nation of Israel still resided in captivity in Babylon. Confucius was a devoted student of ancient Chinese history and philosophy who entered civil service at the age of fifteen. The advice he offered and the society he envisioned never materialized during his lifetime, but it later came to dominate the cultural and religious worldview of East Asian nations such as China, Korea, and Japan. The thought of Confucius, referred to as Confucianism, consisted of hierarchical relationships between, for instance, an emperor and his subjects and a father and his children. It also adopted many Chinese beliefs about the supernatural. Due to the societal upheaval that China experienced throughout Confucius's lifetime, Master Kong strived to bring structure to the disharmony and chaos by assigning and enforcing strict roles to which everyone would conform. Each societal relationship entailed fulfilling clearly defined obligations between members of society.

When Ricci moved to Beijing in 1601, he and others instantly began entertaining curious visitors from among the mandarins residing in the city. Based in part on the Jesuit policies toward missions, Christianity enjoyed a "golden period" at the very beginning of the Qing Dynasty.[7] This time period, particularly in the second half of the seventeenth century, witnessed the great success of latter Jesuits missionaries like Johann Adam Schall, who was the first Jesuit to meet with a Chinese emperor. In fact, the Shunzhi Emperor, who ruled from 1643 to 1661, greatly respected the German Jesuit and made him an advisor. The emperor favored the Jesuits so much that he gave them land, residence in the capital, a church, and "an annual subsidy from the imperial treasury."[8] Not surprisingly, this led to the growth of the Chinese church from less than 100,000 adherents at the end of the Ming Dynasty in 1644 to more than 250,000 upon the death of Schall two decades later.[9] Emperor Kangxi declared an edict of

---

6. Brockery, *Journey to the East*, 48.
7. Samuel Moffett, *A History of Christianity in Asia*, volume 2, *1500 to 1900* (Maryknoll, NY: Orbis, 2005), 119.
8. Ibid., 2:118.

tolerance of Christianity in 1692 that called for no one to "henceforth offer [the Christians] any opposition."[10]

Well before this time, however, Catholic Christianity had been engaged in internal battles for decades, roughly coinciding with the larger war between the Ming and Qing Dynasties in the 1630s–1640s, the latter of which prevailed. By the 1630s, Dominican and Franciscan missionaries had begun arriving in mainland China. The Jesuits, who were more open-minded when it came to issues of contextualization, were threatened by the presence of other Catholic orders in China that engaged the culture differently. Of course, national identity also played itself out in this battle. Generally speaking, the Portuguese supported Jesuits and bickered with the Spanish, who tended to favor the Dominicans and Franciscans. In brief, the Dominicans and Franciscans followed a conservative approach to missions that tended to exterminate indigenous culture more so than accommodate to it. Daniel Bays suggests that these two orders "brought with them from the Philippines a severe missionary policy" that stemmed from "Spain's harsh philosophy of colonial rule."[11]

The open-mindedness of the Jesuits evidences itself in the fact that in 1706 Emperor Kangxi decreed that "all missionaries would have to undergo an examination, and only those who agreed with 'the policies of Matteo Ricci' [who had been dead for a century; this expression meant essentially "those missionaries who accept Chinese rites"] would receive a certificate (*piao*) which permitted them to remain in China."[12] Christianity limped along for the next two

9. Ibid., 2:119.
10. Cited in *A History of Christianity in Asia, Africa, and Latin America, 1450-1990: A Documentary Sourcebook*, ed. Klaus Koschorke, Frieder Ludwig, Mariano Delgado, and Roland Spliesgart (Grand Rapids, MI: Eerdmans, 2007), 39.
11. Bays, *A New History of Christianity in China*, 121.
12. Ibid., 30.

decades until Kangxi's son, the Yongzheng emperor, who ruled from 1723 to 1735, outlawed Christianity as an "evil cult" or "heterodox sect" that subverted Chinese cultures and values. Christianity would carry this official status for more than two centuries, which greatly hindered the development of Christianity, particularly among the mandarins and the elites of Chinese culture.[13]

Figure 17.2. Christianity in Relation to Chinese Dynasties		
Dynasty in China	Years	Status of Christianity
Tang Dynasty	618–907	Oriental Orthodox Christianity first entered China in the seventh century but was later disestablished in the late ninth and early tenth century
Five Dynasties and Ten Kingdoms Period	907–960/79	Christianity disestablished
Song Dynasty	960–1279	Christianity disestablished
Yuan Dynasty	1271–1368	Venetian Catholic Marco Polo (d. 1324) worked for Kublai Khan in the thirteenth century; Catholicism entered China during this dynasty and East Syrian Christianity also experienced some success
Ming Dynasty	1368–1644	East Syrian Christianity and Catholicism initially disfavored due to favor among Mongolian Yuan Dynasty; Catholicism later accepted during end of Ming Dynasty
Qing Dynasty	1644–1911	Protestantism first entered China during this dynasty; Catholicism experienced a tenuous relationship with the government regarding the Rites Controversy

The Compatibility of Confucianism with Christianity

As alluded to above, the accommodation policy of Jesuits like Ricci sparked a vigorous debate within Christianity known as the Rites

13. Ibid., 31.

Controversy. The term "rites" fittingly describes this controversy, since Confucianism was concerned supremely with all members of society observing set rites and ceremonies. European Christians debated the role these rites should play in the lives of Asian Christians for centuries. Initially, and especially in China, the debate was an intramural one between different groups of Catholic Christians in the seventeenth and eighteenth centuries. However, it later came to include different groups of Protestants when they entered Asia beginning in the nineteenth century. For our purposes, we will focus on the seventeenth century, as this time period experienced some of the most rigorous discussions and debates, but we will also make mention of some events that occurred in the following century. Matteo Ricci, given his seminal importance in the history of Christian missions to China and in the history of the Chinese Rites Controversy, will serve as the focal point of discussion.

The Jesuits Frame the Issue

Returning to the question before us, we seek to answer the following: is Confucianism compatible with Christianity? Naturally, this question consists of several sub-issues relating to Confucianism and Christianity. Daniel Bays categorizes the sub-issues in these three ways: first, whether established Chinese terms for the name of the Divine and the soul should be used by Christians or whether existing Christian (European) terms should be used instead; second, whether the different rites or ceremonies such as burning incense and bowing to ancestors (for instance, by means of ancestral tablets) are civic and cultural practices that complement Christianity or religious practices that compete with it; and, third, whether the spiritual effects of Christian ceremonies such as Mass or the Lord's Supper can be applied to the deceased and non-Christian relatives of Asian Christians, and whether Christians can participate in festivals and feasts in commemoration of non-Christian deities.[14] For our part, we will focus on the first two clusters of concerns, though it must be remembered that all of them are related to the larger issue of the compatibility of Confucianism with Christianity (and of secular culture with the Christian faith).

The first cluster of concerns that Catholic missionaries encountered in East Asia centered on ways the missionaries should translate Christian concepts like God, soul, and religion to the Chinese people. When deciding how to refer to the Christian God, for instance—which was the most debated of this particular cluster of issues—missionaries like Ricci opted for, among others, the Chinese term *Tian*, which is often translated as "Heaven" and which carries a spiritual connotation. In his tract titled "On the Various Sects in China that Contradict Religion," Ricci praises the Confucian classics for possessing a high understanding of the divine being, named "King of Heaven."[15] Rather than rejecting the Confucian understanding of this divinity and starting from scratch, it was Ricci's method to infuse a Christian meaning into existing Chinese terms and ideas. He believed that the Chinese made the best out of the natural reason God had given them throughout their past, and that it was then preferable to use these indigenous concepts rather than introduce new and foreign terms.

As expected, the method Ricci and others employed underwent great criticism among other European missionaries and theologians. In fact, even Ricci's successor as Superior General to the Jesuit mission in China, Niccolo Longobardo, rejected the use of the terms *Tian* ("Heaven"), *Shangdi* ("Lord on High"), and *Tianzhu* ("Lord of Heaven") to refer to the Christian God (*Deus* in Latin) as a result of

---

14. Ibid., 28.
15. Matteo Ricci, "On the Various Sects in China that Contradict Religion," cited in *A History of Christianity in Asia, Africa, and Latin America, 1450-1990,* 34.

their non-Christian overtones.[16] Those who disagreed with Ricci's questionable methods sent word back to Christian leaders in Europe, who generally followed a more conservative approach to Christian missions. A papal decree in 1742, for instance, which contained Pope Clement XI's pronouncement from 1704 from the former decree *Cum Deus Optimus*, rejected the use of *Tian* for God while accepting the term *Tianzhu*.[17] As the actual decree states, "The terms *Tien* [a variant of *Tian*] and *Xang Xu* (highest emperor) . . . should be fully rejected."[18]

Second, although Confucianism had existed for centuries, it became the official "religion" of China during the Han and Six Dynasties. In the year 59 CE, at the same time the apostle Paul was writing letters to newfound Christian churches around the Mediterranean, Emperor Ming ordered sacrifices to be offered to Confucius in all schools. By 657 Confucius was worshiped as the perfect teacher and sage.[19] Centuries later, when Catholic Christianity entered China, Confucian practices like these divided the church since the Jesuits largely asserted that these practices were merely civic ceremonies while the other orders generally interpreted them as idolatrous acts of worship.

For his part, Matteo Ricci and most of the Jesuits tolerated these Confucian practices (by this time, more accurately called Neo-Confucianism) among the mandarins as essential cultural ceremonies that did not violate the Christian religion. Ricci regarded even the sacrifices to Confucius as civil in character; they contained no religious sentiments. Many of these types of ceremonies, in fact,

---

16. Michela Fontana, *Matteo Ricci: A Jesuit in the Ming Court* (Lanham, MD: Rowman & Littlefield, 2011), 291.

17. Cited in *A History of Christianity in Asia, Africa, and Latin America, 1450–1990*, 40.

18. *Ex quo singulari*, cited in *A History of Christianity in Asia, Africa, and Latin America, 1450–1990*, 40.

19. Xinzhong Yao, *Confucianism and Christianity: A Comparative Study of Jen and Agape* (Brighton: Sussex Academic Press, 1997), 29.

stemmed from the very important Confucianist concept of filial piety, which is concerned with how a son (and by extension a child) must dutifully respect and show deference to one's father (and by extension one's ancestors). For our purposes in this section, we will focus on "ancestor worship" or "ancestor veneration," which is inherently related to filial piety.

In brief, what Jesuit missionaries like Ricci recognized was that ancestral veneration, when living descendants honor their dead ancestors by bowing at their graves, before ancestral tablets, or by burning incense to them, was the fabric that held Chinese culture together. And when one attempted to neatly pull away this thread, as the Dominicans and Franciscans were doing, all of the rest of the yarn was completed attached to it. In Confucian thought, an indissoluble bond existed between the ancestor and the descendant. It was the descendant's duty to make sacrifices to one's ancestors. To refuse this duty threatened the peace of the ancestor's spirit and simultaneously invited curses from the spirit and hindered blessings on the descendant. In short, refusing this ancestral rite brought shame on the family by disrupting the harmony naturally existing between Heaven and Earth, and thus society as a whole.[20] And if mandarins who converted to Christianity were to reject these rites, so believed the Jesuits, Christianity as a whole in China would be jeopardized.

The Dominicans, Franciscans, and Papacy Respond

When Dominicans like Juan Morales arrived in China in the 1630s and witnessed the rites the Jesuits allowed their Chinese converts to continue observing, they severely criticized their Catholic brothers' tolerance of such superstitious practices. Part of this stemmed from the reality that the Dominicans and Franciscans tended to work in

20. Ibid., 32.

the countryside with the lower class of Chinese who were more prone to superstition than the educated mandarins who performed required ceremonies more perfunctorily than the common people.[21] Either way, Morales summarily constructed a list of twelve questions concerning the allowances of the Jesuits and set sail for Rome in 1640, arriving three years later and seeking papal support of his anti-Jesuit stance on Confucian rites.[22]

The pope at that time, Urban VIII, agreed with Morales. He objected to the observance of Confucian rites. The pope's successor, Innocent X, upheld the verdict in 1645. The Jesuits, however, refused to back down. They sent their own legate to Rome in the seventeenth century. Surprisingly perhaps, the new pope, Alexander VII, took the side of the Jesuits in 1656 without referring to the former papal decisions. Yet more clarity and an increasing consensus (this time, against the Jesuits) came in 1704 upon Clement XI's firm ruling on the matter. This pontiff issued a papal bull that was strongly against observing Chinese rites:

> [B]elievers in Christ cannot under any circumstance whatsoever be permitted to preside over, assist or participate in the celebrations of the offerings that are brought by the Chinese to Confucius and to the ancestors in the yearly ceremonies of the equinox, because these celebrations are tainted with superstition. Likewise it is forbidden for these same believers to carry out ceremonies, rites and offerings in the Confucian temples . . . to honor Confucius each month at the new moon and full moon. . . . And furthermore it shall not be tolerated that the above mentioned Christians help or take part in any sort of offering, rite or ceremony, together with the pagans or separately, at ancestor shrines in private houses, at the graves of the ancestors, or at the graveside before the burial of the deceased, as would usually be done to honor them.[23]

21. Charbonnier, *Christians in China*, 251.
22. Ibid., 221.
23. *Ex quo singulari*, cited in *A History of Christianity in Asia, Africa, and Latin America, 1450–1990*, 40.

Pope Clement XI upheld this stance in his 1715 bull titled *Ex illa die*, and Pope Benedict XIV also made a decree against the practice in 1742 in the papal bull *Ex quo singulari*. Such unified and assertive papal decrees made it clear to Catholic missionaries that accommodation was not an option. Asians who converted to Christianity were to conform to papal law and not to participate in the syncretization of the Christian religion. The only concessions that the papal decree allowed were the continuance of the Chinese term *Tianzhu* for God and the observance of civil ceremonies that contained no vestiges of religious superstition.[24]

Despite papal decrees that eschewed religious syncretization of Confucianism and Christianity, Chinese emperors scoffed at the way the popes responded to this controversy. One of the most vocal Chinese emperors during the Rites Controversy was the Manchu noble Kangxi, who was well educated in Confucian culture. He reacted angrily to the pope's pronouncements against Chinese rites. His response to Clement XI's bull in 1715, for instance, though later than the century on which this chapter focuses, fully captures his downright annoyance at the official decree:

> Reading this proclamation, I have concluded that the Westerners are petty indeed. It is impossible to reason with them because they do not understand larger issues as we understand them in China. There is not a single Westerner versed in Chinese works, and their remarks are often incredible and ridiculous. To judge from this proclamation, their religion is no different from other small, bigoted sects of Buddhism or Taoism. I have never seen a document which contains so much nonsense. From now on, Westerners should not be allowed to preach in China, to avoid further trouble.[25]

24. Bay, *A New History of Christianity*, 129.
25. Cited in *A History of Christianity in Asia, Africa, and Latin America, 1450–1990*, 40.

As a result of the papal stance on the issue, Christianity dwindled. In fact, Pope Clement XIV actually suppressed the Jesuit order in 1773. Had the popes sanctioned Jesuit practices and promulgated a more accommodationist policy, the history of Christianity in China may have turned out very differently. In the end, however, the papal decrees did not at all end the controversy surrounding whether well-entrenched Asian practices such as bowing to ancestors, venerating ancestral tablets, burning incense, and participating in non–Christian holidays comported or competed with Christianity.

Figure 17.3. Catholic Groups and Representatives Weighing in on Christianity's Compatibility with Confucianism	
(Roman Catholic) Groups	Specific Representatives
Jesuits	Matteo Ricci; Johann Adam Schall; Ferdinand Verbiest
Dominicans	Thomas de Sierra; Juan Morales
Franciscans	Antonio de Santa Maria (Anton Caballero)
Popes	Clement XI; Benedict XIV

These debates about ceremonies and rites continued for two hundred years. But change eventually came. In response to the different historical position in which Asian Christianity found itself between the two great World Wars, Pope Pius XII relaxed the restrictions of the former papal decrees in his 1939 bull titled *Plane Compertum*, declaring that some of these Confucian practices were indeed civil or cultural rather than religious. (It should be noted that upon the Qing Dynasty's collapse in 1911 in China, the Confucian cult virtually disappeared.) The bull stated, in part:

> It is abundantly clear that in the regions of the Orient some ceremonies, although they may have been involved in pagan rites in ancient times have—with all the changes in customs and thinking over the course of

centuries—retained merely the civil significance of piety towards the ancestors or of the love of the fatherland or of courtesy towards one's neighbors.[26]

Today, Christians from such heavily Confucianist cultures as China, Japan, South Korea, Taiwan, and Vietnam struggle to maintain their primary identity as Christians with their concomitant culture as Confucianists. As for Korea, Confucianism eventually became the dominant philosophy and religion of the Choson Dynasty. Under this long-lasting and powerful dynasty, Confucianism assimilated itself fully into Korean culture, so much so that "by the eighteenth century [Koreans] were the most Confucian country in East Asia."[27] In Japan, however, the rites controversy was less pronounced, in part because Christianity never developed a strong presence in Japan as it did in China and Korea.

Conclusion: Christianity and Confucianism Uncomfortably Aligned

At the heart of the Rites Controversy was a question that still evades consensus today: was Confucianism a religion or a philosophy? Put simply, the Dominicans, Franciscans, and the popes regarded Confucianism as a religion, while the Jesuits viewed it more as a philosophy. All in all, the Chinese Rites Controversy was a public relations disaster between Europe and China, and it also deeply divided the body of Christ. Daniel Bays summary of the debate perhaps remains the best word on the matter: "The pope was the better theologian, and the Jesuits were better missionaries."[28] That is to say, the papacy, as the guardian of the purity and integrity of

---

26. *Plane Compertum*, cited in *A History of Christianity in Asia, Africa, and Latin America, 1450–1990*, 100–101.
27. John and Evelyn Berthrong, *Confucianism: A Short Introduction* (Oxford: Oneworld, 2000), 5.
28. Bays, *A New History of Christianity in China*, 129.

the Catholic faith, protected the uniqueness of the Christian religion by refusing to accommodate its message while the Jesuits, as the contextually savvy missionaries of the Christian faith, recognized that this religion would never integrate into Chinese culture if dressed in European garb. In the end, the papacy proved the stronger voice, and the Jesuits were suppressed. This likely hindered the growth of Christianity in China for about two centuries until the church was revived during the twentieth century.

18

Is Conversion Necessary to Be a Christian?

It was the year 1741. On a cold October day in New England, a farmer named Nathan Cole lay squirming in spiritual agony on his bed. For the past year, this thirty-something year old had been agonizing over his deplorable spiritual state. In the fall of 1740, the greatest celebrity in the English-speaking world, Anglican revivalist George Whitefield, had ignited a fire in Cole's heart, declaring that he had to experience the new birth of personal conversion if he wanted to live in heaven for eternity. Although Cole had grown up attending church and doing everything expected of a Christian man at that time, Whitefield convinced Cole that his unregenerate heart was weighing him down like a boulder on a spiderweb. So distraught was Cole, he later conveyed in his journal, that "it seemed to me as if I should sink into the very ground every step." He confessed that "hell fire was most always on my mind; and I have hundreds of times put my fingers into my pipe when I have been smoking to feel how fire felt—and to see how my body could bear to lie in hell fire forever and ever."[1]

Fortunately for Cole, the pain of burnt fingers was soon suppressed by the restorative salve of personal conversion. While shrieking in spiritual agony on his bed, Cole wrote, "God appeared to me and made me cringe." Not knowing whether he was "in the body or out," God convicted him of his sin and offered divine saving grace. Overwhelmed and overpowered, Cole converted on the spot. And at that very moment, as he lay warming his limp body next to a fire on his bed, his spiritual torture had ended. "My heart," he exclaimed, "was broken; my burden had fallen off my mind; I was set free, my distress was gone, and I was filled with a pining desire to see Christ's own words in the Bible." Turning to the first verse he set his eyes on, Cole met Jesus in the Gospel of John: "I am the true vine, and my Father is the husbandman." Grabbing the Bible like a mother does her newborn child, Cole wrapped it up "under [his] chin and hugged it; and it was sweet and lovely."[2]

The Question of Conversion

The personal conversion of Nathan Cole on his bed in October of 1741 was characteristic of a new movement that was barnstorming across the English-speaking world. Now often called evangelicalism or the evangelical movement, this new form of Protestantism was a powerful force changing the way countless men and women understood Christianity and their personal role in the conversion experience. As historian of evangelicalism Thomas Kidd writes, "Evangelicalism. . . inaugurate[d] new emphases on the discernible moment of an individual's conversion, or the 'new birth,' and the simultaneous conversion of many individuals during revivals."[3] In

1. Nathan Cole, "The Spiritual Travels of Nathan Cole," in *The Great Awakening: A Brief History with Documents*, ed. Thomas Kidd (Boston and New York: Bedford/St. Martin's, 2008), 62–63. Note: I have made a few minor corrections in accordance with modern spelling and grammar.
2. Ibid., 63. Note: I have made a few minor corrections in accordance with modern spelling and grammar.

this chapter, we will examine the writings of the most prominent heralds of the rising evangelical movement in the English-speaking world, with an eye toward their responses to the following question: must all believers undergo an individual conversion experience?

A Short History of Evangelicalism

The evangelical movement was a product of the Protestant Reformations of the early 1500s. Before this time in the West, the Catholic Church had been the only authorized form of Christianity. The Catholic Church was unified by means of its lawfully ordained bishops who oversaw the valid observance of the seven sacraments. The Protestant reformers, however, questioned the authority of bishops (especially that of the bishop of Rome—the pope) and rejected five of the seven sacraments. As early as 1520, Martin Luther had argued that the only two Christ-ordained sacraments were Baptism and the Lord's Supper, maintaining that the pope was the Antichrist who inculcated believers into idolatry and untruth. The new and emerging Protestant bodies shared several theological tenets, including belief in only two sacraments (those two mentioned above), justification of an individual by faith alone rather than by performing good deeds, freedom of conscience in matters such as marriage, diet, and vocation, and emphasis on the authority of the Bible over against the authority of popes, priests, or saints.

In the seventeenth century, many of the new generation of Protestant theologians began constructing theologies centered on individual salvation and sanctification. A so-called "religion of the heart," fixated on personal faith, took shape in Germany among Pietists and in England and America among Puritans, Baptists, and some Anglicans. In the early eighteenth century, a German Lutheran

3. Thomas Kidd, *The Great Awakening: The Roots of Evangelical Christianity in Colonial America* (New Haven and London: Yale University Press, 2008), xiv.

Pietist named Count Ludwig von Zinzendorf allowed a large group of Bohemian, German, and Moravian immigrants to live on his land in order to practice their Protestant religion undisturbed. A revival soon broke out among the community. Zinzendorf himself came to be counted among the community, and the so-called Moravian Church developed under his influence. Not only were the Moravians the first group of Protestants to initiate consistent foreign missionary teams but they were also among the first to accentuate the new birth expected of all believers.

It was a number of "unconnected events"[4] among Christian groups like the Moravians and others that anticipated the evangelical movement across Europe and the English-speaking world in the first half of the eighteenth century. In colonial America, Congregationalist and Presbyterian forms of Protestantism were the two dominant forms of Christian expression. Calvinist or "Reformed" in theological orientation, these closely related church communities held many doctrines in common, yet both began to languish in popularity as evangelical revivals increased from the eighteenth century onward. With each new evangelical revival, communities became less concerned with heady theological abstractions in the forms of confessions and catechisms and more concerned with heart-felt, emotional responses to charismatic and evangelistic preaching.

The distinguishing feature of the evangelical movement was its belief that each believer had to undergo a genuine personal conversion experience, commonly called "the new birth." God was directly accessible and worked person by person. There was no need for bishops, sacraments, or churches to mediate between God and the individual. Although such terms as "conversion" and "salvation" were in use since the first century after Christ, the Catholic and Orthodox

4. Noll, *The Rise of Evangelicalism*, 70.

Churches understood conversion or salvation to be mediated by God's Spirit *through the sacraments*. Such were the means Christ instituted for the salvation of his church. It was the evangelicals in the early eighteenth century, however, who most prominently connected saving faith with an individual conversion experience independent of intermediaries. Because of humankind's great sin against God committed in the Garden of Eden (and recommitted in the hearts of all individuals), people had to personally believe that Jesus died on the cross to save them from the consequences of sin—an eternity in hell. For evangelicals, each person had to *feel* transformed based on a finite change of heart based on simple faith. As Gilbert Tennent, an Irish-American Presbyterian pastor, famously preached in a sermon in 1740 titled "The Danger of an Unconverted Ministry," even pastors who had not undergone conversion themselves were destined for hell, and he admonished the parishioners attending churches led by the "unconverted" to flee for their lives and find a church led by a regenerate pastor.

John Wesley (1703–1791)

John Wesley was one of the earliest and greatest of preachers during the emergence of the evangelical movement. Born the son of an Anglican minister, Wesley was a life-long member of the Church of England, later becoming a priest after his studies at Oxford University. As a young man, Wesley had come to accept the common teaching at that time that "I could only be saved 'by universal obedience, by keeping all the commandments of God.'"[5] But as much as he tried to follow God's commandments outwardly, he still felt "near death" inwardly. Inspired by devotional Christian

---

5. John Wesley, "Journal," in Timothy Smith, *Whitefield and Wesley on the New Birth* (Grand Rapids, MI: Francis Asbury Press, 1986), 54.

books, he launched an aggressive campaign of personal reform as he prepared for ordination in the Church of England. In addition to daily contemplation and weekly fasting, he "began visiting the prisons, assisting the poor and sick in town, and doing what other good I could."[6] If ever there was a pious and morally upstanding young man, it was John Wesley. But, as of yet, he had found no rest for his soul.

In 1735, he and his younger brother Charles embarked to the United States. John was to be a missionary to the Indians in Savannah, Georgia, though he effectively served as a pastor to the Europeans who immigrated to the new colony. The primary reason he cited for serving as a missionary in colonial America was that of personal salvation. "My chief motive," he resolutely penned to a friend in the fall of 1735, "is the hope of saving my own soul."[7] It proved a much harder task than he imagined, though the experience was a sort of birthing pains of salvation. After arriving in Georgia, Wesley had an eye-opening conversation with a Moravian pastor named August Spangenberg. Wesley was dumbfounded by two very direct questions the Moravian pastor asked him: "Have you the witness [of the Spirit] within yourself?" and "Does the Spirit of God bear witness with your spirit that you are a child of God?"[8] Based on this interaction, and contrary to what he had been taught in the Church of England, Wesley began pondering whether he could be assured of personal salvation through direct encounter with the Holy Spirit. During his three years of failed ministry in Georgia, Wesley wrestled spiritually with God, being resigned to a "vile, abject state of bondage to sin." Returning to England in 1738, he confessed to "being in

6. Ibid., 56, 55.
7. John Wesley, "To a Friend," *The Works of the Reverend John Wesley*, vol. 6 (New York: J. Emory & B. Waugh, 1831), 609.
8. Quoted in John Wesley, *A Real Christian: The Life of John Wesley* (Nashville, TN: Abingdon, 1999), 42.

imminent danger of death" on account of his lack of assurance that he had been saved. As he wrote in his journal, "I well saw no one could, in the nature of things, have such a sense of forgiveness and could not *feel* it. But I felt it not."[9]

John Wesley's conversion experience is among the most well-known and beloved of the Protestant tradition. It offered a simple model for so many subsequent evangelicals to follow. After years of agonizing whether he had undergone an authentic conversion experience, his doubts were finally relieved. "By late April, 1738," historian of American Christianity Timothy Smith writes, "John Wesley came to a clear understanding that the new birth was an instant experience of forgiveness."[10] What's more, such an experience was normative of the Christian life and not simply limited to the time of the apostles, as was often taught. Wesley had certainly come to this conclusion before this time, but perhaps his failure as a missionary in Georgia prompted him to recognize his shortcomings in the sight of God. Whatever the case, his account of his new birth was not only the turning point in his own life but that of millions of individuals that he would influence over the centuries:

> In the evening, I went very unwillingly to a society in Aldersgate Street, where one was reading Luther's preface to the Epistle to the Romans. About a quarter before nine, while he was describing the change which God works in the heart through faith in Christ, I felt my heart strangely warmed. I felt I did trust in Christ, Christ alone for salvation; and an assurance was given me that He had taken away *my* sins, even *mine*, and saved *me* from the law of sin and death.[11]

Although Wesley had preached countless hundreds of times about Christ and led a spiritually vigilant life that would put any Christian

---

9. Wesley, "Journal," in Smith, *Whitefield and Wesley*, 57.
10. Smith, *Whitefield and Wesley*, 51.
11. Wesley, "Journal," in Smith, *Whitefield and Wesley*, 59.

to shame, he now had direct assurance that he was a child of God. He was confident that each person likewise could, and should, expect such assurance, though he stopped short of inflexibly declaring that no one could be saved unless he was certain of his or her conversion experience. Wesley's sermons immediately reflected his spiritual experience. His concern to observe the commandments of God continued, but always under the primary conviction that people had to be born again. In the fall of 1738, a complaint was lodged against John (and his brother Charles) to the bishop of London for preaching "'an absolute assurance of salvation.'"[12] a notion regarded as fanatical at that time among Anglicans. Wesley's preaching invitations were drying up due to his emphasis on assurance that one was saved, but he persevered. In one sermon, titled "Marks of the New Birth,"[13] Wesley laid out several tangible ways individuals could be assured that they had been converted, including evidence of the fruit of the Spirit in their lives and confident assurance that one had been personally transformed. Defying the classic Christian traditions of Catholicism, Orthodoxy, and Anglicanism—which maintained that Christ saved people by means of the sacraments—Wesley boldly admonished readers:

> Say not then in your heart, I *was once* baptized, therefore I *am now* a child of God. Alas, that consequence will by no means hold. . . . To say then that you cannot be born again, that there is no new birth but in baptism, is to seal you all under damnation, to consign you to hell.[14]

Wesley maintained belief in the new birth throughout his uncommonly long lifetime, but he differed from many other evangelicals by promoting a second personal conversion of sorts that often accompanied the first one. Just as controversial (or at least

---

12. W. L. Doughty, *John Wesley: Preacher* (Eugene, OR: Wipf & Stock, 2015), 32.
13. John Wesley, "Marks of the New Birth," in Smith, *Whitefield and Wesley*, 110.
14. Ibid., 119.

misunderstood) in his own time as in ours today, Wesley believed in what has variously been called "Christian perfection," "entire sanctification," or "heart purity." In his work titled *A Plain Account of Christian Perfection*, Wesley described this second conversion as the moment when (mature) Christians are cleansed from all sin and unrighteousness, so "that they are now in such a sense perfect, as not to commit sin, and to be freed from evil thoughts and tempers."[15] Wesley understood justification, one's first conversion experience, as "the cleansing [of] us from the guilt of sin,"[16] while entire sanctification, one's second conversion experience, entailed the removal of the desire of sin (though, to be sure, sinning was always possible). Wesley supposed both of these personal experiences to be finite in time, the second experience of which enabled a person to choose never to sin again.

George Whitefield (1714–1770)

George Whitefield was a personal friend to both John Wesley and his brother Charles. Although they shared the same passion for evangelization and conversion, Whitefield and Wesley parted ways over the issue of Christian perfection and universal redemption. As a Calvinist, Whitefield recoiled at Wesley's endorsement of Christian perfection. One's sin nature, Whitefield held, could never be removed in this lifetime. He also rejected Wesley's belief that salvation was equally available to everyone, instead contending that only the elect were predestined for salvation and thus a genuine conversion experience. Both strong-willed and popular among their audiences, neither ever retracted his views on these matters, and their

---

15. John Wesley, "A Plain Account of Christian Perfection," in *The Works of the Rev. John Wesley*, vol. 11 (London: Wesleyan Conference Office, 1872), 378.
16. Ibid., 11:378.

friendship suffered as a result (though not fully ending, as Wesley preached at Whitefield's funeral).

Figure 18.1. Argument among the Calvinists

A significant debate among Calvinist theologians in the eighteenth century raged over *when* God predestined the elect to salvation and the reprobate to damnation. Supralapsarians (*supra lapsus* is Latin for "before the fall") held that God made the decree *before* Adam and Eve sinned. Infralapsarians ("below the fall"), by contrast, argued that God made the decree *after* Adam and Eve sinned in the Garden of Eden.

Conversion, or what Whitefield and others commonly called "the new birth," was foundational to his preaching. As Whitefield replied to a conservative group of New England clergymen in the fall of 1740, just a month before he was to provoke anxiety in the heart of farmer Nathan Cole, "It [is] best to preach the new birth. . . and not to insist so much on [denominational] form: for people would never be brought to one mind as to that; nor did Jesus Christ intend it."[17] Historian Frank Lambert cites Whitefield's assertion that "most members of the church were 'destitute of a true living faith in Jesus Christ,' relying only a 'headknowledge,'" devoid of any saving faith.[18]

For Whitefield, the new birth was a definable moment in time when God regenerated an individual by faith in Christ by the work of the Holy Spirit. As a Calvinist, Whitefield taught that such regeneration only occurred through the work of God *among the elect*, though he admonished all people to strive to live morally, contemplate their sin, and prayerfully read the Scriptures. Whitefield himself was fully convinced that his own soul was destined for hell had he not undergone personal conversion, despite the fact that he ardently prayed, gave alms, sang psalms, devoured biblical and

---

17. Quoted in Mark Noll, *The Rise of Evangelicalism: The Age of Edwards, Whitefield and Wesley* (Downers Grove, IL: InterVarsity Press, 2003), 15.

18. Frank Lambert, *"Pedlar in Divinity": George Whitefield and the Transatlantic Revivals, 1737-1770* (Princeton: Princeton University Press, 1994), 15.

devotional writings, received the sacraments, and avoided any forms of ungodliness. Whitefield's own conversion experience, dramatically described in his highly publicized journals, was prompted after Charles Wesley gave him a devotional book to read while at university. For Whitefield, it was the beginning of a year-long fight with Satan. As Whitefield wrote, "a ray of Divine light was instantaneously darted in upon my soul, and from that moment, but not till then, did I know that I must be a new creature."[19]

Joining Charles Wesley's Holy Club at Oxford, the members of which were mockingly called "Methodists" by other students because of their methodical—almost fanatical—religious zeal, Whitefield was spiritually whipped into shape, he wrote proudly, "like a good soldier of Jesus Christ."[20] Whitefield followed a rigorous routine of fasting, prayer, churchgoing, prison visiting, Scripture reading, and strict observing of acts of charity. But by openly throwing his lot in with the Methodists, his college peers grew to despise him. For a whole year, he suffered spiritual agony over the welfare of his soul, distracting him from his academic studies and leading many at the university to question his mental state. As Whitefield's biographer Harry Stout writes, "Whitefield was living through the travails of the Pauline 'New Birth' so convincingly that he could feel every stage from the depths of despair to the heights of supernatural deliverance."[21] This year-long spiritual anguish led to seven weeks of medically prescribed bed rest, which culminated in his conversion experience. As he wrote in his journal after almost two months of sickness:

---

19. George Whitefield, *George Whitefield's Journals* (Edinburgh and Carlisle: The Banner of Truth Trust, 1978), 47.
20. Whitefield, *Journals*, 47.
21. Harry Stout, *The Divine Dramatist: George Whitefield and the Rise of Modern Evangelicalism* (Grand Rapids, MI: Baker, 1991), 25.

One day, perceiving an uncommon drought and a disagreeable clamminess in my mouth. . . . I cast myself down on the bed, crying out, 'I thirst! I thirst!' Soon after this, I found and felt in myself that I was delivered from the burden that had so heavily oppressed me. The spirit of mourning was taken from me, and I knew what it was truly to rejoice in God my Saviour. . . . Thus were the days of my mourning ended. After a long night to desertion and temptation, the Star, which I had seen at a distance before, began to appear again, and the Day Star arose in my heart. Now did the Spirit of God take possession of my soul, and, as I humbly hope, seal me unto the day of redemption.[22]

Years later, Whitefield fondly remembered the exact place in Oxford "where Jesus Christ first revealed himself to me and gave me the new birth."[23] The year was 1735. Whitefield placed this date alongside his physical birth in 1714 as the winner in the contest of birth dates.

Whitefield was a changed man. His conversion experience, writes biographer Arnold Dallimore, "was the supreme turning-point of his life."[24] Though an ordained priest in the Church of England, Whitefield eagerly preached in non-Anglican pulpits and in the countryside alike, sharing the message of the new birth with hundreds of thousands of people across the English-speaking world. No matter how good, upright, or holy a churchgoing person was, Whitefield maintained, personal conversion was the entrance exam to heaven. Historian Frank Lambert argues that Whitefield, though borrowing heavily from Puritan and biblical writers, "constructed his own meaning of the conversion process"[25] in distinct ways. First, as mentioned above, Whitefield cared little for denominations, instead subsuming all traditions of Christianity under the theme of the new birth. Second, "Whitefield emphasized the immediacy of the new

---

22. Whitefield, *Journals*, 58.
23. Quoted in Arnold Dallimore, *George Whitefield*, vol. 1, *The Life and Times of the Great Evangelist of the Eighteenth-Century Revival* (Westchester, IL: Cornerstone Books, 1979), 77.
24. Dallimore, *George Whitefield*, 1:79.
25. Lambert, *"Pedlar in Divinity,"* 21.

birth," asserting that individuals could personally undergo conversion "in a finite moment" of time.[26] It was an experience, in other words, that could be dated with as much accuracy of time as one's physical birth was. Egging people on to resolve when they were converted, Whitefield collected and published numerous testimonies of individuals who experienced the new birth at a specific moment in time. Finally, in contrast to the common sentiment of Puritanism, "Whitefield assured his followers that they could know for certain if they had experienced the new birth."[27] One's conversion was not a secret among the heavenly host, but a truth palpably evidenced in the heart and life of the individual. And it could be known with virtual certainty.

The primacy of the new birth can be easily discerned in the titles of several of Whitefield's early sermons. Before he went on a massive speaking tour in colonial America, "The Nature and Necessity of Regeneration," "The Indwelling Spirit, the Common Privilege of All Believers," and "Marks of the New Birth" had each been printed, paving the way for new-birth messages to be heard by eager American audiences. In one of his most famous sermons, "The Nature and Necessity of Regeneration," originally printed in London in 1737, Whitefield declared the "doctrine of regeneration, or new birth" to be "the hinge on which the salvation of each of us turns."[28] "You must be informed," he told his delighted readers, "that nothing short of a thorough, sound [personal] conversion will avail for the salvation of your soul." The "broken reed of an external profession" means nothing if it is not matched by a genuine conversion experience that will no doubt "put us to some pain."[29]

26. Ibid.
27. Ibid., 22.
28. George Whitefield, "The Nature and Necessity of Our Regeneration or New Birth in Christ Jesus," in Smith, *Whitefield and Wesley*, 65.
29. Ibid., 75–76.

Jonathan Edwards (1703–1758)

Jonathan Edwards descended from the equivalent of Puritan royalty. His maternal grandfather, Solomon Stoddard, was a leading figure in seventeenth-century colonial America. He served as the minister of the prestigious Northampton Church in Massachusetts for fifty-five years after assuming the pulpit in 1670. While minister at the church, he controversially adopted what was called "the Halfway Covenant." Up until that time, it was standard Puritan practice to only grant membership to adults who could persuasively describe their conversion experience to the elders, regardless of whether that person had attended that church since birth and otherwise led a moral life. In defiance of this practice, Stoddard granted membership to upstanding churchgoers by affirming a church covenant. These half-way members were granted the Lord's Supper and their children were allowed to be baptized (though the children could not receive the Lord's Supper). One of Stoddard's daughters, named Esther, married a young pastor named Timothy Edwards, the father of the more famous Jonathan. Both Solomon Stoddard and his son-in-law Timothy, who pastored in Connecticut, ardently prayed for revivals in their church communities.

Jonathan Edwards, though perhaps an unusually solemn child, inherited both the cunning intellect and the hearty revivalism coming from his father and grandfather. Trained at Yale, Edwards excelled in his academic studies and eventually joined his grandfather at Northampton Church as an assistant until finally assuming leadership over the congregation in 1729. It was not long before revival swept across many churches in New England, including in the Connecticut River Valley where Edwards ministered. As a Puritan pastor, one of Edwards' key duties was to help his parishioners prepare for conversion, for it was believed that each of the elect would undergo such an experience at some point in his or her lifetime as evidence of God's sovereign regeneration—though the experience typically occurred within the existing framework of the church's ordinances. Puritan pastors observed that the preaching of the law and hell was a sure-fire way of inciting fear, guilt, and consternation in the hearts of the elect for breaking God's holy commandments, which ideally prompted the elect to repent of their sins and accept God's forgiveness through Christ's sacrifice on the cross. This was the agonizing road toward conversion that Edwards himself had to take as a pastor before he could help others follow it. His conversion experience, emotionally gut-wrenching and drawn out, occurred in May or June of 1721, while he was a seventeen-year old graduate student at Yale. In characteristic Puritan fashion, Edwards remarked how God "brought me nigh to the grave, and shook me over the pit of hell."[30] Confessing his great sins that offended God's righteousness, he "made seeking my salvation the main business of my life." Having experienced several moments of spiritual assurance and victory in the past, he still sensed that his soul had not been fully converted. This began to change in the late spring of 1721. As Edwards wrote in his "Personal Narrative":

> From about that time, I began to have a new kind of apprehensions and ideas of Christ, and the work of redemption, and the glorious way of salvation by Him. I had an inward, sweet sense of these things, that at times came into my heart; and my soul was led away in pleasant views and contemplations of them. And my mind was greatly changed, to spend my time in reading and meditating on Christ; and the beauty and excellence of His person, and the lovely way of salvation, by free grace in Him. . . . I know not how to express otherwise, than by a calm, sweet abstraction of soul from all the concerns of this world; and a kind of vision, or fix'd ideas and imaginations, of being alone in the mountains,

30. Jonathan Edwards, "Personal Narrative," in *American Lives: An Anthology of Autobiographical Writing*, ed. Robert Sayre (Madison and London: The University of Wisconsin Press, 1994), 127.

or some solitary wilderness, far from all mankind, sweetly conversing with Christ, and wrapt and swallowed up in God.[31]

As a pastor active during a time of revival, Edwards dedicated much of his thinking and writing to identifying genuine and counterfeit characteristics of conversion. In good Puritan fashion, he even kept a personal tab in a diary about how godly or ungodly he was each month to note his progress in the faith. In 1737, in response to the revival that had taken place in Northampton Church in the early years of that decade, Edwards wrote *A Faithful Narrative of the Surprising Work of God*, which detailed the large number of personal conversions taking place before his eyes. This book was wildly popular, influencing both Wesley and Whitefield, and spurring them on to preach about conversion and the new birth. During the next decade, Edwards' penetrating analysis of the revival and conversion continued with the publication of *Distinguishing Marks of a Work of the Spirit of God* (1741), *Some Thoughts Concerning Revival* (1742), and *Religious Affections* (1746). In the last book in particular, which was one of Edwards' most important works, he argued that it was too simplistic to assert that Christianity consisted of either reason or emotions. Instead, it consisted of both and more—what he called the "affections" or the will. It was necessary for holy affections to bring about an "evangelical humiliation," which he defined as "a sense a Christian has of his own utter insufficiency, despicableness, and odiousness."[32] "The whole frame of the gospel," Edwards continued, was meant to illustrate the odiousness of humanity in the face of God's beauty, prompting one to accept and acknowledge Christ's redemption on the cross. Such was conversion or the new birth, the absence of which meant that churchgoers "have

---

31. Ibid., 128.
32. Jonathan Edwards, "Religious Affections," in *The Works of Jonathan Edwards*, ed. Edward Hickman, vol. 1 (London: John Childs & Son, 1839), 294.

no true religion regardless of the profession they may make and regardless of how high their religious affections may be."[33]

Conclusion: Personal Conversion Necessary

The question of whether each individual believer had to experience personal conversion in order to be truly saved erupted in the eighteenth century in the English-speaking world, and it continues in many churches across the world influenced by the evangelical movement. The three most prominent preachers of this doctrine in the eighteenth century, Wesley, Whitefield, and Edwards, raised the act of conversion to new levels of importance, though they differed in other ways. Whitefield was the bridge linking them together, being the only one who personally knew both Wesley and Edwards. Like Wesley, Whitefield was willing to preach anywhere, anytime, and under any condition. When combined, Wesley and Whitefield preached across most of the United Kingdom and colonial America. Like Edwards, Whitefield was a fervent Calvinist, who believed that Wesley's Arminian convictions robbed God of his sovereign glory. Only the elect were predestined for salvation, Whitefield and Edwards maintained, and Whitefield was horrified at Wesley's teaching on Christian perfection (Edwards died before Wesley's views on this matter were popularized). Edwards, the most intellectual of the three, was more discriminating when it came to judging between true and false conversion. Like a spiritual surgeon, he dissected people's beliefs, actions, and motives upon professing conversion in order to determine whether their experience was truly genuine.

When combined, the influence of these three men on the subsequent history of world Christianity can hardly be exaggerated.

---

33. Edwards, "Religious Affections," in *Works*, 294. Note: I have made minor changes in accord with modern language.

As historian Douglas Winiarski writes about Whitefield, "while the Anglican evangelist shared many of the Calvinist sentiments of his seventeenth-century predecessors, he telescoped the Puritan notion of conversion as a lifelong pilgrimage into a single transformative event: the descent of God's Holy Spirit into the bodies of the regenerate faithful." Although this applies primarily to Whitefield, both Wesley and Edwards deserve credit for the popularization of conversion experiences from the eighteenth century onward. Because of their influence, it became extraordinarily common in many Protestant communities—and in several circles, absolutely mandatory—for individuals to "identify the specific time and place of their conversions,"[34] changing the way millions of Christians would think about salvation and God's role in society.

---

34. Douglas Winiarski, "Religious Experiences in New England ," in *Modern Christianity to 1900*, ed. Amanda Porterfield, vol. 6, A People's History of Christianity (Minneapolis, MN: Fortress, 2010), 226.

19

Does Evolution Disprove Christianity?

It was the year 1859. An amateur naturalist from the English countryside whose industrious father had once scolded him for being more interested in catching rats than in taking seriously his academic studies had just published one of the most influential books in modern history. Although he had done the bulk of the research for the book decades before while sailing the globe as a companion to the captain on a ship called the *Beagle*, this gentleman naturalist was reluctant to publish his findings, possibly out of fear of upsetting Victorian English society or else of being proven wrong and marring his reputation. Whatever the case, upon hearing that an acquaintance was about to publish scientific findings similar to his own, the country gentleman hastily wrote out what he had been casually mulling over for more than twenty years.

Upon hearing the controversial idea advanced in the 500-page book that the amateur naturalist published in 1859, the wife of the bishop of Worcester reportedly exclaimed, "Descended from the apes! My dear, let us hope that it is not true, but if it is, let us pray that it will not become generally known."[1] Unfortunately for the bishop's wife, the book was wildly successful. Not one copy of Charles Darwin's *On the Origin of Species* remained on the shelf for more than a few hours after the first edition was released on November 24. A second edition immediately followed, which was eagerly read by the general public and the professional scientist alike. Less than two centuries later, the book still remains in print.

The Question of Evolution and Christianity

Charles Darwin's publication of the theory of evolution by natural selection was a scientific breakthrough of epic proportions. As Darwin's fellow friend and scientist Thomas Huxley remarked, "It is doubtful if any single book, except [Isaac Newton's] 'Principia,' ever worked so great and so rapid a revolution in science, or made so deep an impression on the general mind."[2] In addition to greatly impacting the general public, Darwin's book also sent shockwaves across the Christian world. As historian of Darwinism Peter Bowler describes, some "declared Darwin to be the most dangerous man in England. If evolutionism implied that humans were merely improved apes. . . where was the divine source of moral values?"[3] In this chapter, we will examine nineteenth-century Christian responses to Darwin's theory of evolution by posing the question of whether, or to what degree, contemporary Christians regarded evolution as a threat to their theological beliefs. Stated pointedly, does evolution disprove Christianity?

---

1. Patricia Horan, "Foreword," in Charles Darwin, *The Origin of Species* (New York: Random House, 1979), v.
2. Thomas H. Huxley, *Selected Works of Thomas H. Huxley*, 2 vols. (New York: Appleton & Co., 1893), 2:286.
3. Peter Bowler, *Evolution: The History of an Idea* (Berkeley: University of California Press, 2009), 177.

A Short History of Evolution

The history of evolution is a chapter in the longer story of the triumph of science during the so-called Scientific Revolution. Based on developments in such academic subjects as astronomy, biology, botany, cosmology, genetics, geology, and zoology, scientists began offering a compelling alternative to more traditionally held beliefs about planetary and animal origins. "The growth of scientific knowledge," explains historian Sally Mitchell, "had a major impact on the way people thought about the world."[4] Such scientific interest dawning at this time was not confined to the halls of the academy; by the nineteenth century, many non-professionals had adopted science as a hobby, collecting shells, catching insects, and classifying plants during their leisure hours. This growing interest in science led to remarkable discoveries by amateurs and academics alike when it came to plants, rocks, animals, and humankind. Collectively, these discoveries cast a shadow over the traditional biblical stories about creation and a creator God.

The theory of evolution was increasingly advanced during the eighteenth and nineteenth centuries. The dominant view of natural science at this time was that scientific discovery affirmed God's handiwork in nature. Many Anglican clergymen were amateur or expert scientists whose findings only bolstered their faith in the Divine. William Paley's *Natural Theology*, published in 1802 and read widely by scientists (including Darwin), "taught that science could be used to understand and appreciate God's creations while providing direct evidence for His existence, wisdom, and goodness."[5] However, evolution posed a potential threat to this way of thinking

---

4. Sally Mitchell, *Daily Life in Victorian England* (Westport, CT: Greenwood Press, 1996), 84.
5. Ian Hesketh, *Of Apes and Ancestors: Evolution, Christianity, and the Oxford Debate* (Toronto: University of Toronto Press, 2009), 5.

by suggesting that organisms evolved independent of divine fiat or divine intervention.

Charles Darwin's grandfather, Erasmus Darwin, was one of the first to theorize about evolution. Based on his medical training and experience, he favored the notion of the transmutation of species, believing that all living organisms were interrelated and evolving from earlier life forms. However, Erasmus did not suggest a suitable mechanism for such a theory. In the first decade of the nineteenth century, the French zoologist Jean–Baptiste Lamarck argued that all species had descended from other species. More widely known than Erasmus Darwin, Lamarck regarded acquired characteristics as the primary mechanism for the evolution of species, famously arguing that giraffes acquired their long necks by stretching them to acquire food in the branches of trees generation after generation. Lamarck also entertained the possibility of the spontaneous generation of new species, a vestige of divine creationism that was increasingly falling out of favor with the European scientific community for the explanation of different species.

It was not until the middle of the nineteenth century that evolution began gaining more widespread popularity. A bestselling book titled *Vestiges of the Natural History of Creation*, published anonymously (but written by Scottish journalist Robert Chambers) in London in 1844, popularized the idea of evolution among Victorian society. Grand in scope, the book argued from a layman's point of view that everything in existence, including stars, planets, animals, and humans had evolved from earlier forms. A little more than a decade later, Englishman Alfred Russel Wallace made some interesting discoveries of organisms during his research in Asia. He formulated a theory of evolution that was similar enough to Charles Darwin's to prompt the latter to publicize his views alongside Wallace's at a small societal gathering at the end of 1858. Fearful of seeing a man who had only recently stumbled across a suitable mechanism for evolution outshine what he had been working on for years, Darwin worked feverishly to consolidate decades of research into his *On the Origin of Species* in the fall of 1859. What distinguished Darwin's work on evolution from that of earlier evolutionists was the mechanism of natural selection. In the book, Darwin argued simply but powerfully that species evolved from earlier species by adapting to new circumstances over the course of millions of years. Those organisms successfully adapting to new environments passed to their offspring those characteristics suited for survival, while those organisms not suited for changing environments died out. With enough time and enough geographic variance, all existing species on earth could be explained naturally as evolving from an earlier common living ancestor.

Darwin himself, though coming from a noble scientific lineage, was an unlikely candidate for popularizing such views. He was a product of Victorian English Christianity. He had even formerly entertained a career in the church during his studies at Cambridge. His study of divinity, in fact, was one of the reasons that he was chosen to accompany the captain around the world from 1831 to 1836 on board the *H. M. S. Beagle.* As Darwin noted in his autobiography toward the end of his life, "Whilst on board the *Beagle* I was quite [religiously] orthodox, and I remember being heartily laughed at by several of the officers . . . for quoting the Bible." Yet, over time his faith burned out after years of flickering: "disbelief crept over me at a very slow rate, but was at last complete." Calling the concept of hell as taught by the Bible "a damnable doctrine,"[6] Darwin eventually rejected all vestiges of his earlier faith and instead regarded

---

6. Charles Darwin, "Autobiography," quoted in *Voices of Unbelief: Documents from Atheists and Agnostics,* ed. Dale McGowan (Santa Barbara, CA: ABL-CLIO, 2012), 181. Note: Darwin's strong remarks about Christianity were edited out of later versions of the autobiography out of respect to his wife Emma's feelings.

all of life as a series of random events and processes unaided by the Christian God. Such a theological change, however, was gradual, and not necessarily explicit in his writings, as *On the Origin of Species* routinely assumed a sort of Deistic divinity at work in the world.

Figure 19.1. Select Works of Charles Darwin		
Title	**Date**	**Primary Argument**
Voyage of the H.M.S. Beagle	1839	Travel memoir of the different fossils and living organisms Darwin observed while traveling the world on the *Beagle* from 1831 to 1836.
On the Origin of Species	1859	All of life can be explained as a natural generation from a common source; organisms evolve over time by adapting to their surroundings, the offspring of which are especially suited for survival and reproduction.
The Descent of Man	1871	Humankind has evolved from the great apes.
The Expression of Emotions in Man and Animals	1872	The behavior and expressions of human beings can be shown to derive from lower animals.

The Oxford Debate (1860)

Darwin's theory of the evolution of species through natural selection was destined to generate "immediate response from scientists and a wide range of educated British and English readers."[7] In England, one of the most well-known opponents to Darwin was the learned bishop of Oxford, Samuel Wilberforce, son of the more famous William Wilberforce, a politician who played so important a role in the abolishment of the slave trade in the British colonies. In the summer of 1860, only months removed from the publication of Darwin's *On the Origin of Species*, Samuel Wilberforce entered

---

7. Christian Young and Mark Largent, ed., *Evolution and Creationism: A Documentary and Reference Guide* (Westport, CT: Greenwood, 2007), 71.

into a spontaneous verbal brawl with the English atheist Thomas Huxley at the annual British Association for the Advancement of Science (BAAS). Surprisingly, given the mythological importance this debate generated in the controversy over science and religion, no one recorded all the actual words spoken at the so-called Oxford Debate. Apart from "the few sketchy reports of journalists and letter writers"[8] written at the time, it was a quarter of a century after the debacle that proponents of Darwinism recorded what allegedly happened.

The BAAS had been meeting in England each year since 1831 as a forum for scientists and amateurs to meet and discuss scientific matters. In order to attract a wider audience, the event was open to the public. In June of 1860, the BAAS met for a week at Oxford. One of the last sessions given at the conference convened in the newly built Museum of Natural History in order to accommodate an unusually large audience of around 700 students, professors, scientists, clergymen, and spectators. There were a number of speakers at this session, but it was rumored beforehand that the bishop of Oxford was intending to smash Darwinian thought to pieces when it was his turn to speak. Although Darwin was away receiving water treatment for another bout of his ongoing stomach ailments, many of his friends and supporters attended the session in order to combat the bishop's remarks.

As mentioned above, Darwin's primary opponent at the Oxford Debate was the bishop of Oxford, Samuel Wilberforce, commonly known as "Soapy Sam" because of his smooth speaking skills. Later addressing the scientific audience during this session like it was a cathedral of churchgoers, he waxed eloquent about how evolutionary theory was scientifically wide of the mark. Bemoaning that a rock-

8. Stephen Jay Gould, *Bully for Brontosaurus: Reflections in Natural* (London: W. W. Norton & Co., 1991), 388.

pigeon, for instance, was just what it had always been—a rock-pigeon, nothing more, nothing less—he advanced the argument that Darwin's principles of inductive science went woefully short of offering any substantive evidence. Not only did the fossil record show no sign of evolutionary development, Soapy Sam sermonized, but no breeder had ever successfully produced offspring from different species. He was a half hour into his spontaneous lecture before Wilberforce dropped the infamous line that has since epitomized the debacle. Turning to Huxley, fittingly nicknamed "Darwin's Bulldog," the bishop asked the scientist: Was it through your grandfather or your grandmother that you traced your descent from an ape?

The audience burst into laughter. Having Bishop Wilberforce exactly where he wanted him, Huxley whispered to a friend sitting next to him, "The Lord hath delivered him into mine hands."[9] Now it was Huxley's turn to take the room. Replying that Wilberforce had offered nothing novel or interesting in his remarks, Huxley answered the bishop's uproarious question with an equally notorious response:

> If then the question is put to me would I rather have a miserable ape for a grandfather or a man highly endowed by nature and possessed of great means and influence and yet who employs those faculties for the mere purpose of introducing ridicule into a grave scientific discussion, I unhesitatingly affirm my preference for the ape.[10]

So iconic was the exchange between Wilberforce and Huxley that reports ran wild about how Huxley preferred descent from lowly apes rather than that from religious frauds. As the headline from *The Guardian* exclaimed, "Scientist Would Rather Be Related to Ape than Bishop."[11]

9. Quoted in Hesketh, *Of Apes and Ancestors*, 82.
10. Ibid. There are several versions of this retort by Huxley.
11. Such was the title for *The Guardian*, published a few days after the debacle on July 4, 1860.

It was only natural that reports of the so-called Oxford Debate resorted to labeling and caricature. Wilberforce came to represent a sort of religiously intolerant yokel while Huxley was portrayed as the open-minded and noble scientist. Both portrayals were overly simplistic. As for Huxley, he was not as fearless as we might assume. Later that evening, while many were crowding around him asking for an encore, he replied, "with the look on his face of the [one] who feels the cost of victory. . . . 'Once in a lifetime is enough, if not too much.'"[12] And as for Wilberforce, if reporters had simply read his written comments about Darwin and evolution, they would have put the brakes on their caricature of him as a religious zealot. Within the same year of the Oxford Debate, Wilberforce wrote a public review of Darwin's book that was hardly the product of a fanatic. Recognizing it as a "most readable book; full of facts in natural history, old and new,"[13] Soapy Sam lauded the work in many ways, though he ultimately found it scientifically weak. As much as latter-day critics of Wilberforce accuse him of discrediting Darwin based on religious prejudice, Wilberforce carefully declared in the review:

we have objected to the views with which we have been dealing *solely on scientific grounds*. . . . We have no sympathy with those who object to any facts or alleged facts in nature, or to any inference logically deduced from them, because they believe them to contradict what it appears to them is taught by Revelation.[14]

For Wilberforce, glossing over scientific facts for the purpose of saving religious faith was dishonest and insulting to God. Both natural (science) and supernatural (religious) revelation derived from

---

12. Isabella Sidgwick, "A Grandmother's Tales," *Macmillan's Magazine*, LXXVIII, no. 468 (Oct. 1898), 433-34. http://users.ox.ac.uk/~jrlucas/legend.html#r-3.

13. Samuel Wilberforce, "Review of On the Origin of Species" (1860), in *Evolution and Creationism*, 100.

14. Wilberforce, "Review," in *Evolution and Creationism*, 103 (emphasis added).

God, and they could not contradict one another. Nineteenth-century Anglicanism was not twentieth-century American fundamentalism. Wilberforce fully acknowledged Darwin as a Christian man, but also recognized the threat his ideas posed to traditional Christianity. The bulk of Wilberforce's criticism, however, was not religious in nature but scientific. He rejected evolution by natural selection based on scientific reasons, not necessarily religious ones. In fact, many English clergymen interpreted the mechanism of natural selection as the means by which God brought about human beings.

The Princeton Theologians Respond to Evolution

Though originating in England, Darwinian thought almost immediately impacted American culture. Although many scientists, including Christian ones such as Harvard professor Asa Gray, regarded evolution as harmless to Christianity, many other churchgoers in America were suspicious of evolution. In this section, we will examine how one of the most influential theological institutions in America, Princeton Theological Seminary, addressed the growing popularity of Darwin's theory of evolution by natural selection.

Princeton Theological Seminary was founded in 1812 as the chief exponent of Calvinism and Presbyterianism in America. Its influence on American theology was profound, especially during the nineteenth century. At this time, two of its most highly regarded theologians, Charles Hodge and Benjamin Breckenridge Warfield, both responded to evolution in their writings, paving a way for American Christians to understand the relation between Christianity and evolution for years to come.

Charles Hodge was one of the most respected theologians in nineteenth-century America. Teaching at Princeton Theological Seminary from 1822 until his death in 1878, his career spanned five impressive decades, deeply influencing countless pastors, missionaries, and professors. According to scholars Mark Noll and David Livingstone, "Hodge personally had instructed more theological students than had attended any other theological institution in the United States."[15] Although a professor of theology, Hodge understood the world to be the product of a singular and rational God whose creative design was evident in all areas of inquiry. While science was an example of natural revelation and Scripture an example of supernatural revelation, both ultimately came from God, and so there could be no contradiction between the two.

The son of a physician, Charles Hodge eagerly read Darwin's *On the Origin of Species* and sensed an innate obligation to offer a critique of the theory from a theological perspective. His primary response to evolution came in a work titled *What Is Darwinism?* He wrote it in 1874, more than a decade after the first release of *On the Origin of Species* but shortly after *The Descent of Man*, which proposed more radically that humankind descended from the great apes. By this time in American history, the tide had turned in favor of scientists accepting the general theory of evolution, whether Christian or secular. In this way, "The early 1870s constituted a day of decision"[16] for Christian theologians: as a recognized voice in America, Hodge was forced to either publicly embrace some form of evolution or reject it.

Hodge divided his treatise about Darwinism into several sections. His first act was to classify the various theories of the universe into a logical arrangement, very much in conformity with how he classified the Christian faith in his theological writings. Beginning with Scripture, Hodge demonstrated that the biblical understanding of

15. Charles Hodge, *What Is Darwinism? And Other Writings on Science and Religion*, ed. Mark Noll and David Livingstone (Grand Rapids, MI: Baker, 1994), 17.
16. Ibid., 25.

the world recognizes God as an intelligent and benevolent Creator who designed and sustains the universe according to his holy and good will. Nothing happens outside of God's will, and all living beings were made by him, including human beings, who were made in God's image. After making that foundational point, Hodge then went on to classify non-biblical understandings of the universe in order to contextualize Darwin's non-biblical theory of evolution by natural selection. Hodge next discussed various proponents and opponents of Darwinian theory before lastly addressing Darwin's thinking in relation to religion.

The primary argument that Hodge made in his book was less focused on evolution and natural selection and more on the philosophy generating the theory of evolution and the mechanism of natural selection. In contrast to how Wilberforce criticized Darwin's thought, Hodge reasoned that neither evolution nor natural selection could exist if it were not for the prior conviction of atheism. Hodge labeled this conviction or philosophy "ateleology," meaning absence of divine design or teleology (but he stopped short of calling Darwin an atheist). By interpreting Darwinism as completely void of design by an intelligent Creator, Hodge necessarily made Darwinism not only contrary to belief in God but directly contrary to Christianity and biblical truth. Hodge especially zoned in on Darwin's use of the word "natural," lamenting that it was decidedly "antithetical to supernatural." As Hodge succinctly wrote, "Natural selection is a selection made by natural laws, working without intention and design."[17] For Hodge, such a view was untenable for Christians, and thus certainly for conservative Presbyterians who viewed all of life as falling under the authority of a sovereign and rational God. As he concluded in his treatise, "We have arrived at the answer to our question, What is Darwinism? It is Atheism."[18] In this way, Darwin's

17. Ibid., 85.

thinking was deemed completely contrary to Christianity. It was Darwinism or Christianity—but not both.

Not everyone in the Princeton tradition so starkly pitted Darwin's thinking against Christianity. B. B. Warfield, who was called in 1887 to be the next professor of theology at Princeton Theological Seminary after the premature death of Charles Hodge's son A. A. Hodge (who held that position from 1878 to 1886), was a serious student of science who had spent his youth collecting bird specimens and classifying insects just as Charles Darwin had. Although he did not write any book-length treatments on evolution, Warfield fully understood the ramifications of Darwin's thinking on Christian theology and made numerous references to Darwin and evolution in his lectures and in other writings. Surprisingly perhaps, given the stern conclusions made by Charles Hodge, historian Mark Noll remarks how Warfield concluded his 1889 review of *The Life and Letters of Charles Darwin*: "there have been many evolutionists who have been and have remained theists and Christians."[19] Clearly, Warfield left much more room than Hodge did when it came to determining whether evolution or Darwinism disproved Christianity.

In his essay "The Antiquity and Unity of the Human Race," written about ten years after the closing of the nineteenth century, B. B. Warfield sought to discuss the age and the unity of humanity. Though conceding that humankind was made by God, Warfield resisted the Christian urge to regard the genealogies in the Old Testament as chronologies. Frankly, Warfield did not care how old humankind was. As he unswervingly stated,

18. Ibid., 156.
19. Quoted in Mark Noll, *The Princeton Theology 1812-1921: Scripture, Science, and Theological Method from Archibald Alexander to Benjamin Breckinridge Warfield* (Grand Rapids, MI: Baker, 1983), 293.

> The question of the antiquity of man has of itself no theological significance. It is to theology, as such, a matter of entire indifference how long man has existed on earth.[20]

The only reason why he, as a theologian, was forced to deal with the topic was due to the "the appearance of a conflict between the Biblical statements and the findings of scientific investigators." Were it not for "the supposition of simple Bible readers," he explained, there would be no conflict between the Bible and scientifically based dating of an old earth.[21] Several years earlier, in lectures that he gave in the late nineteenth century, Warfield was equally straightforward:

> I do not think that there is any general statement in the Bible or any part of the account of creation, either as given in Genesis 1 and 2 or elsewhere alluded to, that need be opposed to evolution.[22]

In short, Warfield differed radically from former theology professor Charles Hodge. As Warfield concluded in his essay, he reiterated "the antiquity of man is . . . a purely scientific one, in which the theologian as such has no concern."[23] Though suspicious of the techniques of biologists and geologists, Warfield did not see an inherent conflict between Christianity and evolution.

20. B. B: Warfield, "The Antiquity and Unity of the Human Race," in Noll, *The Princeton Theology*, 290.
21. Warfield, "The Antiquity," in Noll, *The Princeton Theology*, 290.
22. Quoted in David Wilkinson, "Reading Genesis 1-3 in the Light of Modern Science," in *Reading Genesis after Darwin*, ed. Stephen Barton and David Wilkinson (Oxford: Oxford University Press, 2009), 131.
23. Warfield, "The Antiquity," in Noll, *The Princeton Theology*, 292.

Figure 19.2. Nineteenth-Century Attempts to Harmonize Genesis 1–2 with an Old Earth		
Name of Theory	Proponent	Description
Gap Theory	Thomas Chalmers (1780–1847)	There was a "gap" between Genesis 1:1 and 1:2, meaning that God could have theoretically created the world billions of years ago (as told in Gen. 1:1), but that the creation of species (as told in Gen. 1:2) was more recent.
Day-age Theory	Hugh Miller (1802–1856)	The Hebrew word *yom* (translated as "day" in English) referred to a long period of time rather than a twenty-four hour time period.
Days of Revelation	Franz von Hummelauer	The seven-day week in Genesis is a week of God's revelation to Adam how God created.

In the end, the Princeton tradition, a powerful intellectual force that so shaped American theology all the way to the present, was more malleable than initially thought. Indeed, both nineteenth-century successors to Charles Hodge—his son A. A. Hodge and B. B. Warfield, not to mention those in the twentieth century who veered considerably away from the conservative stance Charles took—softened the hard talk of their predecessor. As Mark Noll explains, both Hodge's son and Warfield "accepted the possibility of broad evolution, while denying that evolution necessarily involved a repudiation of design in nature."[24] In fact, just two years after his father's death, A. A. Hodge wrote, "We have no sympathy with those who maintain that scientific theories of evolution are necessarily atheistic."[25]

Conclusion: The Supposed Clash Continues

The nineteenth century was a watershed century in the history of science. Recent discoveries in such fields as biology, botany,

24. Noll, *The Princeton Theology*, 146.
25. Ibid., 233.

cosmology, genetics, and geology were seriously questioning long-held assumptions about God's role in the creation and sustenance of the planet. As Anglican clergyman and friend of Darwin, Charles Kingsley, wrote in the middle of that century about the profound changes unfolding, he felt as if it were standing "on a cliff which is crumbling."[26] Darwin's publication of the theory of evolution by natural selection in 1859 both reflected and accelerated the transition from a largely religious scientific mindset to a secular one. By the end of the nineteenth century, there were essentially three different responses available to Christians about how to regard evolution.

On the extreme right side were believers such as theologian Charles Hodge who believed that Darwinism and Christianity were like night and day. On the extreme left side were those like botanist Asa Gray who saw no contradictions between evolution and religion. In between was a large number of Christians such as Bishop Wilberforce or Professor Warfield who variously fused together aspects of evolutionary theory with nuanced interpretations of the Bible and Christianity.

Less than two centuries after the publication of Darwin's famous book, evolution by natural selection is the standard theory of life origins in science. Despite the wide spectrum of thought concerning how Christians have responded to evolution since 1859, there has been a long history of pundits who care for nothing more than to posit a fierce battle apace between evolution and Christianity or, more broadly, between religion and science. As we have seen, such a portrayal began almost immediately after the release of *On the Origin of Species* during the Oxford Debate, and it was popularized in America during the so-called Scopes Monkey Trial in 1925. If anything, such caricatures of religion and science have reinforced

26. Quoted in Hesketh, *Of Apes and Ancestors*, 8.

whatever prejudices these two different fields of inquiry have against one another. And with the clash between evolution and Christianity "still underway,"[27] it will be interesting to watch how the church will address, if at all, the advances that scientists will continue to make. The truth, however, is that there were various Christian responses to evolution in the nineteenth century (just as today). As David Livingstone rightly points out, "the encounter between Darwinian science and the Christian tradition cannot be squeezed into the mold of conflict or cooperation."[28] Instead, it was both—and more.

27. Peter Bowler, *Monkey Trials and Gorilla Sermons: Evolution and Christianity from Darwin to Intelligent Design* (Cambridge, MA: Harvard University Press, 2007), 1.
28. David Livingstone, Re-placing Darwinism and Christianity," in *When Science and Christianity Meet*, ed. David Lindberg and Ronald Numbers (Chicago and London: The University of Chicago Press, 2003), 202.

20

How Does Christianity Look Worldwide?

It was the year 1928. Around 230 Christian delegates had descended on the Mount of Olives in Jerusalem in order to attend a meeting for the newly established International Missionary Council. One of the goals of this Jerusalem Council was to "identify and discuss the fundamental theological issues"[1] arising from the dominant non-Christian religions in each major world zone. By this time in the church's history, it had become increasingly clear that non-Western cultures were undervalued yet vital voices needed to appreciate and understand Christianity's identity amid a dizzying array of diverse religious traditions.

Commenting a year after the council convened in Jerusalem in 1928, Francis John McConnell, the first writer to use the now-ubiquitous term "world Christianity," described the significance of the council in his book *Human Needs and World Christianity* as follows: "Whereas most conferences on world Christianization have been predominantly composed of representatives from [Western] Christianity, the aim at Jerusalem was to keep fifty-one per cent of

1. Cox, "Jerusalem 1928: Its Message for Today," *Missiology*, 9:2, 139–153 (1981): 142.

the delegates as a percentage inalienably sacred to the churches in foreign fields." "The East," McConnell continued, "was to be given its chance to speak out. The leaders from the West had a feeling that the time had come to hear the message from the [East]."[2]

The Question of the East

The International Missionary Council's meeting in Jerusalem in 1928 confirmed a growing suspicion among twentieth-century Christians that balance needed to be restored within the global church. Although the Western and Northern Hemispheres had dominated Christian discourse and mission for a millennium, the Eastern and Southern Hemispheres were now (re)taking their place as equal members of the worldwide Christian movement. One of the implicit acknowledgements in this book has been the disproportionally large role that Europeans have played in the history of world Christianity. Regardless of whether we were in Africa, Asia or the Americas, Europeans were always lurking in the distance or making unannounced appearances. The West's prominence in the story of Christianity is a peculiar historical feature. It was in the East, after all, that Christianity was born nineteen hundred years before the Jerusalem Council convened in 1928. And it was in the East, at the so-called Jerusalem Council, where leaders of the fledgling Jesus Movement such as James, Peter, Paul, and Barnabas convened to discuss, first, if Westerners could join the church and, second, what was expected of these Westernized Christians as they adopted this new Eastern-based Christian religion. Christianity's growth became lopsided, however. Due to unforeseen political, social, and religious developments, the set of Christian scales gradually tilted in favor of Western Europeans.

2. Francis John McConnell, *Human Needs and World Christianity* (New York: Friendship Press, 1929), 7–8.

In this final chapter, twentieth-century documents and events allow us to begin restoring the balance of world Christianity. We have circled the globe and are back in Christianity's land of birth, the East. For the most part, this book has followed where the action of the church seemed to be loudest, allowing one important question from each century to emerge from the chopping block of contemporary discussions, debates, disagreements, and developments. It just so happened that a flurry of activity developed in the West around the turn of the first millennium, meaning that several (though certainly not all) of the questions raised and discussed in this book were monopolized by Christians of European stock. In this last chapter, echoing McConnell's words that "the time ha[s] come to hear the message from the [East]," we will listen to what select voices from the East said in the twentieth century—defining "the East" very broadly as those world zones consisting largely of non-European ancestry, namely, Africa, Asia, and Latin America—the very region, historian Philip Jenkins estimates, that will contain 72 percent of the Christian population by 2050.[3] This survey of what Christians of the East were saying in the twentieth century serves as a fitting conclusion to this book by recognizing the great geographic shift in world Christianity that has only accelerated in the first quarter of the twenty-first century. We may well pose the question of discussion for this final chapter as follows: what does Christianity look like worldwide?

Voices from Africa

The amount of Christian growth in Africa during the twentieth century was staggering. According to the World Christian Database, there were only about 10 million Christians living in Africa in 1900, but well more than 400 million in the year 2000. There are now far

---

3. Philip Jenkins, *The Next Christendom: The Coming of Global Christianity* (Oxford: Oxford University Press, 2011), xi.

more Anglicans living in Africa than in England, the homeland of the Anglican Church; and by 2030 it is estimated that Africa will contain more Catholics than Europe does.[4] According to historian Klaus Koschorke, "the explosive growth of Christianity in Africa during the twentieth century took place mainly outside of the 'historic' churches that originated from Western missions and European mother Churches."[5] In fact, certain scholars believe that there has been more growth in African Christianity since the end of European colonial rule than were was during the centuries-long rule of Europeans.

Historically, Africa is a continent that has struggled vigorously with its own religious identity. As world historian Adrian Hasting explains, "African religion includes three main strands—the traditional, the Christian and the Islamic."[6] Generally speaking, traditional religion was regarded as culturally African, the Christian religion as culturally European, and the Muslim religion as culturally Arab. In the twentieth century, one of the most prominent questions that faced African society was how Africans could adopt Christianity without denying their African heritage. African historian J. N. K. Mugambi describes this time as follows: "the modern missionary movement imposed western culture on the [Africans] who were being evangelized on the assumption that western culture was 'Christian,' while other cultures were dismissed as 'pagan' and 'heathen.'"[7] Oftentimes, the measuring stick of African Christian maturity was how thoroughly Africans adopted European customs and abandoned African ones.

---

4. Jenkins, *The Next Christendom*, 3, xii.
5. Klaus Koschorke, "Introduction," in *African Identities and World Christianity in the Twentieth Century*, ed. Klaus Koschorke and Jens Holger Schørring (Wiesbaden: Harrassowitz Verlag, 2005), 9.
6. Adrian Hastings, *A History of African Christianity 1950-1975* (Cambridge: Cambridge University Press, 1979), 1.
7. J. N. K. Mugambi, "Christianity and the African Cultural Heritage," in *African Christianity: An African Story*, ed. Ogbu Kalu (Trenton and Asmara: Africa World Press, 2007), 453.

Our first voice from twentieth-century Africa that reflects this theme comes from the Nigerian minister Mojola Agbebi, who died in 1917. Agbebi was named David Brown Vincent at his baptism but changed his name later in life to reflect his African heritage. As an advocate of the indigenous leadership of African churches, Agbebi faced an uphill battle since leadership of churches under colonial rule was predominantly European, even though Europeans represented a minority percentage of believers in the churches. Having worked at a variety of European missions, Agbebi began establishing his own African-led and independent Christian churches in the latter part of the nineteenth century. (Later, such churches would be called African Initiated [or Independent] Churches, or AICs.)

Recognizing the vast difference between African-led and European-led churches, he later wrote: "Tastes differ. English tunes and metres, English songs and hymns, some of them most unsuited to African aspiration and intelligence, have proved effective in weakening the talent for hymnology among African Christians. ... [As such,] I have found [it] necessary to advise that for seven years ... no [European] hymn books but original [African] hymns should be used at worship."[8] Noting that Africans and Europeans expressed themselves radically differently in song and dance and worship, Agbebi argued that Africans should feel free to express themselves in the most natural and comfortable ways possible, which meant rejecting European ways of worshiping God.

Agbebi was one of the earliest leaders of the growing African nationalistic movement, which culminated in the middle of the twentieth century during the decolonization of Africa. In a sermon given in 1902, part of which came from the excerpt above, Agbebi

---

8. "Mojola Agbebi: Inaugural Sermon in the 'African Church' (1902)," in *A History of Christianity in Asia, Africa, and Latin America, 1450-1990: A Documentary Sourcebook*, ed. Klaus Koschorke et al. (Grand Rapids and Cambridge: Eerdmans, 2007), 218.

discussed how Arab-led Islam did a better job of respecting the traditional culture of Africans than European-led Christianity did:

> [The name of an African Muslim], though indicating his faith, was never put on in a way to denationalize or degrade him. Islam is the religion of Africa. Christianity lives here by sufferance. . . . European Christianity is a dangerous thing. What do you think of a religion which holds a bottle of gin in one hand and a Common Prayer [Book] in another? Which carries a glass of rum as a vade-mecum to a 'Holy' book? A religion which points with one hand to the skies, bidding you 'lay up for yourselves treasures in heaven,' and while you are looking up grasps all your worldly goods with the other, seizes your ancestral lands, labels your forests, and places your patrimony under inexplicable legislations? . . . A religion which prays against "those evils which the craft and subtlety of the devil or man worketh against us," and yet effects to deny incantation, charms, or spells and Satanism. . . . O! Christianity, what enormities are committed in thy name.[9]

Such a sentiment was echoed throughout many parts of twentieth-century Africa. Just one example comes from the writing of Jomo Kenyatta, who was the prime minister and also president of Kenya during the 1960s and 1970s. In 1938, just a decade after the International Missionary Council in Jerusalem met, he wrote:

> We can see . . . that the early [Western] teachers of the Christian religion in Africa did not take into account the difference between the individualistic aspects embodied in Christian religion, and the communal life of the African regulated by customs and tradition handed down from generation to generation. . . . The agencies of the Western religious bodies, when they arrived in Kenya, set about to tackle problems which they were not trained for. They condemned customs and beliefs which they could not understand. Among other things, the missionary insisted that the followers of the Christian faith must accept monogamy as the foundation of the true Christian religion, and give up the dances, ceremonies and feasts which are fundamental principles of the African social structure.[10]

---

9. "Mojola Agbebi," in *A History of Christianity in Asia, Africa, and Latin America*, 219.

Seeking to embody an African Christian faith, many African Christian leaders incorporated longstanding African traditional customs and practices into the church. These included exorcism of demons, revelation by dreams and visions, dancing, and other more expressive forms of worship.

Steve Biko, a politician in South Africa who founded the Black Conscious Movement, was regarded as a Christian martyr due to his premature death in prison at the age of thirty for opposition to government-sponsored apartheid. Writing in 1973, four years before his death while in custody of the authorities, he published an article titled "Black Consciousness and the Quest for a True Humanity." In the article, he attempted to underscore the commonalities between African religious identity and Christianity independent of European influence:

> African religion in its essence was not radically different from Christianity. . . . It was the [Western] missionaries who confused the people with their new religion. They scared our people with stories of hell. They painted their God as a demanding God who wanted worship "or else." People had to discard their clothes and their customs in order to be accepted in this new religion. . . . Their arrogance and their monopoly on truth, beauty and moral judgment taught them to despise native customs and traditions and to seek to infuse their own new values into societies.[11]

In opposition to the Christianity taught by Westerners, which belittled African traditions, Biko went on to "make the case for Black Theology . . . [,which] seeks to bring God back to the black man and to the truth and reality of his station."[12]

---

10. Jomo Kenyatta: Christianity and Individualism (1938)," in *A History of Christianity in Asia, Africa, and Latin America*, 242.
11. "Steve Biko, Black Consciousness," in *A History of Christianity in Asia, Africa, and Latin America*, 258–59.
12. "Steve Biko," in *A History of Christianity in Asia, Africa, and Latin America*, 259.

Voices from Asia

Although the church in Africa witnessed the largest percentage of growth during the twentieth century, the continent of Asia also made impressive gains in numbers. Between 1900 and 2000, the number of Christians there mushroomed from about 22 million to close to 350 million.[13] Two of the Asian countries that witnessed the most growth in the twentieth century were China and South Korea. In China, the Christian population swelled from about 800,000 in 1900 to about 800 million in 2000, with most of the growth coming from Protestant churches.[14] In South Korea, the number of Christians rose from about 60,000 in 1900 to close 13 million in 2000, by which point it represented about a quarter of the entire population.[15]

Like Africa, Asia has struggled to understand its Asian Christian identity in light of Western colonization and imperialism. There have been significant backlashes against Western missionaries, particularly in East Asian countries like China and Japan. Some other Asian Christians have criticized the inability on the missionaries' part to distinguish between Western culture and Christianity. Writing a couple of years before the turn of the twentieth century, for instance, an Indian Christian writing in the *Christian Patriot* lamented "the way in which the various [Western] missions have tried to perpetuate on oriental soil the peculiar distinctions of the West . . . [which have] wrought real mischief."[16] During the twentieth century, there were many other themes about which Asian Christians debated and spoke.

---

13. Jenkins, *The Next Christendom*, 3.
14. Ying Fuk-tsang, "Mainland China," in *Christianities in Asia*, 151; Moffett, *A History of Christianity in Asia*, 2:469, 474, 488, 500. All of these numbers are approximate. They do not include Christian offshoots or the Orthodox Church, as they are not recognized in China.
15. Moffett, *A History of Christianity in Asia*, 2:545, 553; Andrew Kim, "South Korea," in *Christianities in Asia*, 217.
16. "Voices of Indian Christians (1897/98)," in *A History of Christianity in Asia, Africa, and Latin America*, 93.

In India, where a longstanding tradition in the South persistently claims to have been evangelized by the Apostle Thomas in the first century, radical changes in society have occurred during the last century. Within the church, there has been ongoing conflict among the major Christian groups, broadly defined as Evangelicals or Charismatics, Catholics, Mainline Protestants, and St. Thomas Christians. Naturally suspicious of one another, Indian Christians from these different groups maligned each other and attempted to convert members of other groups to their own traditions. But according to historian R. E. Frykenberg, the "most continuous and ceaseless of all ongoing arguments and conflicts" among Indian Christians has been that related to issues of "cast, culture and acculturation."[17] Such were the conflicts that emerged when Europeans arrived in the late fifteenth century, which persisted throughout the twentieth century. In the early 1900s, for instance, an "indigenization movement"[18] took shape that sought to combine the best of the native Indian (Hindu) traditions with Christianity. Out of this religious marriage, Christian ashrams formed that allowed dedicated Christians to pursue wandering religious practices so common within Hinduism. The ashram, a sort of monastery that encourages spiritual mastery through yoga, study, and meditation, came to represent a stage of maturation within the Christian life.

In 1921, a founder of the Christukula Ashram in North Arcot, explained that to "some rare few . . . [members of the ashram who look at it as a new form of Christian Community overcoming the barriers of race, class, caste and sex] the presence of God is so real that without depending on any human companionship they go everywhere as wandering prophets or Sadhus [saints] of the

---

17. R. E. Frykenberg, "India," in *A World History of Christianity*, ed. Adrian Hastings (Grand Rapids and London: Eerdmans, 1999), 182.
18. "Christian Ashrams: 1921," in *A History of Christianity in Asia, Africa, and Latin America*, 92.

Kingdom."[19] Among Christian Sadhus in the twentieth century, the best known was Sadhu Sundar Singh. Born in 1889 in the Punjab Region of India, Singh was brought up into the Sikh religion, an Indian faith that merged the best features of Hinduism with Islam. Singh embodied the struggle in India to live out the Christian life in the context of a majority religious culture that was Hindu and, in his immediate region of the Punjab, Sikh. As a meeting at the World Missionary Conference meeting in South India stated in 1938, "In Europe and other Christian countries, Christians see Jesus only. In the unique situation in India . . . we see Jesus in the company of other founders of religion or saviors of men—Buddha, Rama, Krishna."[20] At the age of sixteen, Singh became a Christian Sadhu, wandering from village to village, healing the sick, miraculously surviving many persecutions, preaching about Jesus, and praying.

In one of his many writings, Sadhu Singh entered into a dialogue with a spiritual seeker about Christianity in relation to the dominant religions and philosophies in India. The following excerpt was written in the 1920s:

Seeker: Sadhu-ji, some say that to encounter God we must fulfill some special devotional exercise of contemplation. What does contemplation really mean?

Sadhu: The wonderful peace and calm we experience in prayer does not come from our own thoughts or imaginations, but from the presence of God in our souls. The vapor rising from one small pond is not enough to form large rain clouds and drench the thirsty land. Such large clouds can only come from the mighty ocean. Peace cannot be found in our own subconscious minds, our own concentration, but only in the boundless ocean of God's love.[21]

19. "Christian Ashrams: 1921," in *A History of Christianity in Asia, Africa, and Latin America*, 92.
20. "The 'Rethinking Christianity in India' Group," in *A History of Christianity in Asia, Africa, and Latin America*, 110.
21. Sundar Singh, "Conversations," in *Sadhu Sundar Singh: Essential Writings*, ed. Charles Moore (Maryknoll, NY: Orbis, 2005), 65–66.

Dressed as an Indian holy man, barefoot and penniless, it is believed that Singh was martyred in Tibet in the year 1929.

Voices from Latin America

Together with Africa and Asia, Latin America became one of the largest regions of Christian presence during the twentieth century. Among Christians worldwide, the church in Latin America increased from about 62 million in 1900 to well more than 500 million in 2000.[22] In the twentieth century, while Latin American society was experiencing many violent uprisings and government takeovers, the church was undergoing explosive spiritual growth. Although the modern Pentecostal movement is often traced to the United States during the first decade of the 1900s, recent historians have recognized that Pentecostalism was not tied to any one geographic locale. While the Azusa Street Revival was aflame in Los Angeles, for instance, many Latin American cities were also touched in similar ways by the Holy Spirit. As historian of Pentecostalism Allan Anderson exclaims, "The growth of Pentecostalism in Latin America has been one of the most remarkable stories in the history of Christianity."[23]

Anderson estimates that, "by the end of 1910," Pentecostal missionaries were already leading revivals "in at least nine Latin American countries."[24] Many of these missionaries hailed from Chile. There, in the city of Valparaiso, "many unusual and ecstatic manifestations" transpired, including "weeping, uncontrollable laughter, groaning, prostration, rolling on the floor, revelatory visions, singing and speaking in tongues."[25] It was in Brazil, however,

---

22. Jenkins, *The Next Christendom*, 3.
23. Allan Anderson, *An Introduction to Pentecostalism: Global Charismatic Christianity* (Cambridge: Cambridge University Press, 2013), 72.
24. Allan Anderson, *To the Ends of the Earth: Pentecostalism and the Transformation of World Christianity* (Oxford: Oxford University Press, 2013), 172.
25. Ibid., 173.

where Pentecostalism would become widespread in Latin America. According to many estimates, Brazil contains the largest number of Pentecostals of any country in the world, claiming 15 to 20 percent of the global population.[26] The first Pentecostal church in Brazil is dated to 1910, when Italian-American Luigi Francescon led a revival among Italian-Brazilians, which eventually encompassed the Portuguese-speaking populations of the country.

A similar revival occurred in the northern part of Brazil among Baptists in the city of Belém. Swedish-American Baptists Daniel Berg and Gunnar Vingren entered that northern Brazilian city in 1910 as missionaries. They were soon expelled from the Baptist church because of their Pentecostal teachings. Commenting on the Pentecostal bodies of believers that separated from the Baptist church, Berg reports that:

> One evening the local [Baptist] preacher appeared in our simple premises. When he opened the door, a wave of song and prayers struck him. We got up and invited him to take part in our improved Service. He refused . . . and accused us of sowing doubt and unrest. . . . Gunnar Vingren got up and declared that . . . we wanted unity among everyone. If only everyone had the experience of the baptism of the Spirit, we would never be divided. . . . The local preacher . . . said that the Bible did indeed speak about Baptism of the Spirit and also said that Jesus healed the sick. But that was in those times. He said that it would be absurd if educated people of our time believed that such things could happen today. We had to be realistic—he continued—and not waste time with dreams and false prophecies.[27]

At the meeting, Berg later explained, eighteen members of the church left with him and Vingren, sparking the Pentecostal Movement in the northern part of Brazil.

---

26. Ibid., 177.
27. "Brazil: Beginnings of the Pentecostal Movement," in *A History of Christianity in Asia, Africa, and Latin America,* 372.

Although Pentecostalism originated within Protestantism, it eventually spread to Catholic Churches across most every Latin American country. Because it was oftentimes Catholics who were attracted to and later joined Pentecostal churches, the Catholic Church's embrace of the gifts of the Spirit minimized the mass exodus that had occurred within Mainline Protestant churches. But the swapping of ideas between Protestants or Pentecostals and Catholics went both ways. Even though many Protestant churches now accept many tenets of so-called liberation theology, it was the Catholic Church that gave birth to this new theological movement. In the second half of the twentieth century, the Catholic Church in Latin America was coming to grips with widespread poverty, injustice, and social unrest that had plagued that region of the world for so long.

It was at a conference of Catholic bishops in 1968 in the city of Medellín, Colombia that "liberation theology" was born. Broadly defined as "an interpretation of Christian faith out of the experience of the poor,"[28] and with an eye toward protesting social inequalities caused by the way societies are often organized in the West, liberation theology favors the side of the oppressed and downtrodden rather than that of the wealthy and powerful. Liberation theology was the product of Latin American application of Vatican II, a momentous council in the Catholic Church in the 1960s that sought to breathe new life into Catholicism by addressing the concerns of the modern world. The bishops meeting in Colombia were bold in their application of Vatican II to the violent, oppressive, and unstable region of Latin America. They pledged to "bring . . . a distribution of resources and apostolic personnel that effectively gives preference to the poorest and most needy sectors" of the church.[29] They also

28. Phillip Berryman, *Liberation Theology: The Essential Facts about the Revolutionary Movement in Latin America* (New York: Random House, 1989), 5.
29. "Liberating Education as an Answer to Our Needs," in *A History of Christianity in Asia, Africa, and Latin America*, 396.

instituted what they called "base communities," which were small groups of lay Catholics intended to promote solidarity among the poor and provide a forum to address their daily concerns by means of reflection on Jesus and the Bible. It was an immensely successful concept.

One of the advisors of the meeting of bishops in Medellín was Peruvian priest Gustavo Gutiérrez. Though not a bishop, Gutiérrez was the architect of liberation theology. His writing of a book by the same name in 1971 propelled *la teología de liberación* onto a national stage, later inviting criticism from the papacy. Six years later, one of the other most prominent voices of liberation theology, Óscar Romero, became the archbishop of San Salvador in El Salvador. Romero was an outspoken critic of the Revolutionary Government in El Salvador due to its widespread human rights violations. A month after becoming archbishop, in March of 1977, a good friend and fellow priest of Romero's was assassinated for working with the poor and denouncing the silencing of priests, propelling Romero to side even more with the poor and to condemn the current regime. In February of 1980, Romero delivered an impassioned speech:

> It is, then, an indisputable fact that, over the last three years, our church has been persecuted. But it is important to note why it has been persecuted. Not any and every priest has been persecuted, not any and every institution has been attacked. That part of the church has been attacked and persecuted that put itself on the side of the people and went to the people's defense. . . . Persecution has been occasioned by the defense of the poor.[30]

A month later, while performing mass, Romero was assassinated. In 2015, Pope Francis declared Romero a martyr and a saint, giving

---

30. Óscar Romero, "The Political Dimension of the Faith from the Perspective of the Poor," in *Radical Christian Writings: A Reader*, ed. Andrew Bradstock and Christopher Rowland (Oxford and Malden: Wiley, 2002), 279.

official sanction to what many Christians in the international community had already believed for decades.

Conclusion: A Shift in Gravity

Since Francis John McConnell's first use of the term "world Christianity" in the 1920s, an entire industry of Christian scholarship has converged around the idea of a center-free or polycentric church, in which no one region represents *the* church. Increasingly, Christian leaders from the East and South are reconnecting to their ancient pasts and reformulating their own identities independent of Western and Northern influence. In fact, some scholars believe that the pendulum of power and influence has now swung in favor of Eastern and Southern Christians. Due to swelling secularization in European-dominated cultures, in contrast to vibrant growth in the global East and South, it has been argued that the time has now come for Christians in the former regions to take a learning posture from their brothers and sisters in the East and South.

However we respond to the changes taking place, it's now clear that the West no longer dominates Christianity as it once did. According to statistics from the World Christian Database, Europe is the only continent expected to undergo a decrease in its Christian population over the course of the next few decades, while North America will trail noticeably behind Africa, Asia, and Latin America.[31] Due to a variety of social and religious circumstances, the influence of Western Christianity is going through an extensive process of realignment. This trend, which began in earnest in the twentieth century, has only intensified in the early twenty-first century. In a matter of decades, Africa, Asia, and Latin America will represent more than 70 percent of the worldwide Christian

31. Jenkins, *The Next Christendom*, 3.

population. Percentages are not everything, of course, but with people come ideas, power, and influence. With Eastern and Southern Christians beginning to occupy the driver's seat of world Christianity, the questions *they* ask and answer will likely impact and influence Western and Northern Christians in ways that were scarcely imaginable even a century ago.

Who Will Define Christianity in the Years to Come?

In the first decade of the twenty-first century, Gambian-American scholar Lamin Sanneh wrote a paradigm-shifting book called *Whose Religion is Christianity?* Consisting of more than one hundred questions related to world Christianity, the title of the book posed a provocative question that gets to the heart of the Christian faith in today's religious marketplace. With such a diverse assortment of Christians stemming from thousands of different traditions across all parts of the world, who gets to define Christianity? And, for the purposes of this book, who gets to decide what questions will be framed in the decades (and centuries) to come?

The short answer to this question is that Christianity finds itself in a period of great transition—the likes of which compel us to inquire what unites the disparate Christian groups active in the world today. Despite historic creeds and carefully nuanced confessions, there is no international and agreed upon arbiter in charge of deciding who is in and who is out of the worldwide "church." Christianity, to the chagrin of many of its leaders and practitioners, is a fluid movement and open-ended club, consisting, in its most recent estimates, of around 45,000 different traditions. Decidedly disjointed and increasingly fragmented, Christianity ostensibly belongs to the Catholics and to the Pentecostals just as much as it belongs to the Brazilians and to the Nigerians. Indeed, one of the peculiarities of the Christian religion is that many of those who profess to be Christians have already predetermined that many others making the same claim are not fellow members of the body of Christ.

This reality has become sharper in focus with the passing of each century of the church—and each chapter of the book. To be sure, there were innumerable questions that Christians asked in the first century, but one of the most urgent ones had to do with the relationship between "any who belonged to the Way," as the book of Acts describes early followers of Jesus, and Judaism, Christianity's mother religion. As we learned in Chapter 1, this was a pivotal question that cast a wide net over the small yet still geographically widespread church in the first century after Christ. It appeared to be a question that most every Christian group asked in one form or another, though, significantly, not every group answered it in the same way. Likewise in the remaining early centuries, the church, though spreading its geographic and theological wings, still raised similar questions regarding authority and leadership, what to do with backsliders, deciding who Christ was, and discerning the relationship between Christianity and culture.

Over the centuries, however, as the church became more and more heterogeneous, the questions one sector of the church posed did not always reflect the questions other sectors of the church were asking. And if they did, different groups sometimes reached different conclusions. Thus in the sixth century, as the church collectively pondered what it meant to be holy, Syrian Christians interpreted holiness one way while Irish Christians, for instance, interpreted it another way. And in the tenth century, as Western Catholics struggled to determine whether they were living in the end times due to their proximity to the millennial year of 1000, Eastern Orthodox believers did not raise the same question since they used a different calendar.

Christianity, whether planted alongside a spiritual river or embedded in the hostile terrain of the desert, is a living organism that thrives, survives, or perishes depending on its setting. It is organically related to the context in which it finds itself, and raises theological questions based on its unique circumstances and social location. In the Middle Ages, for example, the grandeur, power, and wealth of the European Catholic Church prompted itself to ask the extent, if any, of its ownership of newly discovered territory and of the people inhabiting the lands it was fast discovering. Later on, finding itself uncomfortably outnumbered in the East and unfamiliar with Asia's religious heritage, the same Church asked whether the ancient religious traditions of China were compatible with those of Christianity. As the worldwide church entered the modern world, its ever-dividing traditions congealed into their respective forms, only seeming to harden in relation to each other.

Nowadays, the global church is undergoing an extensive alignment process. When it comes to geography, ethnicity, and theology, the church is incredibly diverse. The center of gravity is shifting from the West and the North to the East and the South. People groups once marginal in the story of world Christianity are rising in importance. And Pentecostalism is growing at a meteoric pace. Still, although society is changing rapidly in many parts of the world, it is hardly changing at all in others. What's more, there are a whole host of social factors such as access to medical care, birth and death rates, educational opportunities, political structures, and unemployment that shape the development and characteristics of Christianity in any given region of the world.

Is there any real unity in the church today? And what questions will Christians in the remaining years of the twenty-first century ask? It's impossible to say for sure, but if history's taught us anything, it's that the church will continue to struggle with issues related to doctrine, culture, politics, and faith among its adherents. Consider the following real-life scenarios and questions of Christians in the early twenty-first century:

An Orthodox priest at the Patriarchate of Constantinople proudly greets a group of travelers (in Greek) in Turkish-speaking and Muslim Turkey. Lamenting how the Greek Orthodox population of Istanbul has dwindled to only a few thousand after boasting a population of hundreds of thousands centuries before, he asks, "How long until our political rights will be lost and the church will no longer exist here?"

An evangelical businessman in a gray suit in Indonesia facilitates a meeting in a city skyscraper. Daydreaming about transforming the largest Muslim society on the planet one Christian business venture at a time, he asks, "What's stopping Indonesia from becoming the largest Christian country in the world?"

An elderly Catholic woman totters to her home parish in a medieval city in central Italy. She's been making the same walk to the church for eight decades. When she enters the church, she blesses herself with holy water and bows in reverence before the altar. After praying silently and adoring the crucified Lord located in the front of the sanctuary, she asks, "Will there be anyone willing to worship at this church when I'm gone?"

A female pastor at a Mainline Protestant church in the United States is under censure for performing the marriage ceremony for a same-sex couple that attends her church. In open defiance of the denomination's policy, she asks her elder board, "Are we willing to risk rejection from our denomination in behalf of our beliefs?"

Due to globalization, we are acutely aware of the circumstances churches face from all parts of the globe, and the important questions these churches are asking vary from region to region and from tradition to tradition. Because the church is always reacting to society at large, the questions posed during the rest of the twenty-first century and beyond will no doubt continue to change with the culture, sometimes aligning with questions asked by other churches but many times not. In this book, we have explored twenty questions that shaped world Christianity, the responses of which stabilized and guided the global church during times of controversy and contention. As Christianity becomes more diverse, more fragmented, and more geographically widespread in the years to come, the sky is the limit in terms of the types of questions its leaders will ask. Perhaps changing times will elicit different responses to some of the same questions asked centuries before. Or perhaps not. Only time will tell. As you reflect on the twenty questions raised in this book, how do you think the global church will respond to societal changes in the twenty-first century? And what will be the principal question(s) of the era in which you live?

Index

CPSIA information can be obtained
at www.ICGtesting.com
Printed in the USA
FSHW021256091219
64898FS